Praise for Tom Hirschfeld's
Business Dad

"Juggling responsibilities at work and home is a reality for millions of parents. . . . Using business philosophies, strategies, and anecdotes, the book offers solutions that not only make perfect business sense, but that work, too!"

— *Business Times*

"Tom Hirschfeld makes a convincing case that the same skills can help you succeed as a parent and as a businessperson. . . . With humor and insight, Hirschfeld does parents and careerists both a service."

— Peter F. Drucker, *American Way*

"This smart, straight-shooting work could very well be required reading in all graduate schools of business and is a welcome addition to the small but growing number of books in parenting aimed primarily at fathers. . . . The content is remarkably free of the self-centered, cliché-ridden tips found in most books on business. . . . Even the most unregenerate workaholic dad will understand Hirschfeld's basic message: 'Fatherhood, more than business, is almost always what shapes a man's personal legacy. Simply stated, it is the most important job we'll ever undertake.'"

— *Publishers Weekly*

"Very readable . . . the concepts apply to any parent who wants to make the most of every segment of life, with the ultimate goal of raising healthy, adjusted kids."

—Juliet J. Holden, *Dallas Child*

Business Dad

HOW GOOD BUSINESSMEN CAN MAKE GREAT FATHERS

(AND VICE VERSA)

Tom Hirschfeld

with Julie Hirschfeld, Ph.D.

LITTLE, BROWN AND COMPANY

BOSTON   NEW YORK   LONDON

Originally published in hardcover
by Little, Brown and Company, 1999
First Little, Brown paperback edition, 2000

LIBRARY OF CONGRESS CATALOGING-IN-PUBLICATION DATA
Hirschfeld, Tom.
Business dad : how good businessmen can make great fathers (and vice
versa) / Tom Hirschfeld with Julie Hirschfeld.
p.   cm.
ISBN 0-316-21950-9 (hc) / 0-316-21915-0 (pb)
1. Fathers.   2. Parenting.   I. Hirschfeld, Julie.
II. Title.
HQ756.H564   1998
306.874'2 — dc21   98-54279

10 9 8 7 6 5 4 3 2 1

Q-FG

Printed in the United States of America

This book is dedicated to *Benjamin and Leila,*

my on-the-job trainers,

and to my late father, *Dr. Leonard S. Hirschfeld.*

Contents

Business Dad

Mission Statement

A SECRET WEAPON FOR BUSINESS DADS

The Challenge

As businessmen and as fathers, we face nowadays what is known in business as a high-class problem: an explosion of opportunity without a single extra hour in the day.

Think of how life has changed since 1960. In business, that was the heyday of the Organization Man, who knew exactly where he fit within his company and his world. In his gray flannel suit, he would catch the same train every morning, do the same kind of work, drink the same number of martinis at his two-hour lunch, and pretty much never have to wonder where his next paycheck was coming from. He had every reason to expect his company and his job to be there waiting for him the next day. Life moved slowly, and the world changed gradually. It was a comfortable existence, all in all, if not the most exciting one.

Today, we have all the excitement we can handle. The natural barriers of time and distance, and the man-made ones of tariff and regulation, are crumbling into dust. For enterprising individuals and companies, possibilities expand every day. Previously unimaginable rewards are there for the taking. But for those a bit slower on the uptake, a bit more complacent or less informed, technology and globalization represent opportunities to *lose*, not win.

And the line between loser and winner seems to get thinner every day. Just when we imagine our careers are going fine—boom!—some fresh thundercloud approaches. It could be a new technology, a new market entrant, or even a new VP down the hall. In this age of dizzying change, the wheel of fortune spins faster the harder we run. Even if we're lucky enough to scramble our way to the top, we've got to keep sprinting just to stay there—and the trickiest part is that the blasted thing keeps changing direction. We can never relax, never coast. Laurels? Nowadays, they wither overnight. Nothing recedes like success.

The only thing between us and the bottom of the wheel is information—but information is part of the problem as well. It used to drift in at a nice, manageable pace, then sit politely until we were ready to absorb it. These days, facts and factoids come hurtling at us like balls from a pitching machine gone berserk. If we don't keep watching and swinging, we're bound to get beaned. What we don't know really can hurt us—we're playing hardball now.

To survive professionally, it seems we businessmen must constantly work harder, longer, and farther away. Despite the Internet and videoconferencing, the airlines have never been busier. The "just in time" techniques widely applied to cutting inventories now seem to apply to human resources as well, so we have less and less control over our hours. Even when we're not on duty, the communications revolution keeps us on call. The "efficiencies" from a decade of downsizing have managed simultaneously to increase our workloads and to dangle a constant threat above our heads. But the travel, the crazy schedules, the job stress—they're all worth it, because we're doing it for the kids.

The kids. Ah, the kids. Don't you love to think of them, home with their moms or nannies, or off in day care or school, just waiting for that moment tonight when we'll walk in the door? If we can only get this draft report circulated by seven o'clock, we should be home before they hit the sack. And even if we can't squeeze in any quality time tonight, there's always tomorrow, or this weekend, right after golf. Sure, we'd love to spend more time with them, but our top priority has to be bringing home the bacon, after all. Luckily, their moms are *terrific* with them. After all, the kids have mostly been Mom's department, whether she has a "day job" or not—though we're good family men and help out whenever we can. After a hard day at the office, we probably wouldn't be that much fun to hang out with, anyway.

Just a minute! What's wrong with this picture? Nothing, except that it's not 1960 at *home* anymore, either. Back then, a good family man basically had two roles to fill with his kids: provider and disciplinarian. Mom handled the rest. But today's approximately ten million businessmen with kids under age eighteen have been hit with what the business books might call a paradigm shift. As a result, the kind of remote-control fathering caricatured above just doesn't cut it anymore. *Success at home, like success at work, is a lot more demanding than it used to be. On the other hand, it's also a lot more rewarding.*

Three related trends have dramatically expanded our job descriptions as fathers. First, our own parents rarely obsessed about parenting or even used the term; they just did it. Now, though, society is much more focused on what parents should do to bring up—but not mess up—their children. People think more about what kids really need, and how parents can affect them for good or ill. Entire industries of books, magazines, and Web sites have sprung up telling parents what to do and what not to do—and some of the advice is even right.

Second, the social infrastructure for rearing kids is—let's face it—rotting. The structured schools, safe neighborhoods, wholesome TV programming, frequent worship, and united families of yesteryear, which *reinforced* the messages parents sent their kids (or even offset parental shortcomings), can no longer be depended on. Schools pay more attention to political correctness and children's self-esteem than to learning, kids get snatched off neighborhood streets, TV teaches materialism and cynicism, spirituality too often comes as an afterthought, and half of marriages end in divorce.

Where once parents could count on society as an ally, now we have to *fight* the culture's low expectations of (and for) our children. So raising kids right has become harder.

But not all the news is bad. The third trend is generally positive, although closely linked to the second: the blossoming of options for men and women about what kind of lives to lead. Mothers enjoy more and better opportunities in the world of paid work, while men have learned that strong and silent don't have to go together. Just as women are no longer seen as lovable incompetents or mere ornaments in the workplace, we men are no longer automatically foreigners in the nursery or the kitchen. We can enjoy richer, deeper relationships with our children than the Organization Man ever imagined.

This loosening of gender roles may give men more choices, but put it together with the newly perceived urgency of our children's needs, and it spells *responsibility*. In a haywire society, successful families don't just happen: parents, both parents, have to make them happen. We dads still have to be providers, but no longer just in the financial sense. We're desperately needed as equal partners in child-rearing, in providing that warm, structured upbringing that could make the difference down the line between Yale and jail. Our wives and the (other) experts tell us that we need to make a true commitment to parenting—to be there for our kids every day, not just physically but also mentally and emotionally.

Do you know your kids' teachers? Their friends' names? Their homework schedules, or how many sweets they're allowed in a day? What are your thoughts about their current disciplinary challenges? And by the way, do you remember your sales deliverable for next quarter? Have you figured out what could go wrong in your revenue pipeline? What are you doing about it? Do you even know who your real competitors are?

Think fast! Now, think faster!

The timing is painful. We're trying not to blow the critical years of our kids' childhoods, while at the same time struggling to build careers in the midst of one of the most challenging business climates ever. Is it any wonder that many business dads feel overwhelmed? In

1979, a national survey found that only 12 percent of fathers said they were experiencing stress trying to balance work and family; by 1989, that figure had climbed to 72 percent. What's your guess for 1999?

Don M., a friend of mine, gives me some clues as to the answer. (I'll protect my personal contacts' privacy by using their last initials, and by changing names in a few cases, but they're all real people, not composites.) Don has just completed his M.B.A. after having started his career in the nonprofit sector. He and his wife don't have kids yet, but he's already wondering out loud if he'll be able to succeed in business and still give them what they need. His own dad was a policeman who worked thirty-five hours a week, and so was home more often than not. Don knows with "a kind of lingering guilt" that he won't be able to match that. Nor is he alone; he says the inevitable conflicts between home and work come up regularly among his B-school classmates.

Business Week described the predicament in a long article in the fall of 1998 titled "The Daddy Trap," with the subhead, "Men face greater expectations at home. But work isn't giving them the slack they need." The article quotes Jeffrey Welch, a New York bank executive who's frustrated by the difficulty of succeeding at both work and fathering. "I'd like to participate more in school or camp stuff, but I can't manage my schedule in a way to allow that. I'm letting go of everything for myself, except for exercise on weekends. . . . I want to be a dad who, thirty years down the road, my kids say, 'Yeah, he was a big part of our life.' And right now, I'm not that."

What can we business dads do to escape the Daddy Trap? The first step, once we recognize the problem, is simple: resolving to give it our best shot. In this age of change, we're used to having new expectations thrust on us, so we might as well take on one more—our expanded responsibilities as fathers. We love our kids like anything, and we want the best for them, whatever this world has to offer. It's certainly not our habit to shirk an assignment or to run from a challenge. Jobs come and go, but family is forever—at least we hope it is. So we're ready to make the commitment.

Unfortunately, deciding to be a good father is only the first step.

Real life is littered with obstacles that make fathering tough for even the best intentioned of us. In combination, these obstacles can make us wonder if our fathering efforts are worth the extra stress, even while we feel guilty for not doing more. (It's like the old joke about the guy who tells the waiter, "This food is terrible—and besides, the portions are so small!") Given the ceaseless demands we face from work, the only thing worse than feeling we're not trying hard enough as dads is suspecting that the efforts we *are* making are misguided, wasted, or even counterproductive. Here's a brief sampling of the obstacles I have in mind. I'm sure you can supply plenty more on your own.

What We're Up Against

• **No training.** Dozens of schools offer M.B.A.'s, but there's no Master of Fatherly Administration. The fact is, we can't prepare for having kids the way many of us prepared for our professional careers. And make no mistake: fathering is tricky work, hellaciously hard sometimes, with more pitfalls and traps than an Indiana Jones flick. We can get training to engineer a merger, turn around a factory, or launch a new brand, but fathering makes all those feats look like cakewalks.

• **No role models.** Bookstore business sections bulge with billionaires — tomes by or about idols like Bill Gates, Michael Bloomberg, George Soros, Michael Eisner, Sam Walton, and Warren Buffett. But where are the heroes of fathering, the shining examples for us to emulate and measure ourselves against?

Mentors make a major difference, as the phenomenon of Silicon Valley shows. Did that awesome agglomeration of capital and brains happen overnight? Of course not. Companies such as Hewlett-Packard, which was founded more than sixty years ago, and Fairchild Semiconductor served as mentors and "fathers" to a whole industry. Where can dads get that kind of guidance today?

Our wives typically grew up being groomed for the role of mother, and their first female role models were their own mothers, who by and large did a pretty good job. Most of us, on the other hand, had dads of the old school (if we were lucky enough to have fathers living with us at all). Some of those dads may have performed fantastically under the *old* rules—lower expectations, shorter work hours, and wives who stayed home. But times have changed, and some of our fathers' lessons no longer apply.

• **No expert status.** Moms begin with all kinds of cultural preparation for being sensitive, nurturing, competent parents. What really makes them experts, though, is spending so much time with the kids, beginning with pregnancy. Sooner or later, the children become their turf. Once that happens, anyone who ventures onto that turf risks correction, reprimand, or worse.

The husbands of expert moms may get caught in a catch-22. The best way to learn is by doing, but the more the knowledge gap widens, the more painful it can be for us to try doing anything. At the very least, we're bound to be relatively inefficient. Also, some moms act so possessive about their kids that it can be tough for less-involved dads to get closer. Worst of all, some dads find it unpleasant to do anything they're not instantly good at—meaning they never learn.

• **No books.** Have you been to your neighborhood bookstore lately? Almost all the books on child raising are for moms—or parents, which in most cases amounts to a code word for moms. There's little that focuses on the contributions that only fathers can make, or on the issues they have to deal with. Most books with "father" in the title target subgroups like single dads, gay dads, or middle-aged dads, as if they're the only ones who need or want advice. Of the few general books for fathers, one of today's bestsellers dates from the Nixon presidency! Even the more recent books were written by psychologists, writers, professors, or fathering activists—not a businessman among them. As a result, the authors tend to gloss over issues that business dads face, and they totally ignore the amazing resources that our hard-won business skills give us. Instead, they write long, long chapters dwelling on things that social scientists care about. Parts can be useful, but the authors seem too seldom to have dads like you and me in mind.

• **No magazines.** Try finding anything about fathering in the men's health or men's life mags. Women are bombarded with parenting articles in the "women's service" magazines, and of course they have their pick of general (that is, woman-targeted) parenting magazines, but there's virtually nothing out there just for fathers, let alone for business dads like us. On the Web, you'll find huge volumes of information for parents, but again written mostly with mothers in mind.

• **No time.** For combatants in today's economy, time is the scarcest commodity. Most of our dads had more time to fulfill their (relatively limited) fathering expectations, because they worked maybe fifty hours tops. The rest of the time, they basically stayed around the house, and we got to see them reading, fixing things, and chatting with the neighbors—letting us observe who they were and how they acted. Today, by contrast, our "day jobs" could go on all day, every day, if we let them. Like our dads, we still need adult time with the women we married, and maybe a couple of hours by ourselves to recharge our batteries. With all those competing priorities, who has *time* to be a father, let alone a good one?

• **No professionalism.** It's an understatement to say that corporate and kid environments are not the same. At work we give a few terse orders, and behold, they get carried out; at home we try the same, and get a tantrum or an adolescent snit for our pains. At work we're told problems so we can solve them; at home we're told problems no one can solve. At work we aspire to order and clarity; at home chaos is rarely far away. At work we're rewarded for focus, intensity, and singleness of purpose; if we try applying those characteristics the same way at home, the only reward we get is rapid burnout. Any business dad can testify, in summary, that reflexively slipping into office behavior with our kids is risky business. The problem is, they just don't act like professionals.

• **No evaluations.** At work and home alike, it's tough to rise above the day-to-day tumult—to get a good overview of how we're really performing. Good employers provide some kind of formal assessment every three, six, or twelve months to make sure that we stay on the right track and that we know which skills need more work.

Our kids can't give us any explicit feedback till they talk, and formal evaluations are never very likely. All we can do is watch how *they're* doing, and guess how we might help them do better.

• **No pay.** Annual assessments are all very well, but in the corporate world nothing talks quite like cash on the barrelhead. Our salaries and bonuses constitute our rewards for a job well done, and in good years they can make all our hard work seem worthwhile. As fathers, by contrast, we tend to see cash streaming out in the opposite direction. Then there's the "soft" compensation at work, like Outstanding Salesman recognition ceremonies and praise from the boss, or the little courtesies and ego boosts we get from our colleagues in the course of everyday interaction. These niceties have not, I'm afraid, made it into the repertoire of most two-year-olds. There *are* many other compensations to fatherhood, but they're not always obvious.

• **No competition.** Face it: one of the forces that drives us at work is the primeval urge to outperform our colleagues, or our college roommates, or our neighbors. The raise and the bonus are not simply feedback mechanisms, but also ways of keeping score. Since boyhood, and probably since the cavemen, we've instinctively asked who's biggest, who's smartest, who's fastest, who can throw the farthest, kiss the prettiest, and possess the most. But in our households, *we're it*. There are no other dads to compete against. Where there is no competition, can there be motivation? Can there be meaning?

With hurdles like those to overcome, you'd think business dads would try to even the odds with as much information as possible. In business, after all, we flock to new bestsellers every month, with such titles as *Crossing the Chasm* or *The Learning Organization*. And yet you may have noticed that most businessmen (yes, it's true) read fewer books on parenting than they do on business.

Why might this be? Is it that books about fathering don't have business dads in mind? That successful businessmen see books on fathering as self-improvement, a genre they haven't much time for? That businessmen absolutely must read what their competitors are reading? Or that, confronted by so many obstacles, some business dads just give up and follow Mom's instructions? I suspect that each of these explanations contains some truth.

This book sets out with the modest goal of helping to change all that. For starters, I mean this to be a book that business dads will actually read. It's a simple idea, yes, but one whose time has come: a book by a business dad for business dads.

What makes this book different? It directly addresses the What We're Up Against obstacles listed above. It uses terms naturally familiar to businessmen, with real-life examples from both the corporate and the child-raising worlds. It explores in detail the particular work-family struggles business dads face, from deadline juggling to paternity leave.

Most important, this book recognizes that *we businessmen have a secret weapon to help us in the struggle to be decent dads*. It shows that our business experience itself, of all things, has graced us with huge reservoirs of untapped fathering skills; that successful businessmen, by definition, have the makings of truly exceptional fathers; and that there exist commonsense, logical methods of unlocking that incredible potential.

The Opportunity

Name any weekday afternoon since your college graduation. Where were you? Probably in the office, or out in meetings, but in any case, working. And that would be true not only of almost any weekday afternoon, but also of mornings, evenings, and even (sad to say) numerous nights and weekends. Since our early twenties, in fact, most of us have spent over half our waking hours either working or training to work. In 1995, *Fortune* surveyed more than two thousand of its readers and found that the average time spent working and commuting was about fifty-seven hours a week. And those were the readers who had time to answer a survey!

The point: *work is by far our most formative adult experience*. Most of us have already accumulated far more hours at the office, or in the office-oriented culture of B-school, than we ever spent awake in college or high school, for example. (When I say "office" in this book, I mean workplaces in general. It could be a farm, a store, or a factory floor without altering the central truths.) That tally doesn't even include the monstrous swaths of time we've spent away from work but reading about it, either in office papers or E-mail or trade magazines, or of course the *Wall Street Journal* or *Fortune* or *Forbes* or *Business Week*. Except for time spent with our own parents, work has been the major influence on our world view and way of functioning. We are, like it or not, creatures of the work environment. As Bruce F., CEO of a fast-growing Virginia training company, told me, "When I get home from the office, I've been using my business skills all day, managing different kinds of people. It's all I have to fall back on. It's who I am."

Can these skills really help us as dads? After all, one of the obstacles I mentioned earlier was that home and office are diametrically opposite in some ways, and that transferring behavior blindly from one to the other is a recipe for disaster. In other, more fundamental ways, however, the two are getting more similar every day. On the home front, things are getting a little more regimented, a little more complicated, as kids' activities multiply and as many of their moms work hours rivaling Dad's. (Last definition: when I say "work," it's just shorthand for paid work. A major reason for this book is that parenting entails work at least as hard as you'll find in any office. Ask any stay-at-home mom why she decided not to "work," and you'll be lucky not to get socked.)

Meanwhile, those working moms are bringing their influence into the office. As anyone outside of academia knows, women are different from men. Many have brought with them to the corporate world a more collaborative, less hierarchical, more psychologically astute way of interacting. Not that women crave power and success any less than we do, mind you. They just define those goals a little differently and have different methods of reaching them. Some try to act just like men in the workplace, but most have blazed their own trails, causing management mavens like Tom Peters to postulate that women are actually better businesspeople. The business magazines have been chronicling the results for decades: as women have risen and proliferated throughout our companies, they have brought with them a sweeping cultural change, one that makes the workplace a little more like, well, like family.

At the same time, the nature of work itself has changed. Communications technology has helped to flatten organizational structures. Thanks to reengineering, business processes have become more integrated and less departmentalized, so teams requiring elaborate minicultures, workflow diagrams, and "groupware" have become the basic fabric of many organizations. Most companies are evolving into "adhocracies," in which the needs of the moment determine who works with whom. Shortages of skilled workers, along with the rising cost of replacing and training workers in a knowledge-intensive environment, are making it ever more important to keep people happy and motivated. The changes go beyond any one corporation: companies and even industries have grown more interdependent, giving rise to webs of strategic partnerships, consulting disciplines like "bionomics," and new models for business relationships such as "co-opetition" and outsourcing.

John Doerr is arguably the leading venture capitalist of the 1990s. He has aided and abetted the early successes of Sun Microsystems, Intuit, Netscape, and @Home—and those are just some of the big ones. When this pleasant, unassuming agent of change talks, smart people really listen, more than they ever did in those old E. F. Hutton commercials. To illustrate the kind of social and industrial shifts I'm talking about, I'm including below a widely discussed slide that John often includes in his presentations at business schools and financial conferences:

OLD Economy	NEW Economy
A skill	Lifelong learning
Managers	Entrepreneurs
Labor vs. mgt.	Teams

Monopolies	Competition
Wages	Ownership, options
Hierarchical	Networked
Sues	Invests
Status quo	Speed, change

As the headhunters keep telling us, the skills that took execs to the top thirty years ago are only a small part of the portfolio we now need, and people skills and information management are playing ever-growing roles. One result is that *skills that help people function in families now help them in the office as well*.

How often have you read interviews with successful women executives, women practically fawned over by the business press, who attribute their meteoric rises to skills first learned at home? It's always the same story. "Once you've survived a birthday party full of four-year-olds," they say, "handling the board of directors doesn't pose much of a challenge." Or, "Once you've persuaded your twins to clean their room, you've got what it takes to reorganize a department." And you know what? They're right.

Pat Fili, president of the ABC television network, provided a recent example in a November 1998 *Forbes* interview. "Does being a mom make me a better manager? Oh, yes. It's perfected my negotiating skills." Sally Helgesen, in her book *The Female Advantage: Women's Ways of Leadership*, takes note of how parenthood has helped women executives.

> Increasingly, motherhood is being recognized as an excellent school for managers, demanding many of the same skills: organization, pacing, the balancing of conflicting claims, teaching, guiding, leading, monitoring, handling disturbances, imparting information . . . As Barbara Grogan [founder and president of Western Industrial Contractors] put it, "If you can figure out which one gets the gumdrop, the four-year-old or the six-year-old, you can negotiate any contract in the world."

Well, what's good for the goose, as they say, is good for the gander. If women can exploit skills and mindsets they learned at their mothers' knees to get ahead in corporate America, why can't we use the skills that work has ingrained in us to become the fathers we want to be?

None of the skills and abilities you need as a father are likely to fall outside your daily work experience, and you've probably read about them at length in business bestsellers like Andy Grove's *Only the Paranoid Survive*, Stephen Covey's *The Seven Habits of Highly Effective People*, Geoffrey Moore's *Crossing the Chasm*, and Robert Cooper and Ayman Sawaf's *Executive EQ: Emotional Intelligence in Leadership and Organizations*. Scott Adams's *The Dilbert Principle*, by contrast, does a great job lampooning managers who lack those skills, portraying them as laughable morons. Pick up any business magazine, and you'll find case histories of successful applications of the skills, together with horror stories about clueless CEOs who forgot them.

Although you may have developed those skills and abilities for business, you may find them even handier at home. Don't get the idea, though, that the skills transfer has to run all one way. As we'll discuss fully in the Dual Titles chapter, the fact is that better dads make better businessmen as well. One simple reason is that better dads are likely to be happier dads, so they function better at work. More fundamentally, though, skills and abilities are like muscles: if you don't use them, they atrophy. Giving your fathering skills good, regular workouts will make them strong and vibrant when you get to the office, where you need them every bit as much.

Whether you're striving to succeed in business, fathering, sports, or war, the key to success lies in your mind more than in your technical skills. And the difficulty of the mind work in parenting really can make the office seem simple. *Forbes* has quoted microchip pioneer Federico Faggin as saying, "It would take all the transistors manufactured by the semiconductor industry in a single year to build something rivaling the complexity of the human brain." Teach yourself to navigate the convolutions of your child's amazing brain, where your success counts more than anywhere else in the world, and you may be pleasantly surprised by how far your newly enhanced abilities also carry you at work.

The Mission

Challenge and opportunity can act like two volatile chemicals: put them together the right way, and something dramatic happens. All it takes is a little experimentation, which I hope this book will encourage. Here is my mission, plain and simple:

- Help good businessmen use their skills to be great fathers, and vice versa.
- Use language that businessmen can relate to, not psychobabble.
- Rely on common sense and experience.
- Address the special issues that businessmen face in trying to be dads.
- Make it fun.

As you may have guessed by now, I'm no certified expert on fathering. I'm not a psychologist, nor do I play one on TV. I have no professional stake in this book, no theoretical axes to grind. Nor am I a professional writer. All I am is a far-from-perfect business dad with a few strong views (well, maybe more than a few) and the chutzpah to put them on paper.

After grad school in economics, I spent eight years doing corporate finance at Salomon Brothers (now part of Citigroup); took a leave of absence to serve as assistant to the mayor of New York City; and for four years now have been enjoying my favorite job yet, as venture capitalist at a firm with more than $6 billion under management. Corny though it sounds, I really do get a kick out of helping small companies grow and contribute to the economy. I have had the privilege of serving on eight corporate boards and two nonprofit boards. (Some of the corporate boards were nonprofit also, but not intentionally!) One great part of this job is interacting with people from just about every industry you can think of, big companies and small, so I've been exposed to lots of fascinating work environments and company cultures.

That's the business part. The dad part is that I've got two terrific kids, Benjamin and Leila. (I am also the proud uncle of three nieces and three nephews, whom I have watched grow up nearby.) I have certainly made at least my share of mistakes, both in business and as a father. I hope in this book to share some of what I have learned and am still learning.

Don't get me wrong: I'm not suggesting you ignore what the experts have to say. After all, they are often smart, sensitive people who've thought a lot about fathering. Some of them lean a bit too far toward theory, as opposed to practice. (Theory and practice have never had much to do with each other. In the 1670s, the Earl of Rochester wrote, "Before I got married I had six theories about bringing up children. Now I have six children and no theories.") Most of their work, however, incorporates extensive conversations with real dads, and includes specific examples we can learn from. Reading about the accumulated wisdom of many dads can be worthwhile, as is reading a book by clever consultants who have distilled the views of many businessmen. I do recommend some titles in the Appendix.

But please keep in mind that most fathering experts are Ph.D. types, and the life experience and outlook of Ph.D.'s are different from those of businessmen—not better or worse, necessarily, just different. As a result, they may find it difficult to express things in ways we would, or to address realistically some issues like the conflicts between work and family. Most important, they do not know enough about your daily life to realize what skills your job may already have given you, or how those skills relate to your tasks at home. That's why I wrote this book.

Thinking about the issues in this book and reading the experts have yielded the unexpected but pleasant side effect of increasing my own confidence as a father. Even more beneficial, however, have been the many conversations I've had with other business dads (and some business moms). Anecdotes and ideas have come pouring forth, reassuring me that the issues have relevance for all of us. Talking through these somewhat personal topics has also turned out to be a wonderful way of deepening those business relationships! I have never failed to learn something, or to be impressed at the conscientiousness and ingenuity these business parents exhibit in the face of daunting challenges. On the specific subject of work-family conflict, I have also benefited greatly from the suggestions of experts such as Marcia Kropf of Catalyst, Jim Levine of the Fatherhood Project, and Deborah Holmes of Ernst & Young.

To some extent, this book stands as a tribute to my late father, Dr. Leonard S. Hirschfeld, who taught his sons, by instruction and especially by example, more than could fill a thousand volumes. Not surprisingly, he stars in many of the anecdotes. If there's anything in this book that hits home, anything that touches on the truth, any glimpse of what it really means to be a father, it probably came from my dad, that warm yet dignified quintessential mensch.

You've probably noticed another name on the cover — a highly experienced, practicing Ph.D. in clinical psychology, no less. Wasn't this book supposed to be written by a nonexpert? Julie, though, is not merely an expert with a specialty in family therapy; she is also my wife. I am lucky that she has been willing to act as a collaborator and in-house quality control manager at each stage of this process — adding balance, providing insights and information, and basically laboring mightily to save me from saying too many things that were completely and outstandingly stupid, dangerous, and wrong.

Julie is about as far from the business stereotype of the theory-driven psychologist as one could imagine. She is deeply pragmatic and utterly grounded in reality, both in her family therapy work and in her private life. I am profoundly grateful to her not just for her many contributions to this book, but also for being my beloved partner for nearly twenty years. Learning from and with her has helped shape the basic outlook that informs this book — making me a better father and, I am convinced, a more successful businessman and human being than I could have been without her.

That being said, this book is mine. I conceived it, I wrote it (with extremely helpful guidance from my editor, Michael Pietsch, and his colleagues), and whatever horrible mistakes Julie has not managed to catch are mine, mine, mine. As a result, this is a fairly personal work. People tend to generalize from their own experience, so what I think holds true across the board may be the opposite of your situation. That depends on you, your wife, your kids, your job, and a host of other factors. I've tried not to be too parochial, but as the saying goes, "The problem with people who know everything is, they don't know anything else." At least I know that I don't know what I don't know—which is a lot. Advice is not "one size fits all," but needs to be adjusted to the dimensions of the user. Take whatever's useful, then, from this book, and leave the rest behind.

You may notice that I've written from the viewpoint of a "traditional" two-parent family, mostly since that's what I know best. If you live apart from your kids, or their mother's not around, or you've got a "blended" family with kids from more than one marriage, I hope you'll still find much in the book that's relevant. If anything, such extra challenges may make the skills described herein even more necessary.

In addition to avoiding academic theory, this book makes no attempt to detail the nuts and bolts of parenting, such as childproofing, toilet training, or recommended-reading lists for six-year-olds. This is a book for business dads, after all, and the most popular business books typically explore people and strategy issues such as management philosophy, information flow, and growth planning, rather than technical fields such as financial reporting, quality assurance, and media planning.

An important note: *please do not infer that mastering technical skills somehow lies outside your scope of responsibility.* Remember that nuts and bolts, however prosaic, are what hold things together. You should definitely take the time to pore through those general parenting books along with your wife, so you can be an equal part of every important child-rearing decision. Otherwise, everyone in your family will regret it.

Consider this book an executive briefing for a huge new assignment. If you got transferred overnight to a new department, wouldn't you want to learn as much as you could about it, to get as many points of view as possible? Maybe you'd seek out others from your old department who'd already been moved, getting the skinny on what's different and what's the same. And once you'd been there for a while, you still might want to compare notes with other old hands, just to make sure you hadn't missed any "best practices." Well, this book is meant to be read in the same spirit, and fatherhood is your strange, wonderful, challenging assignment.

Remember: there may be no such job as professional father, but the most electrifying work throughout history has come from amateurs, those nuts who excel for the sheer love of what they do. (*Amateur* is a French word for lover, after all.) And where can we find greater love than what we naturally feel for our kids? However high the obstacles for business dads may seem, that love will *always* carry us through—if we let it. So let's hear it for inspired amateurs!

Dad, Inc.

Transferable Skills

Today's multinational conglomerate seems about as different from the family as a briefcase is from a diaper bag. The fundamental *principles* of business, however, go back long before the invention of large-scale enterprise, which is primarily an innovation of the industrial revolution. Before then, most commerce was conducted through mom-and-pop business units such as farms, inns, stores, and craft shops, which were small and typically based in or near the home. In those days, just about every industry was a cottage industry.

In the small businesses of yore, women and children were closer to the conduct of business, and men were typically around for more of the child rearing. Okay, maybe the Occupational Safety and Health Administration would have raised an eyebrow at the ten-year-old apprentice handling his blacksmith dad's bellows, but at least fathers had more occasion to spend time with their kids. With the introduction of heavy industry, men began to work defined shifts in big places away from their homes. Everything began to get scheduled; it's no coincidence that the industrial revolution closely followed the invention and proliferation of reliable clocks. A wall gradually arose between men's work lives and their home lives. Today, most Americans work in the service sector, and offices have taken their place alongside factory floors, but work and home lives are still seen as separate and, more and more, as conflicting.

In the fifties, many corporations styled themselves as one big happy family, and the Organization Man felt an almost filial loyalty to the company that had nurtured and matured him. Having a wife and kids helped him climb the ladder, since they were seen as signs of stability. The lines between company and family were blurs, not barricades.

All that has changed as stability has lost its chic, in employers as well as employees. Corporations now lay off twenty-year veterans with a nonchalance that would be cruel if it were more personal, while individuals have quite reasonably responded by swapping loyalty for opportunism. Now that professionals have to manage their own careers as if they were each minibusinesses unto themselves, hard work and flexibility are valued more by employers than constancy. In this age of "personal branding" as career survival strategy, we are all entrepreneurs, whether we like it or not.

Those trends have made children impediments rather than improvements in bosses' eyes. Thirty years ago, it would have been unthinkable for *Fortune* to run a cover story called "Is Your Family Wrecking Your Career (And Vice Versa)?" Yet that very headline was emblazoned on the March 17, 1997, cover, directly over a photo of a crying baby clinging to Mom's and Dad's forward-striding, business-suited legs.

The ironic part is, the transformation of each household into a little enterprise to be managed and planned highlights the basic similarities between families and firms. Yet family is used less and less as a metaphor for business, with the common analogies divided instead among sports, war, and mind games like chess. This is unfortunate, because family is clearly more central to most individuals and to society as a whole.

William Pollack, a psychologist writing in the *Harvard Business Review*, has performed long-running studies of businessmen that measure professional success and closeness with their kids. He has discovered a strong positive correlation between the two, which he attributes to "a considerable overlap between the skills for fathering and corporate leadership." As he explains it:

> Certainly, modern leaders and managers, male and female, need creative vision, emotional flexibility, and independent decision-making capacity, along with the ability to work within systems, creative networks, and teams. They must also be able to rally support and achieve results in the midst of almost constant organizational change. My consulting experience and research have shown that, for men, those very skills are the ones most successfully learned and mastered by the well-adapted father.

If you don't have the *HBR* March–April 1994 issue lying around, don't worry. A cursory glance at the business section of your local bookstore will confirm the same point about what drives success in the corporate world. Most of the books, especially the bestsellers, promise to make you the master of skills such as persuasion, planning, negotiating, values creation, information collection, and working with difficult people. What none of them mention, of course, is how to bring those newly burnished abilities home from the office.

The skills and abilities that business and fatherhood have in common depend on the right combination of temperament, effort, and most of all *habit*. Habit is what determines our actions when we don't have time to deliberate, which occurs all too often both in the office and at home. Habits are so deeply ingrained that they can be tough to learn or change, yet they come into play so frequently that they often make the difference between fame and fiasco. As John Dryden wrote, "We first make our habits, then our habits make us."

The best businessmen, not wanting to rely on habit, have enough self-restraint to avoid managing on autopilot. But sometimes events just happen too quickly, or an issue doesn't seem important enough to think through carefully, or habit kicks in and we don't even realize it. Luckily, most of us have had years of experience and training in which to cultivate the best habits for administering employees. Inside our own households, however, we lack even the nine months our wives get to prepare for managing kids. The crux of this book is that *we can't and shouldn't remake ourselves from scratch to become effective fathers.* Instead, we should take the habits, managerial and otherwise, that we've already internalized successfully at the office, and open ourselves to the idea of using them at home.

What are the specific skills and abilities business dads can apply to fathering? They are best organized according to how we use them. Our lives at the office are basically spent performing four activities: *gathering information, making decisions* based on that information, *executing those decisions*, and *managing others* to do the same. Each activity requires a different set of skills and abilities, which are anything but obscure. They are tools we use every day, and they just happen to be perfectly suited for raising happy, healthy, successful kids.

Skills and Abilities Used in Gathering Information

Information is the lifeblood of every business. Nearly every big company now has a chief information officer, and some (Ernst & Young, for example) even have a chief knowledge officer to boot. Information is so valuable that many corporations have spent tens of millions on vast "data warehouse" systems to store it. You probably spend most of your workday absorbing information in one form or another. But do you pay as much attention to what's going on in your family as in your business? If the answer is no, don't be surprised if you feel smarter when you're at the office.

• **Listening.** This is a basic corporate survival skill. We have to listen to our bosses, our customers, our colleagues, and just about everyone else we encounter on the job. Even if we're bored, listening shows respect, and we might actually learn something important. Why else were we given two ears and only one mouth?

Listening counts even more at home, because our kids often have more important things to say than our associates—and fewer people they can tell.

• **Learning.** Your career either moves forward or dies. Survival requires *continuous* learning—about your products, customers, people, competitors, and industry, and about the other industries with which yours is converging (or colliding). Cobwebs in your brain will block you from winning that next promotion—and, similarly, from being an effective father. Your kids and family, too, change every time you blink. In both business and fathering, keeping up is a whole lot easier than catching up.

• **Experimentation.** Management guru Tom Peters says, "If you're committed to innovation, you've got to have a very high tolerance for risk *and* failure." If you're not making mistakes at work, you're not learning anything; conversely, mistakes are wasted if they don't make you smarter. Karl Marx wasn't much of a businessman, but he had a good point about history repeating itself: the first time as tragedy, the second time as farce. As a father, never failing means you're stuck in a rut—but in your trial and error, tracking results will keep the farce to a minimum.

• **Empathy.** Listening takes you a long way, but actually showing you understand gets you even further. For one thing, understanding helps you make better decisions. For another, if people feel understood (or if they feel that you *want* to understand), they'll tell you more. Not incidentally, they'll believe you care about them and what they say. That's never a bad thing, at home or at work.

• **Management by walking around.** It would be nice if subordinates and children always came to us with their problems and concerns, but they don't. Sometimes they're shy, sometimes they're embarrassed, and sometimes they don't even know something's wrong. Big problems at home or work, like big forest fires, usually start small. If we don't gather data dynamically, scanning for those little signs of trouble, we get blindsided.

• **Critical thinking.** Thomas Watson, the legendary CEO of IBM, never took that famous THINK sign down from his wall. Business situations are rarely black and white, and accepting superficial appearances or jumping to the wrong conclusion can undo twenty great decisions. If you have too little information, keep on asking questions. The more you ask at home or work, the more thought people will know you've put into it, so the more they'll accept your judgment. In both environments, brilliant decisions only *look* simple.

Skills and Abilities Used in Making Decisions

"Quick! What should we do?" Once you've gathered enough information (or as much as you realistically can), it's time to put your image on the line with a bold decision—or not. Sometimes, at home or at work, inaction is a decision in itself. If it's the *wrong* decision, then crisp, vigorous, and clearly explained movement is the only way. Neither kids nor the office troops have much faith in wafflers. That is why *Business Week* quoted a consultant praising General Electric's Jack Welch as follows: "Welch will say yes. Welch will say no. But he never says maybe. A lot of CEOs do, and decisions lay there like three-legged horses that no one wants to shoot."

• **Planning.** In the midst of accelerating change, both short-range and long-range planning count even more. You have to plan for tomorrow (whether your goal is to make a big PR splash at the trade show or to keep the kids occupied in the car for four hours), while also making strategic decisions whose implications lie years away (whether it's selling a minority stake to the Germans or switching away from your kids' school because instruction stinks in the upper grades).

Wherever you're making decisions, you have to strike the right balance between short term and long term. Jack Welch says, "You can't grow long-term if you can't eat short-term. Anybody can manage short. Anybody can manage long. Balancing those two things is what management is." That is equally true of business and child raising. Preventive maintenance is usually cheaper than disaster recovery, and indulging kids' every wish in the short run guarantees they'll be miserable over time.

In business, of course, different people have different time frames. Bond traders' horizons may extend to that day's close of business, investment bankers seldom follow offerings for more than six months after closing, venture capitalists stay involved in their portfolio companies for five or seven years, whereas sole proprietors care for decades. I would argue that the right time frame for raising kids is a lifetime—theirs, not yours.

• **Creativity.** Business books sing the praises of innovation and "out of the box" thinking, with good reason. Not only can they jump-start sales, improve operations, and resolve conflicts, but they make you more fun to work with. Whether you're sitting at your desk or your dining room table, nothing cuts through problems like a sharp idea you somehow pull out of nowhere.

• **Proactivity.** Trip Hawkins wasn't satisfied with his midlevel job at Apple in 1982, but he didn't know quite where to go with his career. One day, while waiting for an opportunity to come along, he took inspiration from a cartoon on his office wall. It showed two vultures sitting on a branch, with one saying, "I'm tired of waiting around. Let's go kill something!" Trip realized he could make his own opportunities and left Apple to become the founding CEO of Electronic Arts, which today sells $700 million worth of video games a year. (He later stumbled at 3DO, but that's another story.)

In business, you don't succeed by reacting to external stimuli like some paramecium on a slide, nor by waiting until you are forced to make decisions. Similarly, father power depends on *action*, not reaction.

• **Comfort with chaos.** Gone are the days of our fathers, when the competitive landscape seemed to shift in geological time. Now the plate tectonics have gone haywire, and companies that are on the summit one day can find themselves under water the next. (Not only in high tech is this true: in his fascinating *Value Migration*, for example, Adrian Slywotzky tells how competition from the Japanese, minimills, aluminum, and plastic whittled Big Steel's combined market capitalization from $55 billion in 1960 to a mere $13 billion in 1993.) Today's business climate is a maelstrom, and thus almost as crazy and confused as most homes with kids.

• **Solving root problems.** You don't have to be a shrink to know that people can underperform for unspoken reasons. If your star saleswoman mysteriously can't sell unit one of your latest product, could it be that she doesn't trust the product manager? These things are essential to know and address directly. Now maybe you're ready to tackle Junior's math phobia.

• **Crisis management.** Managers often score major points by performing well when the chips are down. Staying calm and competent in a crisis, whether your production line has gone down or your child's temperature has gone up, can improve your standing long after the crisis itself has passed. Many people in business remember how well Johnson & Johnson handled its Tylenol scare in 1982 — and what a mess, by contrast, Intel made of its Pentium bug in 1995. By creating the right team spirit, planning, and support network *before* a family crisis happens, you can make the right decisions once it hits, thus minimizing the damage. You and your family may even emerge closer than ever.

Skills and Abilities Used in Executing Decisions

Making decisions is meaningless, of course, if you can't execute them properly. The history of corporate failure is littered with the carcasses of plans that woulda, coulda, shoulda worked, but for lack of follow-through. Murphy's law guarantees that you can't manage a company, let alone a child, from even the best-upholstered armchair.

Achieving lasting success, in your career and in your family, is a decades-long marathon. Like any long-distance race, it requires you to sprint now and then, to take the occasional pit stop, to pace yourself the rest of the time, but above all to stay on course. As with decision making, the skills and abilities for executing reflect a constant balancing act between short term and long term, between sprinting and reaching the ultimate finish line, between getting it done quickly and getting it done right.

• **Efficiency.** The only way to make the most of a scarce resource like time is to dole it out more rationally — that's why they call it "rationing." Prioritization, organization, and disciplined time management can make the difference between mediocrity and excellence. They count even more for our home life, since we spend much less time with our kids than at the office.

• **Reliability.** It's hard to accomplish much without being trusted. People need to know that you're honest, you follow through on promises, and you're consistent in your views and practices. If that requirement is self-evident at work, it should be even more so at home. Kids need a father who's dependable, a dad they can count on.

• **Self-Restraint.** It's hard to control a company or a family until you've learned to control yourself. That means thinking before you speak, considering others in addition to yourself, and doing what feels right instead of what feels good. Self-restraint actually makes a lot of selfish sense: you will avoid doing anything hasty or short-sighted, and you'll set the right example for people *you've* got to live with.

• **Delegation.** A key part of executing decisions at work is knowing when to let go. Some tasks are too critical to delegate, whereas others would actually take longer to explain and follow up on than to do yourself. Similarly, as a father you face constant temptation to save time by delegating child rearing to your wife, nanny, TV set, or computer, but some things simply need a dad.

• **Negotiation.** As those ads in the airline magazines say, "You don't get what you deserve, you get what you negotiate." It doesn't matter whether you're dealing with people on the same team or not—everything in business is a transaction, and transactions must be negotiated. Family is different, thanks to your kids' love and respect for you, your power over their lives, and the virtues you try to instill, but let's face it: those three don't work every time. When all else fails, the only way to direct their behavior is negotiation.

• **Respect.** Businesspeople have pretty good radar for contempt and condescension. If you give associates reason to suspect you of either, you will find them strangely uncooperative. Likewise, if you treat kids with respect (which you can do without treating them like adults), they'll reward you by acting more respectable. If you skimp on the respect (by ignoring them, talking down to them, or calling them names, for instance), be assured they will notice and react. In the car, for example, "Young man, I'd like you to put your feet down this minute!" works better than "Get your feet off the back of my seat, you brat!" Kids who are treated like Rodney Dangerfield will act like him, too.

Skills and Abilities Used in Managing Others

No dad is an island, and the same goes for businessmen. You can gather all the *information* you like, make the wisest *decisions*, and deliver the finest individual *execution*, but you'll still fall flat on your face if you fail to *manage* others well. Once you rise above entry level, you can't avoid the terrible vulnerability of depending on other people to do things for which you will be held accountable. If your subordinates consistently underperform, sooner or later *you* get penalized. Society treats parents the same way; if your children become felons, people will wonder what *you* did wrong. The Greek philosopher Diogenes, who took this to extremes, actually would strike a father if his son swore. Though that attitude may not have gotten Diogenes invited to many parties, it persists in diluted form today.

• **Motivation.** Paychecks may put food on the table, but they're not enough to get the "above and beyond" efforts you need from your people. The need for nonmonetary incentives has spawned an entire industry of motivational posters, mugs, and tie clips, but even they are just meaningless bric-a-brac without inspirational management. If you're the CEO, you've got to make it stand for Cheerleading and Excitement Officer. This is great training for motivating your kids, who don't even get paychecks, and whose allowances go only so far. They'll need every pep talk you can muster if they're going to tackle that grueling, lifelong steeplechase known euphemistically as the pursuit of happiness.

• **Authority.** Your title of Vice President or Dad may give you the right to lay down orders, but as you've discovered by now, getting them obeyed is another matter entirely. That depends on the authority that people sense in you. Wielding discipline fairly, with clear positive and negative incentives, is one means of establishing your authority. Listening, empathy, reliability, and self-restraint are others. Without authority, you can't resolve conflicts in the office or at home, and you can't get what you want when you want it. Where would that leave you?

John P., a former Navy man who has two grown daughters and now sells unmanned aircraft to various governments, tells me that authority does not come automatically even in that supposedly authoritarian enterprise, the armed forces. "People have this stereotype of the armed forces as some dictatorial environment, where everyone does what you tell them. That's just not so. I don't care where you are — in the military, in business, or in parenting — you can't get people to do what you want without personnel skills."

• **Tolerance.** Being the disciplinarian has its place, but you also need to know when to let the little things slide. Irritability and rigid perfectionism cause too many distractions for everyone, and they don't do wonders for your authority either — as demonstrated by Captains Bligh of the *Bounty* and Queeg of the *Caine*, both from books with the word "mutiny" in their titles. At work, a bit of patience saves you frustration and employee turnover; at home, it may save your family.

Any businessman who's managed creative types, such as art directors or software engineers, comes well equipped for dealing with toddlers or adolescents. Just as creative types define themselves partly as *not* being like us "suits," toddlers and adolescents will do whatever they can to build and protect their identities independent of us, their awful parents. And yet, they imitate us too, and sometimes have crushes on us. The quickest way to convert the amazing energy of both kids and creative types away from control battles and toward positive feelings is to mix firmness with a bit of tolerance and understanding.

• **Values.** Every company and every family has a culture, knowingly or not. As manager and father, you help decide whether to preside over a strong culture that fits with the values you believe in, or a weak, default culture whose values are random. Which do you think is likely to work better?

• **Mentoring.** Mentoring at work is morally right, especially if you've benefited from it on your way up. Also, it's smart, since you get better work product and build a steady base of support. Both statements apply tenfold to helping your kids—not helping them to become what you are or wish you were or hope they'll be, but rather helping them to become all *they* can be.

• **Team building.** Managers become former managers if they can't guide their people into functioning as a team. It's even harder getting two siblings to cooperate, but it's more important, since you're preparing them for life in a world full of potential friends or rivals. The psalmists weren't thinking of just the nuclear family when they wrote, "Behold, how good and how pleasant it is for brethren to dwell together in unity!"

• **Leadership.** Leadership is that intangible, incalculable mix of vision and charisma that impels people to scale glass mountains, fill bottomless pits, and hack their way through forests of thorns—in short, to achieve the most absurdly, preposterously difficult tasks imaginable. IBM, for example, was a shambles when Lou Gerstner took over and declared, "The last thing this company needs is a vision." Yet now it has ascended like a phoenix from the ashes, soaring on the wings of, yes, a vision, Gerstner's vision, of the network computer as a tool for "eBusiness."

Families need leadership just as desperately as companies, but in neither case does leadership happen overnight. You must lay the groundwork of trust, establish your legitimacy, and make sure you and your followers share the same basic ideas. Education is thus both a function and a foundation of leadership. As John F. Kennedy wrote in the speech he never got to deliver on November 22, 1963, "Leadership and learning are indispensable to each other."

So there you have them: the top skills and abilities without which smart businessmen act dumb, Mr. Right makes the wrong decisions, executives can't execute, and managers can't manage.

Consider this question: where do you find yourself using the skills and abilities more—at home or at work? If you are like most of us, you're stronger in some at home, and in others at work. You may even be using them in both places, but with varying degrees of consciousness. Because murky emotion saturates so many conversations with your kids, though, chances are you're more conscious about applying the skills at work. If you've flourished with them there, wouldn't it be a waste not to leverage them in the other half of your life? Bring 'em on home.

So Why Are the Boss's Kids a Mess?

Given that critical thinking is a key part of gathering information, I assume that a logical question may have occurred to you by now: if business skills work so well at home, why are there so many *über*-businessmen who fail miserably with their kids? *Fortune* has highlighted this discrepancy in a blunt cover story entitled "Why Grade 'A' Executives Get an 'F' as Parents." We all know businessmen who schedule late meetings and out-of-town appointments with relief rather than reluctance, whose "face time" goes way beyond the company's expectations, who tighten their lips or sigh when asked about their kids, and who never talk about them voluntarily. Their extra hours and zeal may make them more successful than average, at least in the short run, while their kids go from bad to worse. Does that give the lie to the whole idea of transferable skills?

The superficial explanation is that their extraordinary career commitments leave less time and energy for home, but in most cases that's putting the cart before the horse. *Business dads who feel comfortable with their kids find ways to make time for them, and often advance more rapidly at work as well* (see the chapter called Dual Titles). If these Men of Steel really felt competent as fathers, you can be sure they would invest more of their time in that role. This returns us to the question: if they're such hot stuff in the conference room, why can't they perform in the playground?

The short answer is that fathering is like business—only much harder. (Did anyone ever tell you fatherhood was easy? If so, you may want to find out what planet he or she came from.) As Fred Rosen, combative former CEO of Ticketmaster, complained to *Forbes*, "You go to the office and people do whatever you say. You go home and say, do this, and the kids just look at you like, no."

Losing generals are notorious for "fighting the last war," blindly deploying whatever tactics worked last time around, and neglecting key changes in terrain, technology, or the enemy. If you march home and do exactly what produced the right results in the office, you're going to get routed.

The classic Hollywood example of that mistake is made by George Banks, the clueless banker dad in *Mary Poppins*—actually a pretty subversive flick for its day. George begins the film spouting false parallels such as "A British bank is run with precision. A British home requires nothing less!" Needless to say, his kids fear and distrust him until the lady with the umbrella sets him straight. But there are all too many real-life examples, as well—like Joe K. Joe is a successful movie executive who told me, "Sure, child raising is just like business. When my daughters ask me for something, I make them give me a kiss before I say yes." In business, it may work never to give without getting something in exchange (a doubtful assertion itself), but that strategy will certainly fail at home.

The following table summarizes the adjustments that most dads need to make in adapting their business skills to home use. As you will see, nearly all the skills and abilities listed above need to be pumped up beyond "industrial strength" for heavy-duty fathering.

Skill/Ability	At Work	At Home
Gathering information		
LISTENING	Your colleagues can typically make themselves understood.	Kids often communicate nonverbally.

LEARNING	Trade papers, company memos, and other knowledge sources cross your desk regularly.	Apart from on-the-job training, you must seek out most data.
EXPERIMEN-TATION	Risks are limited, and results are easily quantified.	The downside can be traumatic, and you may never know if the experiment worked.
EMPATHY	You share your colleagues' frame of reference.	You wouldn't understand. It's a kid thing.
WALKING AROUND	Passing by colleagues' cubicles on the way from the water cooler seems perfectly natural.	Entering a teenager's bedroom uninvited can be foolhardy.
CRITICAL THINKING	Intellectual curiosity helps you.	Probing deeper can be taken as an affront.

Making decisions

PLANNING	Your colleagues are basically known quantities.	The only thing predictable about kids is rapid change.
CREATIVITY	The only skill that is harder in the workplace.	Kids instinctively reward creativity.
PROACTIVITY	Business rewards bold strokes.	Kids have so many needs that even just reacting can be a challenge.

COMFORT WITH CHAOS	Chaos may lurk, but it is usually polite enough to wait outside your office. Your training helps.	Chaos lives with you and demands your attention at inconvenient times. There is no training possible.
SOLVING ROOT PROBLEMS	Colleagues usually admit the real issue if pressed.	Kids often can't tell you what the real issue is.
CRISIS MANAGEMENT	Crises come and go. You're used to them by now.	In home crises, "life or death situation" is not always a metaphor.

Executing decisions

EFFICIENCY	Colleagues reinforce your effort with their own. They respect efficiency.	Kids are not built for efficiency. They neither understand it nor trust it.
RELIABILITY	Mood swings at the office can usually be hidden.	Kids make a science out of studying your moods.
SELF-CONTROL	You've learned to be on best behavior.	Isn't home where you can be yourself?
DELEGATION	You've got secretaries, staffers, subordinates, interns . . .	Fatherhood can't be delegated.
NEGOTIATION	Both sides tend to act rational.	Emotion surfaces often.
MORAL SUASION	People see your point of view.	Kids seem to go from not understanding you to rejecting you.

RESPECT	Adults appreciate your respect.	Kids think respect means letting them do whatever they want.

Managing others

MOTIVATION	You can offer money, recognition, perks, and time off.	You never know when your approval will cause them to do the opposite of what you want.
AUTHORITY	There's an implicit contract. Insubordinates can be fired.	Kids never asked to be born. Firing them is not an option.
TOLERANCE	Subordinates try to act compliant and respectful.	Kids know just how to annoy you and delight in pushing your buttons.
VALUES	Business values are somewhat circumscribed.	Parents are held responsible for teaching their children all possible virtues.
MENTORING	Protégés take your advice to heart, or appear to.	Kids take your advice for granted, or appear to.
TEAM BUILDING	Subordinates see the logic of working together.	Remember Cain and Abel?
LEADERSHIP	Your colleagues share your basic agenda— growing the business, getting paid, and having fun.	Your agenda includes your kids' lives, on which they have their own views.

The skills and abilities in the table are essential for success at home and at work, but they're generally harder to apply at home. Logically, this means your best strategy for succeeding at home is to leverage off the progress you've made at work. *The key is not to act exactly the same in both places, but to apply the same principles to each.* Don't think that because Michael Jordan bombed at baseball, you can't succeed in *both* of the most important roles in your life.

The Org Chart

Your Assignment

When I was at Salomon Brothers, CEO John Gutfreund used to exhort us troops to "be ready to bite the ass off a bear" when we came into work each day. Demanding as our work may be, power fathering requires an even greater level of determination. Luckily, its rewards more than match the demands it makes.

Okay, we're determined, and we know that we as business dads have special secret weapons available to us in fathering. The next issue for many dads is, what exactly are fathers supposed to do? How do my wife and I split responsibilities? In corp-speak, where do I fit in on the organization chart?

You may not realize this, but even young kids learn to draw fairly accurate org charts. They may not look exactly like the charts you see at work, but, like most communications from kids, all that's required is a little translation. Here is a typical family org chart as it might be rendered by a five-year-old whose father is out of the loop:

That's fairly clear, isn't it? Kids draw important things to be bigger and more central on the page. This dad may stand six feet four, but in his kid's life, he makes a small impact. Kids love to draw: it gives them new ways to express themselves. If this kid's dad were to see this picture, maybe a coin would drop and he'd get the message.

To see the same division of parenting responsibilities expressed in more businesslike adult terms, take a look at the conventional organization chart below:

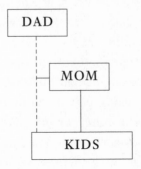

Dad seems kind of off center, doesn't he? And notice the dotted line indicating remoteness. This drawing approximates the positions many dads held under the old paradigm described in the first chapter, where Mom had principal responsibility for the kids, and Dad could be a good family man just by bringing home the bacon and swatting the kids when they needed discipline. Apart from some baseball training if he had a son, the nurturing part of parenting was simply not Dad's job.

The TV show may have been called *Father Knows Best*, but many dads didn't feel they needed to know much at all about their kids' daily lives. If that org chart had titles spelled out, Mom would be both chief executive officer and chief operating officer. In some matters Dad may have had final word as chairman of the board (and was certainly considered the head of the household), but his input into parenting was often minimal. In extreme cases, his executive role was reduced to VP of finance and compliance. Is that the position you want to occupy in your family?

In some ways, it was easier in the old days. Mom and Dad knew their places, so they didn't have to think about what was expected of them. Now we can all choose, so the division of labor depends on complex, ongoing negotiations among all parties concerned. Men are getting mixed signals from society: some people demand more of fathers than they used to, while others still view us as appendages. It's Mom, after all, not Dad, who gets top billing in America, along with baseball and apple pie. As recently as 1998, a major study by the National Institute of Child Health and Human Development, which tracked the impact of differing amounts of child care on toddlers' development, included "time spent with father" in the definition of "time spent in child care"!

How, then, to navigate fatherhood in today's climate? Many of us, unfortunately, were taught that the nitty-gritty of parenting was women's work—that taking part in it would be somehow unmanly and could in fact compromise our masculinity. That is part of the reason men's magazines have few articles on parenting, while women's magazines are filled with them. Some men still view kids as "a women's thing," sometimes even as "something she wanted" (biological clocks may have something to do with that). When such men are forced by circumstances or maternal exasperation to watch the kids for a few hours, they nervously say they're baby-sitting or call themselves Mr. Mom, just to show that this is not really their responsibility. They love their kids, but only within somewhat narrow limits.

Personally, I think that a dad who insists he's only baby-sitting for his own kids is one sad example of wasted opportunity. My guess is that you wouldn't be reading this book if you disagreed. Unless the only mention you want your kids to hear of you all day is, "Just wait till your father comes home," you would probably rather see them draw an org chart something like this:

Or, to put it in a form that McKinsey & Co. might prefer:

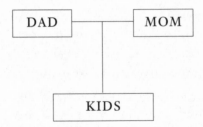

Parenting is a joint responsibility. Numerous studies of kids who have absent fathers show that the odds are stacked heavily against them, even after adjustment for factors like family income and education. Even when the father is physically present but relatively uninvolved, child-rearing experts like T. Berry Brazelton say there is a negative impact on kids' IQ, sense of humor, self-esteem, motivation to learn, and other important qualities.

The truism that two heads are better than one seems tailor-made for child raising, especially when one head is male and the other is female. Let me be perfectly clear: *being a good father does not mean learning how to mother.* Mothers are wise, mothers are wonderful, mothers are essential, but mothers are not the only parents—or the only *kind* of parents—that children need. Men and women have different ways of looking at things, as our workplace experiences demonstrate every day. Kids who are exposed to only one way, or brought up according to only one way, miss out big time. Here are a few reasons why.

Fathering Is a Man's Job

• **Dads get physical.** Roughhousing gives kids a chance to be both silly and cuddly, a winning combination to which dads are naturally disposed. It never hurts to have that kind of additional, nonverbal path toward intimacy. "Guy things" like wrestling and bouncing on the bed (and, later, playing hoops or catch together) also help boys' and girls' physical development. Kids are not so different in this respect from tiger cubs, which spend hours in playful scuffling that actually helps them practice deadly serious skills such as stalking and pouncing.

Getting physical, by the way, exemplifies perfectly why *being an involved father does not have to mean giving up an ounce of your masculinity.* Some men are concerned that acting too "nurturing" will somehow smooth their rough edges or make them less attractive to their wives. That fear may have some basis if they try to act like Assistant Mom, but not if they are true to their own natures as fathers.

• **Dads are strong.** There's a heartbreaking story about John F. Kennedy Jr. shortly after his father's funeral, when he was still known as John-John. He asked William Haddad, a family friend, "Are you a daddy?" When Haddad said yes, John-John said, "Then will you throw me up in the air?" He missed his dad, and needed something he thought only a daddy could give him.

Men typically have the upper body strength to hoist their kids high and let them imagine the giddy joy of flight. Dads can walk a mile with a child on their shoulders, a child looking down on the passing world from a vantage point of total security. Kids' lives are shadowed by the knowledge that they're weak and small, so experiencing firsthand the strength of a dad sworn to protect them gives them a warm and wonderful feeling. Even old Sigmund Freud wrote,

"I could not point to any need in childhood as strong as that for a father's protection." At age two, my son, Benjamin, was never more upset than on the day he saw me lift his six-year-old cousin onto my shoulders. That was *his* special place, and he couldn't bear the thought of sharing it.

• **Dads provide balance in protectiveness.** Kids are born adventurous into a world full of peril. Many moms, with their extra nine months' investment to protect and millennia of social conditioning behind them, tend to come down on the side of caution in restricting exploration. Kids need Dad to say, "Oh, let her walk along the top of the wall. It's not too high, and I'll catch her if she falls." (Your wife's instincts, however, may be right. Business dads make their living by taking calculated risks, but the downside is much greater when your kids' safety is on the line.)

• **Dads discipline by the rules.** It's important for both parents to be consistent in how they apply discipline (see the Conflict Resolution chapter), but gray areas often leave room for judgment calls. In those cases, some experts believe that mothers tend to make greater allowances for extenuating circumstances, the reasons or intent behind a transgression, whereas fathers tend to stick to the letter of the law. Both approaches are valuable: kids learn sensitivity and mercy from their mothers at such times, but absorb from their fathers the respect for rules that any social being requires.

• **Boys need male role models.** Boys identify with dads, all the more as they distance themselves from Mom to stake out their male identities. Without dads as models, boys risk one of two extremes, either becoming overly aggressive or failing to learn how to stand up for themselves. Boys will watch you in everything you let them: how you solve problems, how you handle frustration, how you take responsibility, how you treat women. Unless you somehow convince them otherwise, their unspoken M.O. will be, "When in doubt, do like Dad."

• **Girls need male role models.** At least once a year, I read a tribute to Dad from some world-class woman executive, who credits him with showing her how to think and act in business and in life. Studies show that girls with involved fathers perform better in math, logical reasoning, and other "male" fields. You are also your daughter's role model in another, equally important sense: as proto-type for a future husband. Girls grow up seeing their fathers as stan-dards for male behavior, so if you want her to marry well and have a happy life, act like the kind of guy you'd want her to pick. (This will also tend to make your grandchildren resemble you more!) Give her the warmth, admiration, and respect she deserves and she'll look for a husband who loves her enough to do the same. By contrast, if you act dishonest or remote or unsupportive, she will think all men are like that and adjust her expectations accordingly.

• **Kids need role models.** Not everything you pass on to kids relates to gender (yours or theirs). Virtues like honor, compassion, dignity, love, and self-discipline come not from Mars or Venus, but from Earth and Heaven. The more exemplars kids have of these virtues, the better. If you're truly involved, then you and your wife can reinforce each other's lessons, and also show the young ones how two people of goodwill lead their lives together.

Business dads seem to be particularly important role models for children who end up going into business themselves. In the 1998 edition of *The Fuqua Report*, a biennial survey of graduates from five top M.B.A. programs, the future tycoons were asked to name "the individual you most admire in the world." Dad led the pack with 11 percent—down from 16 percent in 1996, but still the clear leader—followed by Bill Gates with 5 percent, Mom with 4 percent, and Warren Buffett with 3 percent! Those same graduates were asked to rank their priorities in life, and the first six were refreshingly non-monetary: marriage, health, ethics, career, leisure, and children. Dad must have been a good influence.

Adjusting to the Job

Children need us in different ways at different times, but at no time is their need a greater shock to *us* than when they've just arrived. Wordsworth wrote about babies, ". . . not in utter nakedness, / But trailing clouds of glory do we come / From God, who is our home." I agree with this 100 percent, but can't help recalling also that our

two youngsters came in utter confusion, trailing caravans of para-
phernalia, which quickly transformed our apartment into something
resembling a maternity ward the day after a cyclone. Benjamin, with
typical baby timing, was born two days before a major investor conference that I had conceived and organized. His arrival turned our
world upside down, and neither home nor work has ever been quite
the same since. Then, just when I thought we were getting the logistics of parenting down pat, along came Leila to rearrange our
lives all over again.

Natural selection has made babies incredibly cute, with big eyes
and a devastating repertoire of coos and gurgles, so that adults would
care for them until they could fend for themselves. Don't let those
winsome qualities fool you, however. Babies are basically long-term
house guests with terrible hygiene and a habit of making insistent
demands at the wrong time.

For us business dads, they also present a new and scary set of
challenges. We are conditioned to spend our lives responding to, or
anticipating, external stimuli, and eventually we develop a kind of
"to do" addiction. We have perfected the knack of using every spare
moment to maximum advantage, but babies have nothing *but* spare
moments, in which "advantage" is hard to quantify. Babies progress
in tiny increments, which only fathers who spend a lot of time with
them can catch or appreciate. Drive-by dads may notice so little improvement that they wonder whether they're wasting their time.

Moreover, executives who excel at racing around all day fighting
fires may draw a blank when confronted with a baby, who requires
so little (feeding, changing, putting to sleep) and yet so much (soothing, playing, singing, loving). Accustomed to a life filled with "action
items," where we *are* what we *do*, business dads must learn to be
without doing—less action, less itemizing.

The feeling of being at a loss with babies manifests itself in different ways. Some business dads may feel interested but incompetent, others may feel frustrated because the job seems never to be
over, whereas others may conclude with a sneaking guilt that their
babies are just a tad, well, boring. It's ironic, but outside their natural habitats business dads can exhibit attention spans not much

longer than their children's. Many fall into the trap of withdrawing and letting their wives step in whenever there's no right answer to the businesslike question, "What do I do next?" (In other words, for most of their children's infancy.) They reason that they'll reengage once the kids can put a few words together, when there's enough intellectual content to hold their adult attention.

This is, I repeat, a trap. Men who fall into it suffer, because they miss the chance to build up trust with their babies and with the tigress moms who guard them. Knowing that they can do things like calm a crying fit gives dads a warm inner confidence, building a core of self-assurance for the rest of their parenting careers. Dads need the chance to find their own groove with each child, to become a Master of Baby Administration. Otherwise, their babies will regard them as pale imitations of the real parent, and this attitude may remain stubbornly ingrained past infancy, making itself come true if the relationship never gets off the ground. Fathers who sit out their kids' babyhood not only miss some tremendous pleasures, but also find their ignorance increasing inexorably, relative both to the skills their offspring require and to their wives' sum of knowledge, which compounds daily owing to their higher rate of interest in the kids.

If you had the gift of clairvoyance and *knew* that a certain project would eventually give rise to your company's future flagship product, and you had a chance to get involved during the early, messy stages, would you turn down that opportunity? Would you say to your colleagues, "Why don't you guys run with this for now, and give me a call when it gets really interesting?" If so, I can give you the number of a good career suicide hotline. Business dads all know well that early ownership of a key project can turn hired hands into multimillionaires — either within the original host company (Ethan Penner with asset securitization at Nomura, and Ray Ozzie with Notes at Lotus) or in offshoot ventures (Marc Andreessen with Web browsers at Netscape, which he cofounded after leaving the National Center for Supercomputing Applications, and Kim Polese with Java at Marimba, which she cofounded after leaving Sun Microsystems).

Well, in families you *do* have that clairvoyant knowledge about child raising, which is the enterprise's major project—the one that will determine its future. That is definitely one project where you will be well served to get in on the ground floor.

Just knowing that you should get involved right away, though, won't make it easy. From the moment they invade your home as little strangers, your kids need you desperately. How do you feel about that awesome responsibility? How does it feel to have another human being utterly dependent on you for current and future happiness? Although most dads have some feeling of "It's nice to be needed," there may also be an element of "I feel trapped. What happened to my life?" That claustrophobia is normal and understandable, but it is also something that we all must work through. The fact is that having kids is scary and hard and dreadfully, permanently inconvenient.

Take some time, then, to mourn your lost freedom. Learn to let go. Be honest with your family members, so you can recruit them as allies instead of guiltily seeing them as jailers. Don't expect to make the transition easily or quickly, but don't give up, either. Most of all, don't forget that you're not the only new parent in the household. If you and your wife can simply acknowledge each other's new problems as parents, chances are they will become more manageable. Each of you will feel better at having made a clean breast of it, and each of you will know how the other most needs help. At the very least, you can bolster each other's morale. Keep your sense of humor, and try reminding each other, as Virgil's hero Aeneas told his beleaguered men, "Perhaps someday it will be pleasant to remember even this." It was true about tough times two thousand years ago, and it's true today.

Even after we've made the transition to parenthood, though, we can't help feeling occasional resentment for the huge amounts of time and liberty our kids "take away" from us. It often seems the kids' needs inevitably come before ours. We can't take them to the grown-up movies we want to see, we can't concentrate on anything for long when they're in the room, it's hard to have privacy when they're around, and they pretty much determine the kinds of vacations we can take. More fundamentally, there's always something kid-related for us to think about. Parents' work is never done. As bad as it seems with one kid, the difficulty and complexity increase geometrically with each additional one, and our personal desires get crowded out more and more. Julie and I sigh occasionally when we remember how many books we used to read, movies we used to see, and dinners with friends we used to enjoy.

Have you seen the American Heart Association ads that show a bunch of childish get-well cards addressed to Daddy? The tag line is, "You love them so much you'd give up your life for them. But that's not what they want." It's an effective message, but giving up part of your life is, in a sense, *exactly* what kids need you to do—for a while. Don't worry, the time will come all too soon when the children stop being dependent on you, and you never see them enough.

Julie, who at one time taught lecture courses on family dynamics to New York University undergraduates, would occasionally describe the upheaval and rigors entailed in new parenthood. Many students, often males in business-oriented majors, would wonder why anyone in his right mind would choose to make such sacrifices. Being married to a business dad herself, she would ask, "In business, would you expect to get the big returns from small, safe investments—or from the larger, riskier ones?"

Make the investment that real fathering requires, and you will find yourself reaping ample rewards—both present and future.

Your Compensation Package

There's a joke about parenting that echoes those old Emergency Broadcast System announcements: "This job is a test. Repeat, this job is a test. Had this been an *actual* job, you would have received raises, promotions, and some sign of appreciation."

Becoming a father may require nothing more than the right

plumbing, but becoming a successful father is one of the hardest things you will ever attempt. And what does it get you? No fat bonus, no all-expenses-paid boondoggles, not even a gold watch every ten years. Your employer pays you a lot more than some sticky Father's Day card—and for doing what is probably an easier job.

The psychic rewards of work are nothing to sneeze at, either. As I mentioned before, employers are learning the importance of non-monetary incentives, so corporate perks abound. At any moment on a workday, you can bet a recognition ceremony is happening some-where in corporate America. Increasing autonomy and an emphasis on teamwork are making work more enjoyable, even if the hours are longer. In short, it can be easy to feel more competent, popular, and valued at a decent job than with a cranky three-year-old.

Society rewards paid work with dollars and with prestige. The question "What do you do?" at cocktail parties is not intended to elicit the response, "Well, I'm a busy father of three. And you?" Most of us have been taught not only to define ourselves by our jobs, but also to find in them much of our lives' meaning. How can the humdrum toil of fatherhood compete with the glamorous world of wheeling and dealing?

The answer: there are no easy answers. If you don't make an ef-fort, the compensation comparisons are stacked against fatherhood from day one. Do your kids get Hallmark cards with heartwarming messages like, "Sorry I can't be there to tuck you in"? Are they reg-ulars at Grandma Please!, the 900 number that gives them pay-per-minute access to an adult willing to sing songs, tell stories, and help with homework? (I am not making these up!) If so, chances are that being with them will seem a lot more like work than your job does.

Some business dads focus so much on cash compensation that they confuse making a *living* with making a *life*. They may claim the long hours are all for the kids' sake, but what is the toll on the kids? Such dads are going beyond the line we all need to draw between paying for the future and building the future. The kids don't need whatever extra income those extra hours produce one thousandth as much as they need their fathers, and the guys themselves are missing out on the best that life has to offer. They don't seem to understand that *sometimes money just costs too much*.

Perhaps the most notorious examples of driven fathers are those Masters of the Universe, the investment bankers of Wall Street. They can make huge amounts of money, but at what cost to their children? A *New York* magazine article quotes a forty-year-old, who made $5 million in 1997, talking about his outlandish schedule's impact on his family. "They've gotten used to not having you around. You infringe on the life they've had to create for themselves. You're almost an intruder." Another banker's wife is skeptical that money is really the point, since he refused to let up even once he was making $10 million. "Is there a point where he would say that he had reached financial security? I tried to commit him to a number. It turns out it's not really a number."

Many dads obsessed with work and money don't see that work and family success are not mutually exclusive. On the contrary, one major reward of being a good father is that it can help your career. Giving your fathering skills a workout will make those same skills more effective in the office, but the benefits go beyond that, as the encouraging facts below show.

More Power to You!

Happy dads focus better. All parents bring their worries to work with them. Wondering why the principal wants to see you for the third time this semester, for example, is liable to distract you from the Pitkin deal. But the more your children sense your commitment to them, the shorter and smoother their inevitable rough patches are likely to be.

In addition, coming home to happy kids can actually *absorb* stress that you bring with you from work. Now, don't make the mistake of viewing your family as some kind of tranquilizer after a hard-charging workday, because they're every bit as demanding in their own way. If you really engage with them each evening, though, the different type of energy involved often magically shifts your gears, and you may zoom back to work the next morning feeling refreshed and raring to go.

Good dads feel more competent. Remember that line in "New York, New York" about "If I can make it there, I'll make it anywhere"? Fathering's kind of like that. If you feel competent as a dad, you'll probably feel an extra boost of confidence when you go into the office. If you feel *incompetent* at home, it could undermine your self-confidence in the office.

Beloved dads have better self-images. That flood of love from your kids can put you on top of the world just in the time it takes to have breakfast with them. There's nothing like it for putting you at the top of your business game as well.

Kids change your outlook. The more time you spend with kids, the more you absorb their attitude, which often includes an unreasonable amount of optimism; their humor, which features a keen sense of the absurd; and their sense of time, which teaches an unusual amount of patience. These three can actually be useful at work if properly applied.

In your subordinates' eyes, kids can humanize you. My friend Michael H. is the tough chief financial officer of a major book publisher, but he is also the besotted father of two young children. "My people have a terrible habit," he complained over dinner the other night. "When I get really angry with them, they suddenly start talking about my kids, and I get this silly smile on my face."

Your colleagues will notice. Building a close, happy family is not easy. Like any major accomplishment, it can impress those you work with. Just an hour ago as I write this, I was checking the references of a CEO whose company we are considering backing. A former colleague of his, after telling me all the reasons why this executive had been successful at work, volunteered, "By the way, you should know that Mark's personal life is very stable. He's happily married, and he has two wonderful kids that he's devoted to. If you're considering investing money in someone, I think having a stable personal life is relevant."

Fatherhood breeds humility. It's too easy for successful executives, surrounded by underlings who are paid to obey them and who actually admire them (or seem to), to yield to the delusion of superiority. The moment you start to think you're infallible, you are doomed. As Bear Stearns' Alan C. "Ace" Greenberg wrote in *Memos from the Chairman*, "A man will do well in commerce as long as he does not believe that his own odor is perfume. . . . Pride goeth before a rap on the snout." For a swift dose of reality, there is nothing like an evening with the kids. Fred Rosen of Ticketmaster once told *Forbes*, "No matter what you accomplish at work, when you get home you are just Dad. At the office you get a lot of respect; home is a great equalizer."

At work, your compensation provides not only cash, but also an objective measure of success. As a father, you have more indicators to watch, so judging your performance is less simple. What are you trying to maximize—happiness for your kids? for your wife? for your parents? approval from society? It's probably some mixture, which depends entirely on you as an individual. The good news, at least, is that many of those indicators also make *you* happy, and so double as compensation.

It's a good idea to set objectives before any major undertaking, and child raising is no exception. Is your measure of success how well the kids are doing? That's important, but it can be affected by factors outside your control. Perhaps an even more relevant performance measure is how well you know your kids. They may seem fine outwardly, but not to a father who really knows them. Now is also your chance to get close to them in preparation for periods when they need you most. Finally, parenting is easier and more fun when you know your kids well, and (this is important) a measure of success for any job is how much you enjoy it.

When it comes to compensation, fathering is like most worthwhile endeavors: as ye sow, so shall ye reap. Or, in the technical terminology of computer programming, "garbage in, garbage out." Any venture capitalist will tell you that you can't get 40 percent annual returns without taking risks, and you can't get returns at all if you don't invest. Every moment you spend with your kids, every hug you give them, every tantrum you ride out, is an investment in a risky but high-yielding asset.

We're lucky — at least we don't have to carry our children around for nine months before we meet them. But it doesn't take long for good dads to feel they have a lot invested in their kids. In fact, it can sometimes feel uncomfortable having so much of our own happiness freighted in such fragile vessels. There are so many bad things that can happen to kids, so many accidents and missteps, that I sometimes selfishly wish my own children didn't make *me* feel so vulnerable by playing such important roles in my life. It's ridiculous, of course: there's no other way to be a father, and in the end it's always worth it. Warren Buffett quoted Mark Twain by way of explaining his tendency toward big bets: It's okay to put all your eggs in one basket, as long as you *watch that basket carefully*.

If you don't watch your kids carefully enough, you could live to regret it. This may seem unfair, but fathering clearly has a counterpart to business compensation on the *downside*. Failure as a father can give you untold heartache, and there are even equivalents to getting fired (your kids disown you) or going bankrupt (your family dissolves). Your kids will have problems no matter how good a father you are, of course, but will survive them better if they know, deep down, that you are there for them.

Even if all you cared about were money, the cash penalties for faulty fathering are severe. Kids who lose their way in life often need ongoing financial support, so the investment analogy above is not altogether figurative. Do you want them living with you when they're thirty, or even living *off* you? Long-term therapy and rehab clinics don't come cheap, either. Some hapless dads also have had to take extended leave or to resign to deal with their kids' serious problems.

Simple love of their kids, though, is enough to motivate most business dads. When they underperform as fathers, they often do so without realizing it. Many inadvertent slackers experience defining moments, times when they realize they may have been dropping the ball. Perhaps, for example, their toddlers decline to recognize them (at age two, I once greeted my mother with "Hello, lady" after a prolonged absence); their preschoolers consistently refuse to talk to them and insist on clinging to Mommy; their eight-year-olds seem to treat them as nothing but balky ATMs; or their teenagers have completely checked out.

My own epiphany occurred when Benjamin was six months old. Luckily for me, I was forced to be relatively hands-on at the beginning because Julie spent a long time recovering from her cesarean. But I became complacent. Getting back into the swing of work, I neglected to keep pace as a father, beginning with the nuts-and-bolts stuff. One example: when the three of us were preparing for an outing, Julie sometimes asked me to pack the diaper bag while she dressed. I would forget so many things that she eventually had to type a list for me. "What do you want from me—I tried" was my (unspoken) attitude. Julie, unlike some mothers, had difficulty accepting that an apparently capable businessman could become incompetent the moment he entered his own home. I would sometimes turn defensive and criticize her standards, without having the information or experience to do so.

The real crossroads came when I began missing more than "just" the nuts and bolts. As Benjamin began to speak, I was the one who couldn't understand him. As he began to find things funny, I was the one who couldn't make him laugh. As he began to play impromptu little games, I was the one with whom he just didn't click. Despite Julie's best efforts to include me and keep me up to speed, I began to feel like a stranger in my own home.

I remember some long, late-night conversations we had during that difficult period. With help and encouragement from Julie, I decided I wasn't spending enough time with Benjamin to get the most out of being his father. From then on, I made it a point to put him to bed as many nights as possible, and to take morning-to-night responsibility for him at least one day each weekend.

I made the decision from selfish motives, I confess, not out of a sense of guilt or obligation. Perhaps for that reason, the decision is one that I have not for a moment regretted. I'll never be able to spend quite as much time with him (or with his sister Leila) as I would like, but at least I don't feel like a stranger.

Whatever form the wake-up call takes, prodigal fathers eventually realize that the commitment of fathering is more than lip service. It is more than snapshots on the office desk, trophies on the credenza, and a line on the résumé. It is something for them to undertake, not something that just happens to them.

And once they realize that, their lives improve. Here are some reasons why.

Your Inner Paycheck

• **Happiness boomerangs.** If you love your kids, seeing them happier will make you happier. Call it chemical, call it sentimental, but happy kids make for happy dads. When our "investments" are doing well, it pleases us. Not only that, but it pleases our wives, relatives, and other people we care about. It's great for our marriages, and it's great for our lives.

• **Welcome to the center of the universe. You're it.** Your kids are programmed to love you—all you've got to do is give them a chance. The love flooding from your kids (at most ages) will be the headiest mix of hero worship, complete fascination, and perfect adoration that has ever swept you off your feet.

• **You're meeting a challenge.** Fathering is rewarding precisely because it is difficult. Whatever is worth doing at all, is worth doing well, the saying goes. Why do people scramble up cliffs? make their own chairs? master the Japanese tea ceremony? Because those things are challenging, and nothing fulfills one more than a challenge well met. George Leigh Mallory said he wanted to climb Mount Everest "because it is there." Well, nothing in your life is more challenging or more "there" than your kids. And raising them is (usually) a lot safer than scaling Everest or running with the bulls at Pamplona.

The more seriously you take fathering, the harder you'll try; and the harder you try, the greater your satisfaction, not to mention your success. Since that will encourage you to try even harder, this is one of the many "virtuous circles" in fatherhood.

• **You're enjoying childhood all over again.** Children put us back in touch with a part of ourselves that may have fallen into disuse: the playful part, the part that can have fun with hide-and-seek or scissors-paper-stone, the part that can pretend mops are horses and garbage-can lids are shields. Spending time with our kids, really *with* them, can tug us out from under our everyday grown-up burdens and let us relive, if only for a short while, some of the best times of our own childhood.

• **You're having an impact.** Being a good father gives you influence over your children. The better you know your kids, the greater this power will be, and the more likely you are to influence them in long-term ways. The entire world may be different in a hundred years depending on how you instruct your children and what they and their own offspring achieve with that instruction. The Talmud says, "Whoever teaches his son teaches not only his son but his son's son, and so on to the end of generations." As a negative example, England's George V was once asked whether he might not be a little warmer toward his son. "My father was frightened of his father," he replied, "I was frightened of my father, and I am damned well going to see to it that my children are frightened of me." His son was, of course, that royal failure Edward VIII, who abdicated in 1936 after less than a year on the throne.

• **You're catching split-second miracles.** Some of the biggest rewards of fatherhood come in the smallest packages of time. Just exploring the world with your kids, to whom all seems new, can make you feel that, in Elizabeth Barrett Browning's words, "Earth's crammed with heaven, / And every common bush afire with God." The quiet pleasure of feeling your son's sleepy head droop onto your shoulder, or your daughter's hand reach up for yours, can surpass any joy at their achievements. Hearing them make their first jokes, seeing them with their first friends, watching them gain self-assurance, can give you satisfaction beyond any glory that their worldly accomplishments may reflect onto you.

Being involved with your kids—staying alert to their moods,

spending time with them—increases your odds of catching the miracle moments. If you don't stay attuned, then the wonder of their existence, the awe you knew the first time you held them in your arms, may sadly dissipate in the ebb and flow of daily life.

• **You're getting grandchildren.** They're like unexpected dividends, the kind you get when your investments really go to work for you. Do the job right with *your* kids, and they'll probably end up in happy marriages, with reasonably fun kids of their own, whom they'll even let you see from time to time. When you've retired, and the crazy deadlines and meetings and phone calls echo away into memory, you'll have a second batch of youngsters to fill the void. The pleasures of parenthood, with none of the work! What could be sweeter?

Companies get bought and sold, jobs disappear in reorganizations, offices get left behind—but family is permanent, for better or for worse. Do it right, and you're set for life. Do it wrong or not at all, and your failure will haunt you to your grave. Speaking of graves, you have two basic choices for your epitaph: name and dates only, or "loving husband, father, and grandfather." Contrary to the way some people act, "best VP of sales Amalgamated Coolants ever had" is not an option.

The rewards of fatherhood will come in direct proportion to your efforts, so step up your rate of investment, and let those returns roll in!

Delegation

Successful businessmen are used to insulating themselves from tedious or inconvenient work by delegating to those lower in the food chain. Nothing, however, exempts a dad from his child's needs. If anything, the children of high-achieving executives need their dads more than most. The pressure to match their parents' accomplishments is more intense, and the danger of their taking refuge in material comforts, with the accompanying distortion of values, is greater. (Some parents go too far in guarding against this danger. Ron Chernow, in his 1998 biography of John D. Rockefeller, recounts how the magnate's four children had to share one tricycle. "I am so glad my son has told me what he wants for Christmas," John D.'s wife once told a neighbor, "so now it can be denied him.")

So while any work (and parenting is certainly work) can benefit from a mix of delegation and outsourcing, there are limits for even the most high-achieving business dads. The key is in knowing *what*, *when*, *how*, and *to whom* to delegate. On the *what* question, it makes sense to follow the same rule of thumb that corporations do. Don't delegate much that lies within your core competency, defined as what you do well, or your core mission, defined as what only you should be doing. United Airlines and Pepperidge Farms might outsource their data processing work, but you'll never see them asking EDS to fly their planes or bake their cookies. You know what your kids need from you, and you alone; don't duck that responsibility. There may be a role in this world for "virtual corporations," but not for "virtual families."

Let me tell you a story about over-delegation in government. My first day at City Hall, a deputy commissioner took me aside. "I don't think you understand how different the culture is here. We got some engineers working in my department, okay? Their office got a little too warm last week, so they called the maintenance guy. He goes, 'You guys are engineers, right? You just turn this dial on the radiator.' My guys threw up their hands and said, 'No, no, no. We don't want the responsibility!' " This kind of not-my-job attitude, I'm sorry to say, is all too common in the public sector, the private sector, and that ultraprivate sector we call home.

When should you delegate? When you have to, and I mean *have* to. Are you letting the nanny put the kids to bed so you can take a two-legged flight home and score a few more miles? That doesn't qualify as "have to." Or is it because you're filling in for your boss, delivering a major presentation to a hundred industry heavyweights? That probably *does* qualify. You're the only one who can judge the many situations in between.

How should you delegate? The same way you would administer

a major corporate outsourcing: very carefully. Start with clearly defined goals, and make sure your service provider understands what
you expect. Then stay in touch with the project proactively, confer-
ring regularly with both the service provider and the customers
being served (your kids). You must stand ready to "insource" the service, replace the service provider, or at least take corrective action if
you and the customers are consistently disappointed. The sign on
Harry Truman's desk read, "The buck stops here," and the same
goes for any mistakes on your watch, whether you're sending out a
letter with a secretary's typo or letting the baby-sitter substitute TV
for human attention.

Finally, *whom* should you allow to be your proxies? Your parents
and in-laws can be terrific if they're around, depending on how you
feel *they* performed as parents. Schools will play an important role as
your kids get older (see the Human Capital chapter). While your
kids are younger, or outside of school hours, there are various third
parties, such as nannies, sitters, and day-care centers.

Your nanny, if you have one, is key—so key that you should participate as fully as possible in hiring her. Would you let someone else
pick the professional who was going to handle your most important
account in your absence? Not likely. Your "business dad" expertise
in interviewing and hiring applicants should be quite valuable here.
Of course, the more involved you are with your kids, the better
you'll be at helping to choose the right nanny for them.

I've been involved in many executive searches for my portfolio
companies, and the trickiest part was making sure that the candidate's vision and personal chemistry meshed well with the company's. It's the same with prospective nannies. Once you've done the
basics like checking their qualifications and references, you've got
to ask yourself how they'll fit with you and your kids. Does their
philosophy conform to yours? Don't hesitate to pose hypothetical
questions. Julie and I had to hire a new nanny when our son was four,
and we asked each applicant questions like, "What would you do if
Benjamin really didn't want to leave for school?" We were amazed at
the range of answers from seemingly experienced, sensible people,
everything from "I'd bribe him with candy," to "Maybe we wouldn't

go." (The nannies we liked were the ones who said, "I'd want to have coordinated it with you beforehand. I would do my best to change his mood or persuade him, but in the end he'd just have to go.")

Don't move hastily when hiring nannies: if you pick a lemon, the kids will suffer, and you and your wife will bear the burden of having to go through another search. You'll also avoid the psychological and financial costs of not trusting your nanny—for example, the increasingly common hidden-camera-in-the-teddy-bear services, which in New York cost up to six hundred dollars for installation and ten dollars a day for monitoring. Some of those services, astoundingly, let you monitor the camera via the Internet, which only goes to show (to paraphrase H. L. Mencken) that no one ever went broke underestimating the paranoia of the American people.

One candidate for delegation I cannot say enough bad things about is the boob tube. Many parents try to save time or energy by occupying their kids with the flickering screen, which ends up becoming a major source of values, vocabulary, and worldly knowledge. Kids turn to every available source for life lessons, and few are as compelling as TV. Are you comfortable with the Mighty Morphin Power Rangers as mentors for your kids? Ads during kids' TV shows (including ads masquerading as shows) are insidious pied pipers in and of themselves, but even some programming on so-called educational TV is not much better, with its quick crosscutting and countless reruns. The very nature of the medium promotes sloth, passivity, superficiality, slickness, and short attention spans. Use it when you must, but treat it like the drug it is.

Other than that, I think TV is terrific.

Joint Venture Partners

Five Criteria of Highly Successful Ventures

In the world of finance, a joint venture occurs when two companies think they might have synergy, that the capabilities of both partners together will produce more than they could alone. "Synergy" is derived from a Greek word meaning "working together."

In my opinion, the concept of synergy applies even more to parenting than it does to corporate marriages. No matter what you do in business, parenting will be the most important joint venture you ever undertake. You and your wife, if you work together well, can achieve far more in tandem than independently. As Benjamin Franklin exhorted his fellow patriots at the signing of the Declaration of Independence, "We must all hang together, or assuredly we shall all hang separately." Nothing is more of a venture than parenthood (take it from a venture capitalist), and parenthood is about as joint as ventures can get.

In the business world, sad to say, many joint ventures end up failing. The same is true of major mergers or acquisitions like IBM/Rohm, AT&T/NCR, and Matsushita/MCA (maybe companies with three-letter names should avoid merging). Despite the best intentions, they fall victim to poor planning, management conflicts, or clashing cultures. My investment banking experience gave me many examples of joint ventures that did and did not work, enough to come up with five criteria that I think apply just as much to our joint ventures in parenthood.

1. The two companies must know each other (and themselves) well.
2. They must plan and prepare carefully for the joint venture.
3. They must contribute equally to the joint venture.
4. They must figure out the best ways for each to contribute.
5. They must have constructive mechanisms in place for resolving disagreements.

Know Thyselves

The best management teams prepare for a joint venture by doing extensive due diligence, meaning they study each other, and have intimate and thorough discussions about their respective needs and philosophies, both before and during the venture. If you're already a parent, it may be a little late for due diligence before your venture begins, but it's never too late to try deepening your understanding. You may think you and your wife already know each other in the biblical and every other sense, but if you don't go through parenthood understanding yourselves and each other *as parents*, you may be in for some nasty shocks. That knowledge must be continually renewed as you both grow personally and change in your parental roles.

In business, we all have stories about how we found our jobs—or how they found us. Did you always know you wanted to be a businessman, or was it a bolt from the blue? Did it astonish your college roommates, who figured you'd be teaching Sanskrit, reporting from Moscow, coaching the Dodgers, or setting broken bones? Does it fit with your own earlier ideas of who you are? Was this the type of job

your family wanted for you? How much of your working style is derived from what you observed in your own parents?

Was it easy to find your job, or did you send out hundreds of résumés and go through dozens of interviews? Were you sure this was
what you wanted, or did you jump on in because you just had to
make a move, and this was the best option around?

Founding a family is like a cross between finding a job and starting a small business. All that dating through which you found your
wife, which led to your current (and permanent) position as father,
had some similarities to job interviewing. In much of the animal king-
dom, males display themselves openly so that females can choose the
most robust. For Homo sapiens, it's a lot more complicated: men
and women look for compatibility in many different respects.

Now your "interviewing" has paid off, in the biological sense:
you got the job. You're a husband (current or former) and a father.
How does this "job" fit with your self-image? Did you always figure
you'd have kids one day, or did your paternal status come as something of a shock? How was the adjustment to your new title? How
did the transformation from couple to parents change the dynamic
between this little enterprise's two founders?

As a married couple, you and your wife bring together your individual family histories and now share a history of how you came
together—as well as hopes, dreams, and plans for your family's future. (Even if you're widowed or divorced, those initial plans and
wishes are *still* part of your history, of where you're "coming from"
as a father.) All this history, and these hopes and dreams, help determine *the kind of couple you are, which will heavily influence the kind of
family you raise.*

What kind of families do you and your wife come from? What
were your parents like? Did they divorce? What kinds of training
and role models did they provide in their parenting and in their relationships with each other? What "best practices" or family traditions would you like to carry on? What bothered you that you want
to avoid in your own household? Did you receive enough material
comfort, enough encouragement, enough attention, enough love? If

not, how have you each coped with that? How have those issues shaped your expectations of what's good for your own kids—do you want to change the course of family history, or do you feel that what was "good enough" for you both is okay for your kids, too?

How do you and your wife complement each other? Business partners wouldn't hook up if they didn't somehow need each other to succeed. In your parenting partnership, take a look at your individual personalities, needs, talents, and goals, and see how they mesh together. Are you and your wife fairly similar in temperament, or do you balance each other by being opposites? What needs does each of you fulfill in the other? What does each of you appreciate about the other as both spouse and parent? What are your dreams, your visions of the future? How effective are you at pursuing them? What are your values? Does any of the above raise conflict? And how does it influence your thinking about the children you want to raise?

Every business has a culture in which certain behavior and communication patterns are expected. A garment industry "How ya doin', sweetheart?" would go over like a lead balloon at a white-shoe Wall Street law firm. Similarly, your interaction as a couple has its own style. How do you talk together? How do you make decisions? Which issues get talked through, and which are left unsaid? How do you resolve disagreements? What do you really enjoy together? How do you show love? How do you feel about your style of interaction as a model for your children?

Finally, does your wife "work"? Once again, that means work for pay in this book's shorthand. Of women with children under age seventeen, 69 percent work—quite a change from 13 percent in 1950. Only about half of that 69 percent work full time, however, so at-home moms, part-time earners, and full-time earners each account for about a third of the maternal population. Which third has your wife joined?

The answer will have a major impact on the entire family. There's the financial aspect, of course: you and your wife may feel she has no real choice if the family is going to attain or maintain the standard of living she and you have chosen. There are considerations about the psychological effects on the children, which depends on your kids' personalities, on the quality of child care available, on your wife's strategies for minimizing the conflict between work and family, and on your own level of involvement. It is also only fair to ask what effect *your* working has on the kids, since hours and type of work increasingly contain some element of choice for both parents.

In any case, your wife's employment status affects *you* in every part of your life. If she works, you (like her) have less flexibility when it comes to child-related emergencies; you need to interface more with your sitter, school, or day-care center; and you have to take time away from work and yourself in order to relieve her from working the "second shift" alone. Studies indicate that working mothers feel healthier, happier, and more valued (both at home and altogether) than nonworking mothers. But there's no question that when both parents work, everyone pays some price in terms of extra stress and less time together. It's a trade-off only you and she can assess.

If your wife stays home, you have what *Fortune* cynically refers to as the ultimate modern status symbol. You can certainly use her full-time availability to the kids as a source of flexibility in scheduling your own work time, but you should resist the temptation to take that availability for granted or to exploit it by not spending enough time with the kids yourself. Treat it as a way for you to be a better father, not a worse one. Bruce Reese, CEO of Bonneville International and father of seven, showed this positive attitude in a recent *Forbes* interview. "We are fortunate that my wife doesn't have to work. She is the principal reason I get to think of myself as a great dad."

Jim P. is a talented venture capitalist based near Washington, D.C., with boys ages three and one. Before they moved to Washington, Jim's wife was a rising star at a huge Los Angeles law firm, on a clear track for partner. After their first son, she decided that lawyering from 8:00 A.M. to 10 P.M. was no longer sustainable, so she agreed to stop working and move east when Jim's Washington opportunity arose. He emphasizes, however, that her career was just as promising as his, and either of them could have been the one to sacrifice for the other. She keeps in touch with her former colleagues, most of whom have now made partner, and he confides over lunch that they seem to look down somehow on the choice she made. "I've got a sense of guilt—no, obligation—to be an equal partner with her after what she gave up. Sometimes I'll take the kids just so she can be alone. A lot of my peers have the same issue, even if their wives are still working. It's a big issue for us."

Planning and Preparation

Successful partners start preparing themselves long before the venture begins. In parenting, there are huge adjustments men need to make between the beginning and the end of pregnancy. The sooner we make them, the better we will perform after everyone's home from the hospital.

Children change their parents. Issues that never came up between you will suddenly assume great importance, while earlier priorities will fade into obscurity. As you talk through issues like delivery options or names, you will have the opportunity of melding into a parenting team. Nothing forges team bonds like a challenge, and few undertakings are as challenging for couples as having a child.

Our fatherhood really begins at conception, both physically and psychologically. Never mind that the only way we can actually see our children is through ultrasound or the shape of Mom's belly. As soon as we get that gleam in our eye that comes from learning "we" are pregnant, we begin to live out George Herbert's maxim, written in the early 1600s: "The first service a child doth his father is to make him foolish." We have only the vaguest idea of how our lives are about to change, especially if this is our first child. All we know is that we're filled with a tantalizing mix of pride, wonder, love, bewilderment, and dread. Still, it is during these nine months that we will fall into patterns of interaction with our joint venture partner, patterns that can set the entire venture on the road to paradise or perdition.

Preparing for the parenting partnership includes practical duties like making sure your wife gets enough food and rest to safeguard the baby's health, but there are major psychological issues as well. Pregnancy puts your wife at her most vulnerable—physically, because she feels so ungainly (if not nauseated) and is carrying such precious cargo, and emotionally, because she feels less attractive yet more needy. For solid evolutionary reasons (pregnancy having been such a dangerous time historically), her hormones are also feeding her plenty of free-floating angst and insecurity. Now is the time for you to soothe any anxiety she may express, no matter how little basis in reality you think it may have.

Giving your wife plenty of love and attention will convince her that your relationship is stable and secure, a topic of concern (spoken or not) for many pregnant women. You may even want to splurge on one final romantic trip, when you and she can be relatively footloose and fancy-free without a baby to care for. You can also minimize her anxiety by exercising at least as much tact as you would with any valued coworker, banishing phrases such as "beached whale" from your vocabulary. Your wife is already self-conscious enough about her appearance, and you're the one who has sworn to support her through "thick and thin."

Pregnancy is a difficult time for dads, but also a time of opportunity. You don't know what your baby will be like, but you can begin to make the huge mental adjustments necessary for *having* a baby. Not only will you have a new person to relate to, but your existing relationships to nearly everyone else in your life (such as your wife, other kids, and boss) will change dramatically. Luckily, pregnancy has its own ways of preparing us: pregnant women often have enough hormone-driven needs and limitations (physical and emotional) that the help and consideration required from you begin to foreshadow life with baby.

Equal Stakes

For any joint venture to work, the partners must contribute equally in return for their equal stakes. *If you want equal say in what happens to your children, you must assume equal responsibility for them.* The businessman's code word for power, remember, is "responsibility." If you want the power to share in major decisions such as where your kids go to school or what kinds of friends they have, you must invest the time and energy to know them, their strengths, and their needs. Equal power over your children's lives is not a right that survives neglect, but a privilege that must be continually earned.

Some men who earn more than their wives believe that that alone gives them the right to make all the key household decisions, including decisions about the children. They are deluded, however, as deluded as the CFO who believes that holding the purse strings gives him sole power to veto projects. You can't buy parenting ownership with money; in this venture, sweat equity is the only kind. If a husband tries to pull rank based on finance alone, he will provoke either seething resentment or a blow-up, and whatever decisions he forces through are likely to be wrong and unsupported.

Some women actually like the security of a "man in charge," and so may defer to you on important parenting decisions. Some men like to *be* in charge and—surprise, surprise—those types of men and women often find each other. Having your wife defer to you may boost your ego in the short term but carries its own risks. First, you may have agreed at the beginning of your relationship, or when your child was born, that you would be the one who "wears the pants," but the arrangement that worked then may not work now, given the complexities of parenting. Second, effective parenting requires consensus between parents, so proceeding without her true and voluntary buy-in may result in resentment and fissures. Third, deferring to you relieves her of accountability for decisions that turn out badly, leaving you holding the bag in both her eyes and the kids'. Fourth, parenting is a two-person job, and she needs to take ownership every bit as much as you do.

Instead of one side being overbearing or the other deferential, power in a household should most naturally come from "sweat equity." In business, we sometimes talk about "owning" a project. To deserve the credit for a successful project, we must spend time working on it. The more work we do, the greater our ownership. The megaproject of parenting follows the same rules. Are you a full partner in raising your children if you think of your wife as the primary caregiver, whom you "help" sometimes, maybe even by "baby-sitting" the kids for an evening? No. You're not thinking like an owner at all, but rather like a peon in a hierarchy of parenting.

Shakespeare told us that "some are born great, some achieve greatness, and some have greatness thrust upon them." No one, however, is born to greatness as a parent, and no one can thrust it on you. You have no choice but to achieve it, by the sweat of your brow—and with some help from your trusty partner, of course. Unfortunately, that is more easily said than done. Learning to be a good father is hard enough under any circumstances, but sometimes husband and wife themselves unconsciously make it even harder.

It's all about how the two parents see their roles. Most of this book is about us and how we see our responsibilities, but we should not forget about how our wives see themselves and us. Let's face it: society prepares most women to feel that parenting is part of their core identity—a greater part than for most men. Biology reinforces that through women's physical and emotional experiences of pregnancy and its aftermath. Add to that our awe at the pain and drama of childbirth, and we are often content to stand back and let Mom take over as primary parent. "After what she's been through, she deserves it."

Plenty of fathers are secretly relieved to have their wives take over: as we've discussed, we men often don't have a lot of training in the baby department, and *we don't like to look incompetent*. So it works perfectly, maybe, at least in the beginning: Mommy, possessive of her sweet little thing, protectively hovering over every aspect of baby's care, ceding some of the parenting work such as changing diapers, but little of the parenting control. And to be honest, we may not really want that control, because of the responsibility it implies.

But this pattern, if left unchecked, can eventually be devastating to our families. As described throughout this book, kids need both parents' intimate involvement. Not only that, but sooner or later mothers shouldering all that responsibility by themselves get burned out and resentful.

The good news is, it's never too late to change. But as you're thinking about change, ask yourself, do you feel you have to push your way into equal status as a parent? Do you feel as if your wife listens to other moms or to the experts, but not to you? Sometimes a mother consciously or unconsciously crowds out her husband in the parenting department. She schedules important outings without consulting Dad; she withholds key information; she swoops in to comfort the kids without giving Dad a chance to do it himself; she refuses to teach Dad or include him in major decisions. She doesn't push Dad to get more involved when he needs it. In short, everything she does sends the message that parenting is her territory, and that Dad is a visitor.

Do you sometimes get this feeling from your wife? If so, here are some possible reasons.

Room Enough for Both of You?

• **"The baby stops here."** Most moms feel they are the ones whom society holds accountable for their children's safety and welfare. The downside to outsourcing major responsibility to anyone else, particularly someone who's not proven competent, is this: if there's a problem, Mom is still the one who'll get blamed—and she'll blame herself as well.

• **Whose turf?** Your wife may see parenting as her core competency or power base within the family. If you "take over" more responsibility, it could be seen as threatening her territory.

• **She's got to be better at *something*.** If your wife gave up an outside career, she may feel a special need for the kids to be defined as her exclusive job—or one where she so excels that you couldn't hope to do as well, so why bother trying? Couples sometimes collude on this: the unspoken message from the male perspective is that we are too importantly busy to take close interest in kid stuff. I once asked a colleague about how his toddler was adjusting to preschool, and he glowed proudly. "Oh, I'm barely home for all that. You'll have to ask my wife—she's really the expert on all that stuff. She's terrific." Chalk one up for the guy who's got himself that "terrific" status wife!

- **She can *too* have it all!** If your wife is working outside the home, she may feel guilty or upset about missing parts of the children's day, and so she may be all the more possessive about her influence on their lives.

- **Mother knows best.** If your wife spends significantly more time than you with the kids, she may know more about them and feel (with some justification) that your input is less informed and therefore less meaningful.

You may have noticed that competence is a major issue in most of those points. If your wife feels threatened by your competence, that's her problem for both of you to work out. Or maybe she's such a perfectionist that she thinks you're not competent *enough:* you put the baby's undershirt on backwards, or the lunch you made the six-year-old is less than ideal. Which is more important to her, for everything to be done exactly right or for you to be close to your children?

On the other hand, there may be alternative explanations, less flattering to you. *Maybe, for example, you're really much less competent than you think you are.* Before you leap to defend yourself, think carefully. You should be as self-aware at home as you're forced to be at work, keeping in mind that "a little humility makes you perfect," in the words of (believe it or not) Ted Turner. Any good businessman knows his weaknesses and tries to work extra hard to compensate for them.

Frank L., a biotechnology consultant I've worked with, has an M.D. degree, so he thought he knew more than his share about babies. This self-confidence was put to the test when complications from delivery kept his wife in the hospital for several weeks after their first baby was allowed to come home. Frank stationed the crib next to his bed, so he'd be sure to hear if the new arrival needed anything during the night. Newborns usually get hungry and cry lustily several times a night, but we'll never know how many times Frank's son did. Frank, you see, *slept soundly the whole night*. He'd never realized what a deep sleeper he was, he told me a little sheepishly.

So ask yourself, honestly, how perfect a parent you really are. Without even realizing it, after all, dads can be unreliable and impractical. Often, they lack the big picture view and thus do each task in isolation, without seeing how it fits into the overall household schedule or the child's daily routine. Dads get defensive when criticized for a "little" mistake, never understanding how much havoc it has actually wrought. That less-than-ideal lunch, for example, may have given Junior constipation all day if it was too starchy, or diarrhea all night if it wasn't starchy enough. In short, you may have far more to learn as a parent than you realize. (Here, as usual, I am *definitely* speaking from personal experience!)

If you feel left out by your wife, let's look at the situation from her perspective. Would you entrust major decision-making or caretaking power to a sitter who had never read a child-rearing book or magazine, spoken to another adult about child-rearing issues, or spent time with other children?

To put it another way: would you hire an employee who claimed interest in your industry, even if the applicant had no experience, had pursued no education in the field, had never networked, and didn't read the trade journals? Or would you perhaps question not only the applicant's ability to do the job, but also his or her sincerity and motivation?

Or think about this. Wouldn't you feel the tiniest tad resentful if you were suddenly told you had to share your hard-earned professional position and title with a newcomer like that, who would receive universal praise for taking on some of your work load—but because everyone knew you were more experienced, *you* would still receive the blame if anything went wrong?

That is how many mothers feel when their husbands lobby for greater decision-making power regarding the kids. They feel torn: on the one hand, they want the husbands to participate, but frankly they're resentful at men's assumption of a right to have input without having paid their dues in parenting scut work and without having accumulated the knowledge to make informed decisions. It's certainly confusing to us dads—aren't these the same moms who've been complaining about our lack of involvement? Now we're doing something, and look at the thanks we get!

Moms *do* need us to get involved, but in the right way. Although there are plenty of rewards, motherhood can be a tough job on a day-to-day basis. If you are in a power struggle with your wife, it adds to her stress—and you won't be happy, either. There have to be some ways out of this vicious cycle. And, in fact, there are.

Pathways to Equal Partnership

• **Start early.** Beginning with your children's births, remember that you are their *father*, not a part-time employee. Don't assume that your wife knows more than you. Maybe she comes equipped with a few genetic trip wires that help her respond more naturally to an infant's cues, whereas you have to learn by trial and error. In parenting, though, what counts is experience. If you let yourself fall way behind in experience, it's like permitting your stock in a joint venture to get diluted.

Fathers often fall behind even in the first days after childbirth. In order to minimize that risk, make sure you stay current on all the key skills (feeding, burping, changing) and develop your own indispensable talents, such as becoming the god of clean bottles or tending to the diaper pail, your home's very own skunk works (at least in the olfactory sense). Mothers often develop a wonderful intimacy with their babies through breast-feeding. Nothing can equal that early bond, but you may be able to approximate it by giving any supplemental bottle feedings you can (once nursing is well established), including those in the middle of the night.

The middle of the night? Absolutely. Like any job worth doing, fathering does not stop and go by the clock. Some of your first opportunities for developing your skills will inevitably occur when your baby cries in the wee hours. It's actually enlightened self-interest to take your share of such calls, for several reasons. First, your future fathering will be much easier if you pursue a major goal of early parenthood—namely, building your baby's sense of security, the all-important conviction that *help will arrive whenever she might call*. Babies are too young to spoil, so don't withhold what they so desperately need and let them "cry it out." Second, if you permit (or compel) your wife to answer all your baby's calls, she'll be the only one your kids associate with comfort in distress. Third, it's worth getting up just to experience the quiet pleasure of rocking the baby and yourself back to sleep, of feeling that tense little body relax, the breathing even out, and the head loll on your shoulder. Great satisfaction is gained when your tiny creatures need you, call you, and get what they need—and all's right with the world once more.

• **Pay your dues.** Some business dads' instinctive reaction when presented with their first dirty diaper is, "Hey, wait a minute! I'm a successful executive. I shouldn't have to do this kind of scut work! Can't I bond with the kid without wiping his rear end?"

Wrong on both counts. You may have advanced far up the ladder of responsibility at work, but fathering is a different job. When you started in your profession, you probably paid your dues with plenty of mindless, unappealing drudgery. Well, *parenting is always an entry-level job*. The dues you've paid at the office may result in a higher salary and more interesting work, but they mean nothing in parenting. And no, if your salary exceeds your wife's, that doesn't make your time more valuable than hers at home.

Luckily, the scut work (changing diapers, cleaning up vomit, chauffeuring, and so forth) is a more important part of parenting than you might at first think. It usually provides one-on-one time with your child, lets you see him in different situations, increases your overall sense of investment, and gives you standing in parenting discussions with you wife. By tenderly keeping your child warm, fed, and dry, or by depositing him safely at his desired destination, you reinforce his sense of confidence and comfort with you. Show me a dad who's never done scut work, and I'll show you one whose involvement with his kids is almost sure to be superficial.

• **Ask directions.** In your children's infancy and beyond, if you fall behind in parenting skills and knowledge, then *trying* to catch up will always benefit you, *even if you never quite succeed.* Those efforts are extra tough for some business dads because they require asking advice, accepting gentle (or not so gentle) reminders, and otherwise learning from their wives. You may pride yourself on never asking for directions as a driver, but as a father you have no choice if your wife's roadmap is clearer than yours. She'll probably be glad you want to come up to speed. If she isn't, she's not being a team player. The kids are yours too, and if you're feeling left out your wife needs to know. Otherwise, you'll never even approach equal partnership.

It's not easy. You have to be willing to give up some of your male bravado and take responsibility for your relative lack of experience. You've got to be prepared to observe, to learn, to drop your defensiveness when corrected. If you're feeling ashamed that you don't know how to do some task, or worried that you might do it wrong, or guilty that you *did* do it wrong, speak up now. Ignorance may be bliss in the short run, but what you don't know can indeed hurt you (and everyone else in the family) over time.

Even when you disagree with your wife, ask her detailed questions so you can truly understand and learn from her thinking, not just put her on the spot and argue away her point. Start tapping other information sources as well (described in the Knowledge Is Power chapter), and upping your kid activity level. The more interest you show in the kids' lives, the greater your absolute and relative competence will be, and the stronger your position with kids and mom alike. When you know your child's shoe size, the name of his best friend's pet, the weather report for the day of the field trip to the farm, whether Carla scorned him in the playground again, how many of the other kids in his class can ride without training wheels, and how many times he had vegetables this week—or even when you know enough to ask for this information—you'll be ready for your promotion. In a well-functioning marriage, those measures should effect a pretty swift turnaround.

• **Survey the terrain.** If asking directions doesn't work after a trial period of a few months, you may need to look around for other, more subtle issues—with yourself, with your wife, or between you. Have you really followed through on the directions you've received?

Would your wife report your activity and competence level the same way you would? If not, is it because she's still seeing you in old ways, or is there a grain of truth in her observations?

On the other hand, if you think your wife is being unduly possessive because of other issues, you two need to talk about it. If parenting is your wife's only area of perceived competence, for example, it'll be hard for her to relinquish exclusive control no matter how hard you work to earn your share. But how did it happen that she is respected, or respects herself, only for her parenting? Is this an issue she needs to work on individually, or a joint problem? The two often overlap.

If you're lucky, you and your wife have created a true partnership. She is secure: she knows that she's a competent parent, but she also knows not to base her entire self-worth on her parenting skills. She is open to new ideas, including the very notion that *you* have new ideas to contribute. She can recognize a two-person job when she sees it. In short, she's a team player.

You, for your part, are committed to being the best co-CEO you can. You are secure enough to admit what you don't know and to avoid defensiveness when you've made mistakes. You are motivated enough to commit time and energy to information gathering. In short, *you* are a team player.

Go, team!

Division of Labor

Successful joint ventures require a clear understanding of both partners' responsibilities. For corporations, division of labor may be the hardest criterion to meet, because it requires significant continuing effort. For parents, similarly, it's all too easy to drift away from the original plan.

You may find yourself disagreeing about division of labor especially strongly if both of you have paid jobs. In that case, both of you have job-related stress, conflicts between work and family, and a scarcity of downtime. Any change in plans is extra stressful for both of you. Essentially, you are each working two jobs, one at home and one at the office. All too often, how you split the second shift produces real tension. As wage-earners, you may understand each other's lives better and identify with each other more than if you did not both work, but there are also risks of career rivalry or jealousy.

Some couples get caught up in a contest to see whose job is more high-powered and requires more hours—leaving the "loser" to pick up the slack at home. That is obviously the wrong response to the situation. The right response is for dual-earner couples to coordinate even more explicitly on division of labor than single-earner couples. In fact, some two-earner couples plan their child-care schedules four weeks in advance. But explicit coordination is essential for *all* parents. Without it, a dad sometimes believes he is shouldering a greater share than he actually is, risking both resentment on his wife's part and a growing gap in expertise. In 1993, the Families and Work Institute surveyed two-career couples on how they divided child-care work. Of the husbands, 43 percent said they did half the work, but somehow only 19 percent of the wives confirmed that!

Pat Schroeder, the former congresswoman, tells a delicious anecdote in her memoir *24 Years of House Work . . . And the Place Is Still a Mess*. Her husband Jim, a Washington lawyer, told an interviewer that his wife's career meant he had to play a greater role in the household, for example, taking their kids to the pediatrician. "I immediately ran to the House cloakroom and called him. 'For $500, what is the name of our children's pediatrician?' Knowing he was busted, he coughed and said, 'Oh, I was misquoted.' Jim was way ahead of his time, but he wasn't Mr. Mom."

That type of "he said, she said" paradox is common in many marriages, and division of labor is one of the most common issues that generates it. It is no secret that women are generally more empathic than men and so go to greater lengths to accommodate their spouses' and children's needs. Husbands, who often are less involved in the household to begin with, may not realize how much gets done without their ever knowing it. Men also have somewhat lower standards for household and child maintenance (rightly or not), and too often take an attitude of "she wants it, so she can do it." Relations will be better in the long run if husband and wife take the trouble to sit down and discuss what really needs to get done; *then* they can decide who will do what. Explicit discussion can prevent your wife from thinking you are being selfish when you are merely oblivious, and prevent you from thinking she is being obsessive when she is merely taking a bigger-picture view. Whatever the outcome, it's good office politics to at least notice when your teammate thinks you're being lazy or thoughtless, and to talk it through. Such dialogue may also correct the opposite problem, of fastidious husbands who come home in the evening and do not understand what their stay-at-home wives have been doing all day, or why the household can't be in better shape.

All across the country, business dads are shouldering more and more of the household burdens. In 1998, the Families and Work Institute released a survey of 2,877 workers showing that fathers in 1997 were spending half an hour more each weekday, and a full hour more each day off, with their children than in 1977. That's an increase of almost five hours per week! And men's time devoted to housework rose by almost an hour per workday. Some of those claims (self-reported, remember) may result more from changing expectations than from changing reality, but clearly more men are taking ownership in their home lives.

Unfortunately, this new attitude is still far from universal. There's a woman in my office, for instance, who had her first baby a couple of years ago. One morning about seven months later, I saw her coming in looking remarkably haggard, so I asked how the baby was. "Fine," she said, "but she woke up every hour last night." So did she and her husband switch off? I asked. "Ha! Are you kidding? He just kind of zones out till I get up, even if he hears the baby first." My face must have shown that I thought this was not quite fair. "It just takes a minute. All she usually needs is a pacifier." That fellow, whom I've never met, may have maximized his beauty sleep at the time, but I wonder how many sleepless nights his lack of involvement might end up giving him in the long run. In the meantime, his wife was just letting the resentment build up, making the potential eruption even worse.

Here's another case from higher up the corporate ladder. A former boss of mine, part of the triumvirate running a major department at Salomon, boasted to me that he had so far avoided changing his nine-month-old's diaper—even once! I'm always bemused when I hear business dads boast that way. At work, any employee who flatly refused a responsibility would be fired, with cause. So what if your wife doesn't "work"? Her days are still harder than yours (especially if she has other kids to care for and can't nap during the day), so she needs the uninterrupted sleep as much as you do. So what if you get spritzed a little while changing your son's diaper, or don't like the smell? Looking down at him, bouncing smiles back and forth as you lean over, more than makes up for it. In short, insisting that you won't take night feedings or change diapers would devalue your wife's work, betray you as not a team player, reject your baby as a priority, and rob you of many rewarding, intimate moments. I didn't envy that Salomon guy's wife one bit—though I wasn't too surprised. Within the firm, he had long been infamous as no treat to work with.

It's important to split child care fairly. *This doesn't have to mean fifty-fifty:* the precise balance will depend on you and your wife's schedules, stamina, and psyches. You'll know it's not working if you find your wife snapping at you seemingly without provocation, sighing whenever you leave her with the baby, or looking resigned when you leave for work. Resentment is not pretty, and it can corrode even the happiest love nest. An equitable division should also give both of you time and energy for your relationship as a couple, including the sex part. When things aren't coming together between husband and wife, one of the first possible causes marital therapists look for is a lopsided division of parenting work.

By the way, the standard of fairness is certainly not being met if you find yourself deliberately failing in order to evade responsibility:

"Honey, he fell off the changing table again. Can you do the diapers from now on?" Those are not words that a full participant would ever dream of uttering.

As I mentioned earlier, core competency can be one useful standard for divvying the workload with your wife. In our family, for instance, Julie is especially adept at short, time-sensitive tasks; I move more slowly but have more energy for long, protracted chores. There are many things that men can be as good or better at, such as baby bedtime (with their soothing low voices and big shoulders for rocking on), extended outings (with their stamina and ability to pluck the kids up and "airlift" them back home if they get overtired), assembling shelving (dads can work quickly enough to let a toddler "help" with some extra tools but avoid any actual damage), acting as chauffeur, or coaching Little League. Celebrate the differences between you in physique and temperament, and make the most of them. That's what synergy is all about!

The same teamwork principles apply at work. Rob G. founded and still runs one of the largest telephone support outsourcing companies in the United States. If you call an 800 number for technical support, you may well be talking to one of his operators. Rob tells me he realized a few years ago that he needed someone else at his level in the company, so he hired a new president, keeping the CEO title for himself. Where Rob calls himself "excitable and decisive," his president is "calm and deliberate." Rob acts as ambassador, gives speeches, and makes the fast decisions; his president negotiates, raises money, and is important in making the slow decisions. The two men complement each other when they work separately, and balance each other when they work together.

But don't overdo the strict division of labor in child rearing. You and your wife must each be practiced enough to be able to pinch-hit for the other from time to time. If your child finds a mud puddle he can't refuse on a day your wife is traveling, for example, you may have to assume temporarily her title of chief bath giver. Also, dividing responsibilities too precisely can, if you don't respond to changing circumstances, produce the kind of artificial constraints that no efficient labor market can countenance. If the household isn't working right, you shouldn't hesitate to reengineer certain key processes by reassigning responsibilities.

Whatever you do, don't split up the work by each taking a different kid exclusively. You don't want to end up resembling two families in one house. Each of your kids needs a mother and a father. Remember that core competency is only one guideline for division of labor. The other is core mission, the things that only you, or only your wife, can do.

Speaking of core mission, there is one parenting responsibility that only you can fulfill: *taking good care of your wife*. She is so central to your kids' lives that her health, happiness, and well being have major effects on theirs. Taking care of her is something you probably already do habitually, but sometimes she needs even more than your usual TLC. The more conscientious she is as a mother, the more vulnerable she is to "mommy burnout."

This affliction may start out deceptively mild but eventually sucks your wife down into a spiral of dampened spirits, reduced effectiveness, low self-esteem, and perhaps even full-blown depression. Moms instinctively keep on giving to their kids, and the kids just as instinctively keep on taking, until the mom is too exhausted to give any more. The trouble comes when she doesn't realize just how tired she is, so her demands on herself are still high. When she falls short, she begins to question her competence, her morale falls, and so the spiral begins. The trick for you is to recognize the problem before it gets too serious.

Although working moms may seem to lead more time-pressured lives, at-home moms are at least as vulnerable to burnout. Their self-esteem rests on a narrower base of only one "job," so when things start going badly at home they have nowhere to turn for offsetting encouragement. And they've got one of the toughest jobs I know of, handling the never-ending stream of children's needs with precious little adult company or reinforcement.

Luckily, the warning signs of early burnout are not that hard to spot: they include insomnia, inertia, deteriorating grooming, and sudden crying. You'd think that she would ask for help before things got that bad, but some moms don't—so it's up to you, the cavalry, to charge in with reinforcements without being asked. Be attentive enough to notice her distress, just as she would yours. Don't let her be a martyr to the kids—or, for that matter, to you.

I know, you're busy enough already. If she hasn't asked for help, you may wonder whether you really need to volunteer it. As a businessman, you're trained to give only what you're forced to yield at the negotiating table, and to withhold the rest as future bargaining chips. If your wife isn't pressing you to shoulder more of the burden, or even mentions it but neglects to make it a "deal issue," your instinct could lead you to hold back.

But your wife is your teammate, not your opponent. At work or home, teammates don't always know *themselves* what they really need. Consider an analogy to distress in one of your company's divisions, maybe a division that's underperforming but thinks it can work its own way out of the hole. Division management doesn't want to look weak or helpless, or perhaps they don't want to make undue demands on the rest of the company, so they keep digging away even as the hole gets deeper and deeper. Notice how it's the rare manager who reports bad news as quickly as good? It's up to the other executives to detect the problem, gauge division management's ability to address it, and send help before paralysis sets in and the problem compounds.

A burned-out wife is already victim to one vicious cycle, in which the kids get more needy as they sense her distress; don't let her fall into a second one, in which you start to pull away from her and the kids as the situation turns increasingly ugly. Don't retreat into work when she needs you most, but sit down with her and talk through the problem. Together, you should be able to come up with the right solutions.

A mommy suffering from burnout needs several things from you, beginning with the gift of sleep. We're a chronically sleep-deprived society, and mothering is too hard a job to do without enough shut-eye. You can also help your wife tremendously by increasing your share of the housework, perhaps persuading her to lower housekeeping standards somewhat and agreeing to bring in whatever extra hired help the household can afford, at least until she gets back on her feet.

Perhaps even more important is your acknowledgment and appreciation of the heroic job she's been doing, day in and day out. Cosmetics queen Mary Kay Ash has said, "The two things that people want more than sex or money are recognition and praise." Recognition is as simple as listening to your wife closely each evening, sharing what happened in her day, and extending compliments when due. That will bring you the added bonus of catching up on the kids and their doings.

That kind of listening will also help you examine your own attitudes toward household and child-rearing work. If you zone out during every blow-by-blow description of a play date or the mommy politics at the bake sale, then in addition to missing information that affects your kids' lives, you're also communicating the low valuation you place on your wife's central concerns and daily dramas.

Giving your wife whole-hearted support has the not-so-coincidental benefit of improving your relationship, which should in turn improve your fathering. It stands to reason that dads in happier marriages tend to be more involved with their kids: their wives include them more, the kids accept them more, and home is a more pleasant place for them. On the flip side, dads in worse marriages often withdraw or communicate only through fights. They might even find their children acting out in bizarre ways, frantically attempting to bring the two parents together; most kids would rather have parents yelling at them than at each other. A troubled marriage, moreover, may be too weak to respond effectively to the crises that occur all too often in kids' lives.

The moral: keeping your marriage sprightly is a superb investment from everyone's perspective. You will be repaid many times over if you regularly devote time to enjoying each other as adults— to recognizing, celebrating, and renewing all the things about your relationship that made you decide, long before kids came into the picture, that you wanted to spend the rest of your life with this woman.

For every vicious circle, happily, there is a virtuous one. *Just as investing in your marriage will help your kids, investing in your kids will help your marriage—in multiple ways.* First, understanding the children will let you appreciate your wife even more, knowing firsthand what she endures and what she achieves. Second, working as a full teammate with her, on the most important endeavor of your lives, will deepen your relationship indescribably. Third, taking full part in the child rearing will make her life (and her career, if she works) easier, and you will earn her undying gratitude. Finally, never underestimate the maternal instinct, the one that gives moms the superhuman power to hoist Hondas off their kids in emergencies. Love her little cubs, cuddle them frequently, help keep them happy and healthy, be true to your role as a father (not Assistant Mom), and she will adore you with a passion Don Juan could only dream of inspiring.

When Partners Disagree

The final criterion for successful joint ventures is to have constructive mechanisms in place for resolving disagreements. Even the most harmonious of equal partners, after all, do disagree sometimes. As movie mogul Darryl F. Zanuck put it, "If two partners agree all the time, one of them is useless. If they disagree all the time, both of them are useless."

If you find yourself constantly at odds with Mom on philosophical or practical issues of child rearing, it may be tempting to save everyone a lot of stress by simply retreating—withdrawing from the field and letting her do whatever she wants. But parenting is too important for you to quit like that. It's your duty to be fully engaged, even if that means engaged in battle from time to time. Perhaps one of you will convince the other, or perhaps you'll arrive at a compromise, but you have to keep trying until you reach consensus.

Disagreements can actually deepen your commitment to fathering, because there's no better spur for thinking issues through. If you argue for something you believe in, you convince yourself as well as others. The more facts that you and your wife have in common, though, the more likely it is that you'll be able to reach agreement quickly. Just as a corporation's managers go on retreats to think through major topics, the two of you may want a day to yourselves every month or so to work toward consensus on the hardest household issues.

Note the importance of consensus in this situation. Drastically alternating your parenting styles is one of the worst things you can do to your kids, who need stability, not mixed signals. Work through your differences while out of the kids' earshot, so they don't hear lengthy arguments that point up the subjectivity of the rules they're given. If you too openly disagree with each other, you run some major risks.

A House Divided

• **Blurred message.** Marketing experts stress the importance of staying "on message," so that customers do not become confused about your selling proposition. Similarly, sending your child mixed messages can be worse than no messages at all. Without unified leadership, they don't know whom to follow or what's important, and they lose faith in the very concept of rules.

• **Undermined authority.** If kids see that two grown-ups can't reach agreement on a topic, they logically (if simplistically) conclude that at least one must be wrong. Moreover, if one of you clearly doesn't respect the authority of the other (for example, if you slip the kids a candy after Mom said no), then the kids will see no reason why they should respect it either.

• **Ammunition in the wrong hands.** A parental Miranda warning: whatever you say in kids' hearing can and will be used against you. If you have a heartfelt disagreement about the kids in front of them, and they don't like the winning side's view, you're sure to hear the losing side's arguments from here to eternity.

• **Divided loyalties.** Have you ever worked in a company with openly divided management? If you have, you know it's a mess. Fiefdoms develop, employees are forced to choose sides, morale falls to pieces, and nothing positive gets done. Same story at home, only more intense. Kids haven't been alive long enough to develop independent senses of self, so they desperately need a solid base without visible stress fractures. Abraham Lincoln may have meant "A house divided against itself cannot stand" politically, but it certainly applies to families as well.

• **Wrong lessons.** Kids learn from everything they see us do, and they don't miss much. It's okay to let them witness a constructive discussion over parenting issues, as long as they can tell that you respect each other, share basic principles, and have their best interests at heart. In other words, it can be helpful to make an argument, but not to have one. What's the difference? If you have an argument, it often means acrimony and unresolved conflict, with no real consensus at the end. That kind of argument never ends, and it gives kids the wrong model for settling important disagreements.

As destructive as it can be to argue in front of your children, criticizing your wife to them behind her back is even worse. Such disloyalty lowers her standing with your children, blows away their trust in you, and makes them anxious over the health of your marriage. Loyalty is in fact just as crucial if you are divorced, since the children's trust in both of you has already taken a blow. For that matter, this whole chapter applies as much to divorced dads as it does to married ones. Regardless of who has custody, divorced dads need to put even *more* effort into coordinating with moms — trading views about the kids, about their joint responsibilities, and about their own performance as fathers.

Parenting is similar to any joint venture in that disagreements are inevitable, but everyone will be better off if you handle them constructively and privately.

Knowledge Is Power

INFORMATION-BASED FATHERING

Know Your Customer

In one of my first venture capital deals ever, we invested in a wonderful company that provides cable TV and telephone services to truck drivers, in their cabs, at truck stops. The driver pays a monthly membership, which entitles him to twenty channels of cable TV, two-way phone service, and Internet access (via outlets in the parking lot). The company has exclusive, long-term agreements with the country's largest truck-stop chains, and offers a better life to the hundreds of thousands of truck drivers who spend twenty or more nights a month in their sleeper cabs. It's a great company.

After we invested, I joined the board, and the hard work really began. Several times a week, sometimes several times a day, I would check in with the company's excellent management, finding out what they had learned, what they had achieved, or what threats were looming. Phone calls, of course, were just the beginning. There were also board meetings, interviews with potential hires, and trips to unique gatherings such as the annual Mid-America Truck Show in Louisville, Kentucky.

The questions we had to work through together never stopped. How were driver sign-up rates? Once they signed up, how often did they use the service? Where were monthly renewal rates heading? What did market research show that drivers wanted in the channel lineup? How many stops had to offer the service before they felt the network had reached critical mass? Were the new contractors on schedule in building out more stops? And how were relationships with the chains? What did the truck-stop manager in West Memphis think of the new promotion program? Were they any closer to signing up the next big chain? How about sales to fleets? And so on, and so on, and so on.

It's been a fantastic experience and, so far (knock on wood), a successful investment. The reason it's relevant here is that my firm had a lot invested in this company, and the only way to protect that investment was to know as much as possible about all aspects of its environment, its operations, and its prospects. At any moment, we might need that information to brainstorm with management, to make strategic recommendations, to provide key introductions, to pitch in on new fund-raising, or to help find any additional executives they needed. More subtly, knowing that we investors were keeping close track of certain key performance measures motivated management to attend to those measures even more closely.

Information is any good businessperson's stock in trade. Gathering it, processing it, and applying it are our most important tasks. Not just any kind of information will do, either—only detailed, in-depth knowledge. Conceptual understanding may be a good first step, general familiarity a terrific follow-on, but God and the devil both live in the details.

For a good father, love lives in the details as well. *The only way to know your children is to know their fine particulars, and learning those particulars is also the best way of showing your love.* You should know their hopes, their fears, their friends, their foes, their assets, their liabilities, their favorite foods, their latest lingo—in short, everything you can learn without being unduly intrusive.

Know your customer. That's the first rule for every salesperson and every marketer. Businesspeople often take great pains to memorize clients' and colleagues' personal data—their spouses' names, kids' ages, and hobbies. Companies invest huge sums to build demographic and psychographic profiles of their customers, and they often advertise with the unspoken message, "Not only is our product great, but it's great for *you*, because we know what you want." The same rule applies to children, the "consumers" of all our fathering.

As Leonard Lauder, CEO of Estée Lauder, has attested in *Forbes*, knowing your customer creates more value than any cloistered academic training. "We don't hire M.B.A.'s. Most of the people who work here started out at lowly jobs—behind the counter selling our products or working in the office as secretaries or assistants. These people are running the business now. They know what the customer wants."

You know how customer data help you in business, but how about as a father? In fact, the examples offered below show that the benefits are not all that different between the two.

Knowledge Is Power

• **The power to serve.** The best corporate leaders know that a big part of the job is to serve their followers—to supply them with whatever encouragement, information, and resources they need to realize the collective vision. You can't lead, however, if you don't know what people will find most useful. All your most selfless efforts to serve your children, similarly, may be wasted if you don't know what they actually need. How can you tell when your kids need help? How can you guess what will make them happy? How do you know when to give them what they *think* they want? If you don't know them inside out, you may be trying your hardest and still missing the big opportunities.

• **The power to instruct.** Knowing your kids (or corporate trainees) includes understanding what they know and how they learned it. That tells you what they're ready to absorb next, and how you can best present it. You will also need to give them advice at crucial times, when they're about to make important decisions. If you don't know what's going on in their heads, they'll think the advice doesn't apply (and they'll often be right).

• **The power to persuade.** With kids as with employees, the first step to motivating them is understanding their desires. What drives your kids? What rewards will give them the strongest incentives? On those rare occasions when your kids talk back and refuse to see reason (as you see it, anyway), and you don't feel like using punishment or physical force, nothing wins an argument like knowing how the other side thinks.

• **The power to avoid mistakes.** The people at General Motors didn't study Spanish before releasing the Chevy Nova under the same name in Latin America. If they had, they would have avoided the embarrassment of hearing from the laughing, skeptical public that *no va* means "doesn't go." Marketing annals abound with gaffes such as this, and all because companies didn't take the trouble to know their customers. The Swedish launched a U.S. campaign with the slogan, "Nothing sucks like an Electrolux." In China, "Come alive with the Pepsi generation!" was translated as "Pepsi brings your ancestors back from the grave!" In Spain, Frank Perdue's "It takes a tough man to make a tender chicken" came out "It takes an aroused man to make a chicken affectionate." Those were smart companies that didn't do their homework. The least you can do is avoid the same slipshod approach in your own most important market.

• **The power to experiment.** On the other hand, sometimes the only way to innovate is by making mistakes. Learning won't happen, however, if you don't study your child closely enough to recognize the impact of your actions, catching those mistakes as they occur. Post-it Notes might never have been invented if 3M's scientists hadn't paid close attention to that not-quite-sticky-enough-for-tape adhesive.

• **The power to decide.** How often do businessmen refuse great opportunities because they haven't taken the trouble to get the relevant information? It's always easier to delay or say no than to put their reputations on the line with a yes. Apple Computer probably would have been better off, for example, if John Sculley had said yes to clones. At home, by contrast, the easy answer to give is often yes, but parents may not really know what they're agreeing to. Next time your sixth-grader asks if he can sleep over at Mark's house, for instance, knowing Mark's parents will let you make a better-informed decision (even if those all-night toga parties don't bother you).

• **The power to protect.** To ensure your kids' immediate physical safety, you need to recognize when their impulses might suddenly drive them to try something that exceeds the limits of their balance or strength. When they're older and you're safeguarding their moral and social development as well, closeness with them will enable you to spot warning signs that other parents might miss. I know Exxon takes this approach with its tanker captains since that little incident with the *Valdez*.

• **The power to change.** Markets shift, customers change, and companies that can't keep pace become tomorrow's carcasses—a process that economist Joseph Schumpeter called "creative destruction." In the forty-two years between the *Fortune* 500 list's first appearance in 1955 and the 1997 version, thirty-seven of the original top fifty companies have either fallen below that rank or vanished altogether. Norman Augustine, former CEO of Lockheed Martin Marietta, says there are two types of companies, "those that are changing and those that are going out of business." Your children, likewise, are constantly going through their own bouts of creative destruction, in which elements of their personalities submerge in order to make way for new ones. If you don't recognize those radical shifts, you won't change your own behavior or expectations until circumstances force you to, possibly in unpleasant ways.

• **The power to befriend.** Let's face facts: you can never let yourself be a pal to any child or subordinate. Your responsibilities as their senior get in the way. Once your children have grown up, however, when your position of authority is less necessary, a healthy friendship can be one of life's great treasures. It's hard to imagine a closer rapport, since you've known one another since they were born. So even if you can't be friends while you're the kids' "boss," you can lay the groundwork for a golden friendship later on.

Of course, knowledge is more than just power. Your kids are fascinating creatures, bubbling miracles of life that you helped and are helping to create. The more time you spend with them, the more interesting they become. They contain more mystery than the vast reaches of space, more challenges than Scotland's golf courses, more pathos than all of Western drama, more suspense than Hitchcock and Serling together, more comedy than a thousand *Seinfeld*s. *What could be more interesting to a father than his own children?*

Cross-Border Trade

Here is one instance of the power that comes from information. America's second largest manufacturer of white goods, large appliances like refrigerators and dishwashers, is General Electric. GE began the 1990s with no major white-goods presence in Asia, but soon realized that Asia was where demand would be growing the fastest. Rather than applying a one-size-fits-all approach to every country in the region, GE spent months studying each market in minute detail: market size, competition, demographics, culture, and history. Only then did GE design the most thoughtful combination of products, brands, manufacturing facilities, marketing, and retailing for each country. The result? Analysts estimated that GE's Asian white-goods profits for the years 1994 through 1996 totaled $320 million. During the same period, Whirlpool, the largest U.S. manufacturer, *lost* $142 million in Asia.

What does this tell us? GE realized that Asia's societies were not only foreign to what it knew, but also quite different from one another. It therefore designed and executed a very deliberate "smart bomb" strategy of careful research, which provided the foundation for its stunning success. The lesson for business dads is that they can apply the same methods to the foreign cultures within their own homes: the children.

Children, like foreign cultures, have different philosophies from ours (more overtly self-centered), different requirements for personal space (up close and personal), and different noise sensitivities (louder is usually better). One of the biggest differences is their sense of time, which tends to be much more languorous and fluid than ours. Schedules, deadlines, and linear progressions do not come naturally to kids; they didn't to us, for that matter, but we've learned them all too well. Young kids even *talk* more slowly than we do, since they're piecing together sentences from words they may never have uttered consecutively before.

Speaking of speaking, the greatest gap probably lies in language. It's really a combination of differences: the words they don't know, the ones they invent to compensate, the inflections they haven't learned, the pronunciations they lack coordination for, the feelings they can't recognize, the thoughts they can't or won't articulate. Toddlers often say no when they really mean yes, for example; ironically, this is the reverse of what American businessmen often encounter in Japan. Translating from kids and to kids builds a dad's vocabulary just as much as a sojourn in a new country or industry. (Fathering also improves your spelling, for when you want to tell Mom something in a language the kids *won't* understand.)

Your business experience should help you with cross-border transitions. I was fortunate during my eight years at Salomon to work with companies in many countries and industries. Whether I was immersed in a Georgia paper mill, a Hollywood studio, an Italian TV network, or a Japanese video game publisher, one of my favorite parts of the work was learning new cultures, a mind-broadening (and often humbling) experience. From there I went to City Hall, where the culture was even more different: at least everyone in the private sector had the profit motive in common. Now I'm doing venture capital, and my firm has invested in everything from Jiffy Lube franchises to Internet medical services to the Scottish company that brought us Dolly, the cloned sheep. Those adventures across commercial cultures have, I think, helped prepare me for the even greater leap required to mesh with my children.

As with any leap, cultural ones are easier when you start closer together. The advice to "stay close with your kids" is as obvious and as important as "stay close to your customer." Not coincidentally, the principles below show that the methods are similar in each case, but you have one big advantage at home: *you love your kids, and all your best ways of getting close are really just ways of showing that love.*

Don't Be a Stranger

• **Start early.** When dealing with a major customer, it's never too soon in the relationship to meet. Similarly, you will be glad if you get acquainted with your kids as early as pregnancy. Talking to that kid in your wife's belly gets him accustomed to your voice and helps you start the bonding process yourself.

• **Make time.** When I'm doing due diligence on a potential investment, I always see a red flag when important customers tell me the company hasn't been spending enough time with them lately. Studies saying that the average father invests only five minutes a day with each of his children give me the same uneasy feeling. The Dual Titles chapter debunks the myth of "quality time" in detail and discusses ways of making "quantity time." For now, I'll simply note that more is better. It doesn't have to be formally planned: some of the best moments can occur spontaneously while you're heading from the couch to the fridge. Keeping in touch by phone and beeper works okay in a pinch, but face-to-face, one-on-one, is always best. As the old line goes, nothing propinks like propinquity.

My shining example is my own father. He had a lot of responsibilities, and the summer nights he spent playing Ping-Pong with me in our garage, always agreeing to "just one more game," must have taken him away from other things he needed to do. But for decades since and ever after, those hours of lazy chat and volleys will glow in my memory as magical gifts of magical time.

• **"Waste" time.** With customers and coworkers, we sometimes

build relationships by sitting in endless meetings whose only immediate results are the consumption of bagels. At home, the two thousandth game of peekaboo may not be our *first* choice of leisure
activity, but it's still a great investment in trust and closeness. And
the better we know our kids, the less likely we are to be bored with
them at all. "Wasted" time is seldom really wasted.

• **Seize the moment.** "Carpe diem" ("seize the day") really has
two meanings. The common one is to take action now rather than
later; the hidden one is to grab every moment and get the most out
of it that you can. You'll miss those golden moments that make fatherhood rewarding, and you'll miss knowing your kids, if your
mind is always on tomorrow's big meeting instead of on the pint-size
folk you're with tonight. Plan for the big meeting during your work
time, and let it happen when it happens. You'll probably concentrate
better, when it *does* happen, if you have no guilt about ignoring your
kids to distract you.

• **Learn the lingo.** If you're selling to the widget industry, you
have to master widget-ese. In Detroit, you'd better know your cams
from your carburetor. On Seventh Avenue, you won't get far if you
think "bias cut" means the dress designer is prejudiced. In retailing,
you've got to understand that "shrinkage" is not a problem of size 8
becoming size 6. Among yogurt makers, "FOB" has nothing to do
with freight on board or friend of Bill (it means fruit on bottom). In
cellular, the "price per pop" has nothing to do with balloons, sodas,
or Rice Krispies.

Without communication, minds cannot meet. If you know how
to listen and to express yourself within the industry you serve, you
can become the toast of your company. But if you don't or can't, then
you're just toast.

With kids, language skills are just as important. The key is not
to talk down to them, and yet not to converse with them as adults either. This balancing act is so important that I'll expand on it shortly.

• **Use body language, too.** The pat on the back that makes
your customer feel valued comes a lot more naturally when you actually like the person. With kids, hugs of all kinds should *always*
come naturally—quick squeezes, hug-and-kiss combos, and great

big bear hugs that only Dad can give. When my father and I were sauntering back from those Ping-Pong games in the garage, he'd often put his arm around my shoulders—not talking, just walking. I remember those moments as clearly as a delicious dream. It doesn't matter how old your kids are or whether they're male or female; as the author Samuel Osherson wrote, "getting a hug from Dad is like touching home base."

• **Observe them in their social circle.** Whenever I'm doing due diligence on a company, I always make a point of visiting its offices. I like to see the kind of environment the officers have created for themselves, but even more important is the way they interact with their colleagues. I find that those moments are more realistic (more typical, less guarded) than prepared presentations, and so give a truer picture of the company and how it operates.

Similarly, kids behave quite differently with their peers than with us. The more you watch them interacting with other kids, the better you'll understand how they actually view the world. In their friends, you'll also find benchmarks to measure them against. This is all important stuff: in my opinion, the leading reason that most mothers understand their kids better than Dad does is precisely their greater exposure to play times.

• **Show your priorities.** Would you flip through your mail in front of a customer who's been waiting to talk to you? Julie knew a psychology supervisor who was infamous for doing that in front of trainees, and I knew a venture capitalist who frequently did it in meetings with financing candidates. Both eventually lost their jobs.

When you get home from work, don't head straight to the mail or to the fax machine. Sit down with your family and catch up. You may want to change into comfortable clothes first, which might also help to shift your mind-set from office to home. Should you need to decompress before you see your family, try to do it on the way home, not once you're there.

Your kids and your wife will appreciate it when the fact that you've arrived means you're *home*. If you work longer hours than your wife, she and the kids are probably due for a break from one another, whereas you're fresh. Oh, you may be tired, but being with your family is a change of pace for you, requiring a "different flavor" of energy. Doing office work from the moment you arrive, and waiting to play until you and your brood are too tired to enjoy it, would be "bass ackwards." Playing with them *first* will probably refresh you and let you work even better after they're asleep. (That recommendation is for general practice, not for every night. Each evening has its own logistics of travel, commute, kids' schedules, and so forth.)

In my family, we used to have a ritual where I buzzed from downstairs, everyone met me at the elevator, and we'd all have a procession down the hallway to the apartment—from the outside world to the family world. It set the right tone for the evening, and the celebrity treatment was not too shabby for a tired Daddy's mood, either.

• **See beyond differences.** Your customer may come from a different country, or be of a different gender or religion or ethnic background, but letting that get in your way would be self-defeating and possibly illegal. Kids, on the other hand, sometimes seem as if they come from a different solar system. Inside, though, they need your love and understanding as much as ever. Even during adolescence, their dad means more to them than any other guy alive.

• **Reject rejection.** As any master salesman will tell you, "no" is when the selling begins. After your kids have compared you to the illegitimate offspring of Scrooge and the Wicked Witch and heartily wished you dead, it's only natural to stalk off, lick your wounds, and stay away. Who needs that, anyway?

But remember, you're the grown-up and they're not. They won't admit how much they really need you, so it's up to you to keep coming back. Consciously or not, they may only be testing your commitment. Let them know their behavior is unacceptable, but don't reject them because of it. The only way to make things easier is to be there through the hard parts.

• **Enjoy yourself.** Lunch with your customer produces smaller orders if you're so bored that you can find nothing to do but toy with your roll. Customers aren't blind, and they can tell if you see hosting them as an ordeal. Likewise, kids sense it when you treat your time with them as a chore, and that in itself tends to make it one. If you can find something to interest you about your biggest but dullest client, you can certainly find it with those rather fascinating small individuals.

I promised to return to the language issue. How do we deal with the fact that kids communicate so differently? The trick is to meet them halfway: learn enough about their idiom to understand them, but also teach them how grown-ups do it. If there's one thing kids do amazingly well, it's picking up languages.

But how do *we* pick up theirs? There's no Berlitz for toddler-ese, and that old book *Kids Say the Darnedest Things!* doesn't really fit the bill. The ideal would be a little book with one section to translate kid-speak into (adult) English, and another section to translate English into kid-speak. The next best thing is a conceptual guide to translating between the two, which is what I'll offer here. It is, however, still helpful to split this guide into the two parts of communication: what we *hear* and what we *say*.

Let's start with listening. Contrary to some businesspeople's apparent belief, the opposite of "talking" is not "waiting to talk." We may all be born with ears, but using them correctly is very much an acquired skill. Did you know that some hospitals and airlines actually make surgeons and pilots take seminars in how to listen? Given their huge potential liabilities from a missed sentence or two, it makes sense once you think about it. And Starbucks, whose customers can order hundreds of different permutations of size, flavor, temperature, and style of coffee, has for years trained its "baristas" in a specially devised method of listening and remembering.

Which matters more, understanding what our kids are telling us, or getting our coffee made right? (Coffee lovers may need to think about that one for a minute.)

Listen Up!

DO pay attention. This may sound obvious, but it's not easy. Business dads are busy people with a lot to think about, so it's easy to get distracted when your kids are mumbling something or other. Remember, though, that kids are very good at recognizing lack of interest. They won't tell you the big things until you've proven that you're interested in even the most trivial stuff they can think of— which isn't that trivial, once you realize that they are trying to connect with you any way they know how. You have two goals in listening: to understand and to show interest. If you don't pay attention, you'll fail at both.

DO listen "closely." Executives often serve themselves poorly by keeping too much distance between them and their subordinates. Gene L., a consultant I work with frequently, told me about a nightmare trip he once took with a client, who insisted on flying first class. This fellow's junior colleague didn't rate first class but had something important to discuss during the flight. The flight attendants wouldn't let him into first, while the client wouldn't deign to go back into coach, so the poor guy spent the whole conversation hunched by the divider curtain, poking his head around to communicate!

As a refreshing contrast, Intel's Andy Grove keeps his office in a cubicle only a little bigger than everyone else's, out in the middle of the floor. I am convinced this lets mission-critical information reach him twice as quickly as it would in the usual Taj Mahal suite of a *Fortune* 100 president. Other CEOs, such as Paul O'Neill of ALCOA, have more recently picked up on the same idea.

To bring this lesson home: it's hard to hear from four feet above your toddlers' heads, and that distance may discourage them somewhat from even trying. When young children ask you something or when you want to start a conversation, get down to their level. Sit down, kneel down, squat down, lie down, whatever—the operative word here is "down." Unless, of course, you choose to pick them up!

DON'T check your watch. You want your kids to think you have all the time in the world for them. You can tell them when they start if Daddy has to go do something soon, so they're not surprised when you have to cut the conversation short. But while they're actually talking, nothing squelches their enthusiasm like a father who keeps signaling (by checking his watch or drumming his fingers or jumping in to finish all their sentences) that he doesn't have time for them.

DO listen with empathy. Life's realities are often subjective, as the philosopher George Berkeley demonstrated with the following experiment. Immerse your left hand in cold water and your right simultaneously in hot, then dip them both into lukewarm water. Your left hand will tell you the lukewarm water is hot, while your right will insist it's cold! In business and in child rearing, subjectivity means we can never assume other people see things the way we do. That's what makes life interesting.

If we forget to check others' perspectives, we risk acting like those cartoon characters who walk blithely off cliffs, realizing only when it's too late that they're standing on thin air. What we need to establish, in other words, is common ground. That requires empathy, a sincere effort to understand others' feelings. Empathy becomes easier with tools like reciprocation and feedback, but most of all it means what Julie calls "listening with two ears" and showing a *genuine* underlying interest. This process may not lead to agreement on subjective matters, but if nothing else it will help us to comprehend where others differ from ourselves, and so to avoid further misunderstanding.

DO reciprocate. Even children too young for words are very energetic communicators. Encourage them by showing you understand them. If they want something tangible like a rattle, you can encourage their communication by giving it to them. Even better, you can say, "You want the *rattle?*" before handing it over, so they learn the word. Often, though, they are trying to communicate a feeling or just to show you a new facial expression they've made up. At those times, the best thing you can do is be their mirror. Show them on your face the expression they just made, together with the appropriate responsive noise, and they will be delighted. Not only will they know you "got it," but they will also see for themselves what it was you got.

This may sound touchy-feely, but it works, and not just at home. Your officemates each have their own "inner child," after all, and they love it unconsciously when their smiling makes you smile, or when raising their eyebrows makes yours arch in sympathy. Watch yourself at the office, and I bet you'll catch yourself reacting this way automatically, as an instinctive means of "making friends and influencing people." And next time you're on the phone with customers from another part of the country, listen carefully to see if the rhythm or accent of your speech shifts a little toward theirs.

DO use feedback. As kids get older, reciprocation gives way to "the paraphrased return." Take what they tell you and say it back, maybe changing the wording to standard English if appropriate. For example:

"Daddy, we winned the game last morning."

"You won the game yesterday morning? That's great!"

Never adopt teenagers' slang in your paraphrased returns, of course. They use it to be different from you, and you will sound phony using it. The point of paraphrasing is to put things in your own words.

Starbucks has made this technique part of its standard method, having found that repeating every order greatly reduces misunderstandings and errors. At home, paraphrased return brings an amazing total of eight benefits:

- It forces you to pay attention.
- It *shows* you are paying attention.
- It tactfully demonstrates for next time the proper way of saying something.
- It prevents misunderstandings.
- It helps you elaborate for kids what they are really feeling.
- If your kid is expressing an emotion, coming back with the same tone of voice shows that you understand and sympathize, and that the emotion is "okay" to have.
- It lets you ask better questions. Questions from *your* point of view are usually less effective at eliciting the key answers.
- Once you've sympathized, the groundwork is laid for you to take action, whether that be solving an underlying problem that was causing sadness or frustration, or enforcing your will despite your kid's defiance. "Yeah, you don't want to leave yet, do you?

This *is* fun, but we *do* have to go now or we'll be late for picking up Mommy."

DO help out. Kids can't always articulate what they're thinking or feeling. If they've said enough to give you a hunch, supplying a word or completing the thought once they're finished not only shows attention and understanding, but teaches them words they can use next time.

DON'T interrupt. Helping out is not the same as interrupting. I'm sure you can often tell what your kids are saying a full minute before they finish the sentence. Don't finish it for them, though, unless they're really having problems; they need the practice in speaking. Interrupting makes them think you don't have time to listen and is really an exercise of power, which is no more polite at home than in the office.

As a young man, Randolph Churchill was once trying to make a point when his father Winston interrupted with his own views. When Randolph tried to regain the floor, Winston snapped, "Don't interrupt me when I am interrupting!" This should not be a model for father-child dialogue.

DON'T let the media interrupt. If you must have the TV or radio turned on, at least avoid conversing with your kids at the same time. The electronic din can distract them or even drown them out, and they end up competing with it for your attention, which sends them exactly the wrong message about your priorities. Print media need to be held at bay as well: if your kids want your attention desperately when you're reading a newspaper or magazine, have the civility to put it aside at least until you've heard them through or answered their question. Feel free to set aside some "protected time" each day when you can read or watch TV uninterrupted, but don't begrudge your attention at other times.

DON'T let the telephone interrupt. Businessmen use the phone as much as anyone, other than maybe teenagers. The late Texas oilman Jack Grimm once joked that he used his phone so much he wanted it buried with him. But simply needing the phone doesn't mean you have to worship it.

Treat time with your kids like any customer meeting. There are only a limited number of phone calls you can take before you become rude. Staying on one call forever can send them the wrong signal, especially if you've just gotten home and haven't seen them all day. If you're expecting an important call in the middle of your kid time, consider giving your kids advance notice, and try to keep it short. You may want to set aside some "no telephone" periods each week or each evening, such as when you're putting the kids to bed. (With teens, you can then require similar courtesy from them during family times.)

That doesn't mean you should jump off the phone the moment your kids start whining. That would teach the wrong lesson: whining gets results. Instead, tell them not to whine and *don't* hang up, but do try to end the call quickly as soon as they start waiting patiently. (Some parents keep special toys that they let young kids play with only during phone calls, so the kids don't mind calls so much.)

DO listen with your eyes. Even older kids can't or won't put words to everything they're telling you. Use all your senses, not just your hearing, to detect nonverbal cues like facial expression and body language. Yogi Berra once commented, "You can observe a lot by watching." Showing that you understand them with *or* without words gives them a deep feeling of love and security, even if it also (in the case of teenagers) drives them crazy.

DON'T jump to conclusions. No matter how well you listen "between the lines," you may still miss some subtext in what your kids say. Before you reach any dramatic conclusions, make sure you've asked all the follow-on questions you need to. Otherwise, you risk accusations of "You never understand me!"—even (and especially) from kids who really could have expressed themselves more clearly.

DO listen even when you don't like what you hear. Smart technology companies often have internal E-mail discussion groups specifically designed for employees to grouse about management. Sun's is called Bad Attitude, and Netscape until recently had one called Really Bad Attitude. The idea is that management can learn from anonymous postings, and that employees will be more brutally frank than they might be face-to-face. Approach what your children say with a similarly open mind. Correct them if they're wrong, don't tolerate it if they say things in a disrespectful way, but don't close your ears to the possibility that they may just have a point.

The pointers above are all good to master, because how you listen probably matters even more than what you say. Just as in business, the Listener's Law is that the volume of information you gain varies in *inverse* proportion to how much you talk. But learning is not the only goal of communicating: you also care about instruction, persuasion, and expressing your own feelings. Although all that knowledge you've soaked up by listening will heighten your effectiveness in those areas, listening has its limits. Parents need not only to understand, but also to be understood.

Once you've mastered all the dos and don'ts for *listening* to kids, you may find the following helpful for *talking* to them. Put the two sets together and you will know, as a recent book title put it, *How to Talk So Kids Will Listen and Listen So Kids Will Talk*. (By the way, that book, by Adele Faber and Elaine Mazlish, is terrific if you want to explore those topics further.)

The Art of Conversation

DON'T be Mr. Abrupt. Most important business conversations begin with small talk, which sets the right tone for a constructive discussion. When you enter a room where your kids are playing, you'll do better if you establish a connection with innocuous, engaging questions such as, "What are you building?" than if you jump in with an order or accusation that disrupts their mood, such as, "Time to stop that. The store's closing in an hour!" In a business negotiation, I doubt you would march into the other side's office, skip any preliminaries, and shout, "We'll pay $2 million and not a penny more!"

DO be specific. Your questions will get better answers if they are specific, not open-ended. For example, ask "Did you and Jamie play in the pool?" rather than "What did you and Jamie do?" Generic questions usually elicit generic replies. Specific questions get better answers *and* often lead to worthwhile further questions.

DO be Socratic. About ten years ago, Salomon Brothers sent my whole department to an expensive all-day seminar on Socratic selling technique. Socrates, as you may recall, was the Athenian who got into hot water and hemlock for giving young people too many ideas. Plato preserved examples of his mentor's teaching methods in numerous dialogues, in which the old guy gets his points across quite effectively using almost nothing but questions.

The seminar was all about the power of questions. I remember it well, since it made a great impression on me and has proved useful ever since. It taught me to avoid launching blindly into a sales pitch, and instead to begin with something like, "We've come prepared to talk about interest rate swaps, but first we'd like to know what particular concerns *you* want to discuss. Are there any additional topics you'd like to focus on?" And you know what? It worked. I actually learned stuff in those first ten minutes that made the next two hours much more effective. I learned what clients really wanted to understand, what their sensitivities were, and often what they had already decided was the right answer. Plus, they liked being asked what *they* thought for a change.

If you want to teach or persuade your kids, it's better to draw the key conclusion out of them than to impose it top down. "Don't grab Jamie's toys! It makes him feel bad and it's wrong!" is fine, but you might occasionally try something like the following Socratic dialogue. You: "Did you grab that toy from Jamie?" Kid: "Yeah." You: "How would you feel if other kids took your toys?" Kid: "I'd be mad, and I'd hit them!" You: "Would you think they were wrong?" Kid: "Yeah!" You: "So now you understand how Jamie felt." *Then* follow through with the stern talk, together with any punishments you think are necessary.

DO talk about yourself. Kids are curious about everything, but especially about you, since you're so important to them. They may not show it, though, out of shyness, or they may not even know the right questions to ask. Letting them into your world by volunteering information gives them beachheads in your reality, from which they can explore further when they are ready. There are plenty of good reasons for them to understand your life outside home. You're giving them something of yourself, which strengthens your connection with them, helps them understand why you leave them each weekday, and may make them more forthcoming when you turn the tables and start querying them.

DON'T talk when play is better. Even if kids don't seem in a mood to talk, chances are good (unless they're teenagers) that they'll still be up for the intermediary step of playing. Collaborating on a castle of blocks, or shooting hoops, or doing whatever engages them, certainly can break the conversational ice. It also tells your kids, "I like being with you. You matter to me. I'm interested in what you're interested in." Last but not least, it should serve to relax *you* so you don't bring extrinsic tensions into the exchange.

For any of these to work, though, note that in child's play the process counts more than the product. If you've just come from the office, you may have to restrain yourself from being "productive" and "competent" with this castle. For your kids, the fun of putting one block atop another to make a wall probably matters more than getting the towers symmetrical or the crenelations just right. Most of all, they do not feel at all pressed to get the castle finished quickly and would, if anything, rather have it take longer. This is the time to "zen out," to be "in the moment," and to set aside that compulsive efficiency your boss rewards you for.

DO pick your places. Just as you wouldn't discuss your subordinate's raise at the urinals (would you?), you should find the optimal time to broach sensitive subjects at home. Children often have favorite places to open up. It may be in the car going to school, or in the kitchen cleaning up from dinner. The more "quantity time" you spend with your kids, the better you'll observe where their favorite places are. Benjamin, for example, happens to prefer city buses, and "lights out" time just before we say good night. Take note of your own kids' proclivities, and time your heavier discussions accordingly.

DO serve a verbal sandwich. When you think you're about to strike a raw nerve with an older kid, you may want to slap together what the writer Paul Lewis calls a "verbal sandwich." That means starting with something soft and personal (equivalent to a slice of bread), layering on some positive reinforcement (the mayo or mustard, depending on your preference), going on to the meat of the discussion, and closing with something soft again. If your teenager tries to reject your order to stop showing her midriff in midwinter, for example, she'll have to reject the rest of the sandwich as well (compliments on the shape she's in, concerns for her health, admiration for her sense of style, or whatever else you, the chef, select). There still may be an argument, but no one can say you didn't make an effort to render your criticism palatable.

DON'T talk to the walls. A key skill for any effective presenter is knowing when he's losing his audience. Kids have short attention spans, or they may be embarrassed to have done something wrong. They may be sitting quietly without heeding a single word you're saying, so keep eye contact, watch the subtle cues, and yank their attention back when necessary. Depending on the situation, you might use a question to jolt them into rejoining the conversation, or simply the time-honored admonition to "listen when I'm talking to you!" If it happens repeatedly, you may be lecturing too much and listening too little, so switch to Socratic mode for a while. Better yet, just keep the interchange short and sweet. You're not talking for your health, after all, and it does take two to communicate.

DON'T give up easily. Ian W., an entrepreneur I know in Florida, has created about $100 million in value for himself and his private shareholders in the past four years. He is also a widower bringing up two teenagers on his own, and so knows more than most of us about connecting with kids. In that regard, he told me two important lessons business has taught him. First, give due consideration to your kids' viewpoints. "The impulse is, I'm the adult, and I know everything. Teenagers hate that." Second, when you're trying to convince kids of an idea, don't take no for an answer. Find out what their issues are, then address them one by one. "I know every-thing about overcoming objections. In business, I have to overcome ten objections to every deal." And he does, too.

DON'T force it. During their moodiest phases, some kids just can't be drawn out. Listen when they want to talk, let them know you're available, but don't press too hard or they'll clam up even tighter. When you're forced at such times to limit your questions, make sure you've done enough homework through your other sources to achieve surgical levels of precision.

DON'T make one size fit all. Be yourself, but remember which of your kids you're talking to. One might respond to humor, another to sternness, and a third to plain declarative sentences. Don't fall into ruts with any of them, but take particular care not to fall into the same rut with all three.

DON'T "solve" problems by dismissing them. Business dads may be particularly prone to the male habit of responding to our loved ones' sadness or frustration by trying to make the under-lying problem go away. Problem solving is something we get di-rectly paid for at the office, after all. The practical approach works fine if the problem can be solved, as with a Lego toy that just needs reassembly. But if the problem *can't* be solved easily, as with a toy that's broken beyond mending, some men then make the case that it shouldn't be seen as a problem at all. ("Don't be upset about that. It's not worth it.")

That, of course, is precisely what our loved ones (wives or kids) do not want to hear. They want a shoulder to cry on, not an insistence (albeit well-intentioned) that they're wrong to be crying at all, or that their problems are unimportant. And the only thing worse is a frus-trated response from Dad that the problem was their fault to begin with. ("This wouldn't have happened if you'd been more careful.")

If your kids think there's a problem, then there is—whether it has to do with their toys, with their friends, or even with you. Some-times helping them accept it achieves more than trying to belittle it (and with it, them).

DON'T "help" bad feelings by denying them. "I hate my

baby sister." "No, you don't." *Bzzzt!* Wrong answer. All you're doing is discouraging your kid from telling you truths he doesn't think you want to hear. The right answer, O Socrates, is a question. For example: "You hate your sister? How come?" Kid: "She keeps trying to mess up my jigsaw puzzle. It's not fair!" You: "You're right, that's a pain. But remember, she's just a baby, so she doesn't understand yet about right and wrong. Hey, I've got an idea!" Kid: "What?" You: "Let's put the puzzle up on this table, so she can't reach it." That method acknowledges and validates your kid's feelings, and also helps prevent them from getting worse.

DO mean what you say. Just as dogs can smell fear and Alan Greenspan can sniff inflation, kids can sense insincerity. It's one thing to have an ulterior purpose in what you say (assuming it's benevolent), but it's another thing altogether to say something you don't mean. Every time you do that is like another drop of acid eating away at your kids' trust in you.

I've been talking a lot here about the importance of getting to know your kids, and of being available to chat and play with them. I do not mean to give the impression that I think you should be 100 percent available to them whenever you are home. There are several reasons:

- It's not realistic. Both your paid and unpaid jobs are so demanding that you can't erect impervious firewalls between them. Your kids just have to accept that sometimes Dad has work he needs to do or time he needs for himself or Mom.
- It gives your kids the wrong expectations. If they think you can always drop everything to come discuss their toy wish list, their feelings will be hurt even more when the inevitable happens and you can't.
- It gives them bad habits. Even if you could provide your kids "hot and cold running Daddy" by being forever available, that's not how the world works. Accustoming them to hogging the

spotlight will set them up for a cruel rejection once they enter society. At best they'll have trouble readjusting, and at worst they will retreat back into the coddling comfort of home.

- It gives you bad habits. If you feel that being with them *always* requires your full attention and does not permit you to get any work done, you will probably end up spending less time with them. That would also be a shame because seeing you working gives them a good role model.

When Junior wants your attention, don't hesitate to let him know if, for example, you're in the middle of an important conversation, either with Mom or on the phone. Pleasantly but firmly, inform him that you'll be with him in a few minutes, but that he needs to be patient and not interrupt. If he obeys, great. If not, use your full armament of disciplinary tools (see the Conflict Resolution chapter) to make sure this social grace takes root deeply. Most business dads, however, are so harried that they tend to err in the opposite direction, giving too little attention to their kids rather than too much.

Information Transfer

Remember that truck-stop cable investment I mentioned before? We learned a lot by questioning management, but please do not think that management was our only source of information—far from it. Both before our investment and at various points afterward, we spoke to more than fifty truck-stop operators, plus drivers, fleet executives, equipment manufacturers, potential competitors, and others.

It's not that we didn't trust management, but management had no way of knowing what was inside the heads of all those important company contacts. We needed to educate ourselves about the industry, and about how those players really viewed our company. They told us some things they might never have told management. As a result, we got a fully rounded view of the company and its place in the truck-stop environment.

Every businessman needs the same skill—tracking down key information about someone or something from third-party sources. He could be a CEO scoping out a potential acquisition target. He could be a manager conducting a "360-degree evaluation" of an employee, getting input from everyone the employee works with, under, or over. He could even be a "chief knowledge officer" trying to create systems for information to flow freely wherever it is needed, like the "boundary-less" sharing of ideas promoted by Jack Welch within GE. In every one of those cases, the urgency springs from the fact that the *best* decision a company can make is the *best informed* decision.

Fathering requires the same diligence. Even if you give your all to interacting closely with your kids, the fact remains that you spend most of your waking hours at the office or on the road. Their mom, their siblings, their nanny or sitter, and their teachers all see more of your kids than you do, and they also may understand what they see in ways that could benefit you—ways that are not necessarily better than your perspective, but that may be complementary. Because they see your kids in more settings, they also may see weaknesses or strengths that you have not seen.

The information you will gain from the following pointers might be routine stuff like what your kids have been learning in school, whether they had enough greens for lunch (useful if you're giving them dinner), or what their mood might be when you get home. It might also, however, include more urgent matters like a major playground outburst or a spectacular behavioral breakthrough. In either case, it will help you become a better and smarter dad.

Work Your Sources!

Mom. Your wife is the most crucial link between you and your children's world. Even if she works away from home, she may have had six conversations today with sitters, teachers, other parents, and the kids themselves. She will be your best source if you have the right kind of team relationship, but she alone is not enough, for several reasons.

- She would have to be superhuman to remember and tell you everything she herself learned from all the other sources.
- Your time alone with her is scarce enough; why overburden it by funneling all other sources through her?
- You may have your own take on what the other sources have to say, so it's better to hear them directly (when possible).

Nanny/sitter. Your kids' nanny (if they have one) or sitter (depending on how much she's around) is so important that you should really treat her more like a third parent than like an hourly employee. Ideally, you should participate alongside your wife in the "seven C's" of good nanny relations:

- Choose: Be sure you and your wife are both involved in the nanny selection process. You'll get the nanny to commit to both of you, and to understand that she is accountable to both of you.
- Communicate: Help make every handoff to and from the nanny as seamless as possible. Has the baby been changed recently? How many ounces did he have? When was his last nap? And so forth.
- Coordinate: Plan with the nanny what each of you will be doing in the coming day or week. If I have late meetings or travel in my plans, I try to let our nanny know myself.
- Connect: Treat your nanny with respect, and she will respond in kind, becoming a real conduit for connecting with your kids.
- Confer: When your kids have problems, or when you are considering a change in their lives, include your nanny at least partly in parental deliberations. She'll appreciate it, and she may well have insights to contribute.
- Compromise: Remember that your nanny is a person with her own life, maybe even her own kids. If your needs and hers conflict, be reasonable. If you take a rigid "my way or the highway" stance, you may just find yourself and your family having to adjust to a new nanny all over again.
- Compensate: Pay the nanny as well as you can, and foster her

sense of accountability to both of you by deciding on compensation together.

School. Your children will do a huge part of their growing and changing within the walls of school (or day care, for younger kids). You should connect with their teachers as often as possible, learning what's going on in the class and with your kid. If you also get to know most of their classmates by name and face, you will have a clue about the players in their daily dramas.

One way to accomplish all this relatively painlessly is to drop your kids off sometimes on your way to work. Another way is to visit their classrooms once in a while and give little presentations on your favorite hobby or how you earn your living. That accomplishes three goals: it deepens your relationships with teachers and classmates, it provides a glimpse into your outside life, and it raises your children's peer status by making you a class celebrity. Finally, you might consider pitching in on class projects or chaperoning a field trip.

School is more than just the classroom, of course. As your children mature, they will begin team sports, drama productions, and other extracurricular activities. Going to most of their big public events is a must, but you might also attend the occasional practice or rehearsal. That will give you a chance to connect with coaches and arts directors, who may be important figures in your children's lives. Your kids will appreciate it too. (As Milton wrote, "They also serve who only stand and wait.") The same truth may apply to other parts of your kids' lives, such as playgrounds and doctors' offices. Give them some space, always, but cut yourself a window into that space when you can.

Friends' parents. Another reason to attend play dates, practices, and other kid get-togethers is that you will also get to know other parents, who may have valuable insights into your kids' behavior and personalities. Maybe their children went through the same issues last month, or maybe they just have a different way of looking at kids. Some dads may even inspire you with useful fathering techniques, either through dad-to-dad discussions or simply by using them in front of you. (Alternatively, you may learn from their mistakes!) Some very committed fathers form monthly discussion groups, which can be useful forums for hashing out issues their whole gang of kids is going through.

Grandparents. Grandparents are wonderful resources who know your kids, have tons of experience (though they may be rusty), know you or your wife from way back when, and won't be bashful when asked for advice. Don't be embarrassed to solicit their interpretations of your kids' latest craziness when all else fails. You'll have to handle the delicate issues of when and how to accept their advice, but it's often better to have it than not.

The media. Just as you read periodicals for business, don't neglect the reams of advice for parents in magazines like *Child*, *Parents*, and *Parenting*. The experts don't know your kids personally, but sometimes they have an uncanny way of seeming to. Although they are mostly for "parents" rather than dads, they still can be worthwhile. The same is true of parenting bibles such as the *What to Expect* books. I have listed in the Appendix what I consider to be the most useful nuts-and-bolts and "experts' " books on fathering.

Some of the most useful print sources are not on paper. I am referring, of course, to Web sites, of which the best general parenting resources include Parents' Place (www.parentsplace.com), Parent Soup (www.parentsoup.com), and Disney's Family.com (www.family.com). Those may provide useful links for dad-specific sites, such as Fathering Magazine (www.fathermag.com), The National Center for Fathering (www.fathers.com), or FatherNet (www.cyfc.umn.edu/Fathernet/index.html). Talk City (www.talkcity.com) is one of the leading community sites on the Internet (and I'm not saying that just because I sit on its board) and offers many worthwhile chats about parenting issues. Finally, you can use our own www.businessdad.com to trade tips with other business dads, develop your own fathering strategies, and find additional relevant links.

Those are among the major sources for independent information about your kids. As with business consultants' reports, accept what you find useful, but don't automatically defer to these sources' recommendations. Leo Tolstoi betrayed his ignorance of family bliss when he wrote condescendingly that "happy families are all alike; every unhappy family is unhappy in its own way." Every effective parent knows that people and the families they form are *all* different, happy or not, and so must all find their own ways of functioning.

Assimilating hard facts is always worthwhile, but subjective recommendations (including many of those in this book) are trickier. After all, every dad (like every businessman) has a different personal style to which he must be true. *Only you know your kid in a dad's special way, and only you know yourself.* Do what seems right to you, as long as you're satisfied that you have all the requisite information and have *thought* about it in the right way. If you consistently follow that principle, then you'll be on the way to becoming the best father for your kids that (only) you can be.

Human Capital

BUILDING A HAPPIER CHILD

Customer Support

Raising happy children first of all means attending to their basic emotional needs, which can be summarized in one word: LASS. (Come on, this wouldn't be a book for businessmen without at least one acronym! And this acronym actually makes sense, if you're the parent of a girl.) LASS means *love*, *acceptance*, *self-esteem*, and *stability*. They're all nice- sounding words (who could be against them?), but some family "experts" have taken them too far, turning them into a license to overkill. Let me tell you what I think these words should mean for business dads.

Love in the most basic sense means plenty of hugs and cuddling. Studies show that animal babies wither without them, even if they're getting enough to eat and drink. You don't want your kids to take you for granted, but you don't want them to take you for granite either. As a father, you should always employ this policy: when in doubt, give a hug.

King L., a veteran software entrepreneur in central California, has three grown kids who've turned out terrifically, and he recalls that "we always had plenty of hugging and kissing." That was not the way he himself grew up. "My father came from that old school—if you hug your kid, you make him gay." It wasn't until he reached adulthood that King decided to break with family convention. "When I gave him that first hug, I could feel him stiffen. He looked at me kind of funny, but then I could see him thinking, 'Well, if he's married with three kids, I guess he's okay.' I started hugging him every time I saw him, and eventually he came round. By the time he died, he was hugging everyone."

Then there are more elaborate ways of showing love, like spontaneous acts of kindness or an affectionate word just before bedtime (it keeps kids warm the whole night). Empathizing with their problems shows you love them, but remember that empathy is like some people's idea of exercise: you're not doing it right unless it hurts. Empathy's easy to dish out in fair weather, but when those storm clouds gather, you really do feel kids' pain. No truly empathic father can be happier than his least happy child. Empathy means giving up that shield of emotional toughness that serves you so well in business.

I have a rule with business contacts whom I admire and want to stay in touch with. I always call to congratulate them on good news, but I call twice as fast to commiserate and offer help when something goes wrong. Businesspeople remember the loyalty others show when the chips are down, and children are no different. If you make your empathy conditional on whether their distress seems reasonable, they'll wonder what else between you is conditional.

It's hard to show love without the gift of time. Not quality time, but quantity time. Like empathy, your time cannot be conditional, to be withheld if the kids misbehave. Kids will do bizarre things to get your time and attention, and the stakes just go up if you punish them by ignoring them. Brian O'Reilly, in his *Fortune* article "Why Grade 'A' Executives Get an 'F' as Parents," quoted one bitter teenager as remembering, "My dad worried about me from behind his desk."

Love does *not*, contrary to the habits of some very successful businessmen, mean giving your children whatever they want. Indulging them, spoiling them, rendering them unfit for human society is no way to show affection. Love means simply giving them the human warmth they need to grow and flourish. Love means supplying them with the conviction that they are not just special in the abstract but special to *you*, their father, who happen to be one of the two most important people in their lives.

Spoiling, I should note, is sometimes more appropriate in the workplace than at home. Artie Isaac, the president of advertising agency Young Isaac, gave an apt example in a 1998 *Forbes* interview. "At one ad agency I worked for, a top creative person had a legendary deal: a peeled orange was delivered to him at 1:30 P.M. every day. Some people won't give an employee a peeled orange on principle. It might be in your best interest to give your employee that orange. Let him feel special." The reason that employers can profit by spoiling selected employees to the point of insufferability is that their mission does not include raising those employees as functioning social beings. Not so, however, your mission as father.

When an airline wants to show its best customers that they are special, it lets them sit in a magical realm called first class. What is the best investment any airline ever makes, with a return a thousand times its cost? Not computers, not advertising, and certainly not planes. No, it's that little curtain between first class and coach. It drives some people crazy to be aft of that curtain, not because the food or accommodations are that much worse, but simply because they're being excluded. It makes them so crazy, in fact, that they pay thousands of dollars extra for first class, or go out of their way to earn enough miles and stickers for upgrades. That flimsy little curtain must be worth ten times its weight in gold!

All businesspeople, if you think about it, use little curtains like that in their lives. The purpose is the same, to divide what they care about most from everything else. And children, as alert as any frequent flyer, pay great attention to which side of their dad's curtain they're on. Love, then, is simply showing your kids that they matter to you, that they fly up front in your life, and that you are determined to give them first-class treatment. If your boss rides up front while your kids get economy treatment, it's definitely time to up-grade your life.

Acceptance, the second component of LASS, does *not* mean saying everything your kids do is okay, or teaching that trying their best doesn't matter, or even claiming that you don't care about their worldly successes. Sending such messages would do them no favors. On the other hand, this is a rough world, a world full of rejection for children who are still learning their way. Sometimes, struggling in their social or athletic or academic lives, kids must view life as a Sahara stretching out before them, parched and blistering in the day-time, chilly and solitary at night. The least you can do is offer them an oasis of acceptance, *the knowledge that you care about their success but don't measure their worth by it.* If they sense that your acceptance is conditional, that it could melt away in the heat of failure, they will trust it no more than they would a mirage.

Face it. You can't act like "Chainsaw Al" Dunlap in your family life, firing children so you can get a higher valuation for the rest of the family. If you reject your kids when they displease you, if you shoot the messenger, pretty soon all you'll be hearing is good news. I don't know about you, but I'd rather know *all* the news. And diffi-cult or low-achieving children need your acceptance even more than most, since for them it seems, in the words of Roxy Hart in the musical *Chicago*, "like one big world full of no."

Accepting your kids isn't always easy, so the key is to differenti-ate between them and their behavior. You can say they're *acting* un-acceptably or delivering unacceptable *grades*, as long as you make clear you're not writing them off as children. Even when you've had a rough day with them, it's still worthwhile to end it with good feel-ings. Come to think of it, all this is probably pretty good practice for situations at work, when colleagues you respect are doing something the wrong way. Chainsaw Al, by the way, never had children with whom to practice this.

Self-esteem (also known as self-respect) has probably been taken to the most harmful extremes of all the LASS ingredients. Too many educators and parenting experts have focused only on short-term self-esteem (that old short-term–long-term trade-off again!), telling kids that the most important thing is to feel good about themselves. It would be easy to write this off as New Age pablum, a feel-good fad with no real impact. Self-esteem *does* have real impact, however, on every aspect of your children's lives, including their financial futures. Economists have studied its effect on earnings, for example: even adjusting for factors such as schooling, work experience, and skills (which are themselves affected by self-esteem), self-esteem has a substantial effect on paychecks.

Unfortunately, *the self-esteem movement all too often defeats its own goals.* Turning your kids into little egotists is not going to endear them to anyone in the long term, which in turn can't help but give them rotten self-images. If all children are equally wonderful no matter what they learn or achieve, moreover, it lowers the incentive to excel in school or athletics. Some educators claim with a straight face that placing significant value on excellence is elitist. I guess that's why they're not in business. If elitism means teaching all youngsters that they have wonderful *potential* but also the weighty responsibility of realizing that potential, then I am proud to be called an elitist. Once those kids leave the academic cloister and enter the real world, lofty self-opinion unconnected to actual skills or knowledge will hinder rather than help them, and what will *that* do to their self-esteem?

Here is one business dad's working definition of self-esteem: *a feeling of intrinsic self-worth independent of one's abilities, but which does not artificially alter one's judgment of those abilities.* Like so much in business and child rearing, self-esteem requires a balance: the trick is to guide your children between the Scylla of egotism and the Charybdis of insecurity. One way of doing this is leading them to appreciate both the intrinsic worth and the achievements of *others*, so they learn that universal "specialness" and objective standards can coexist.

Self-esteem without the successful meeting of challenges is hollow and must ultimately collapse of its own weight. How your kids approach life's challenges, of course, depends on how you've taught them to think about themselves. Tell them there's nothing they can't try, and they'll prove you right. Remember, effort isn't easy, or else they wouldn't call it "trying." If your kids have poor self-images, not only might they fear failure too much even to make attempts, but also they will misbehave in other ways to prove that their low self-opinion is correct. Show them respect (not respect between equals, but the respect due any human being) and they will treat themselves and others the same way; show them contempt, and they will feel and act contemptible. In other words, treat children as your juniors, not your inferiors.

An active father can't help but be influential in his kids' lives, but that doesn't force you to be domineering. They'll be best served if you let them make their own decisions, strive toward their own goals, even tilt at their own windmills. Parents who try to protect their children by doing everything for them actually hurt their children's self-esteem in the long run. Don't frantically keep them from mistakes; just teach them how to learn from those mistakes, how to get over them, and how to avoid them in the future. If you're over-protective, overbearing, or over-anything, they'll perform *under* their potential over time—and know it.

Neither coddle nor humiliate them when they fail, but let them know they're capable of better. Teach them an optimistic way of explaining both their losses (they didn't do well *this* time, but they can improve with effort) and their victories (they have real skills, and their efforts are paying off). Help them to learn from their mistakes, not to pretend they never happened. If you want them to have positive self-images, teach them to examine the true causes of their failures, so they don't generalize and become convinced they stink at everything.

Demonstrate that you value them *and* their achievements. Direct praise never hurts, but don't overlook the power of praise delivered indirectly, since it's even more likely to be believed. I'll give you an example. My father was a fine periodontist, with a practice that extended for almost fifty years. As you know from your own dental experiences, he had many captive audiences each day: patients gaping in his chair, poor souls who could not talk but had to listen. Occasionally my brothers and I would meet those brave people, who would recall nice things my father had said about us. We knew perfectly well that he loved us, but the fact that he had shared his pride with third parties warmed our hearts. So, although it's poor taste to brag excessively about your children, it doesn't hurt to say something positive behind their backs once in a while. Sooner or later, it's bound to get back to them.

Stability, finally, is rare in this world of accelerating change, but especially rare for children, who themselves change more frequently than one would think possible. Given that their own minds and bodies are morphing constantly on the way to adulthood, they really need the other parts of their lives to be as predictable as possible. When your teenager moans, "Dad, you're so predictable!" it's really a hallelujah of unconscious gratitude. *If self-esteem gives kids security in themselves, stability gives them security in their surroundings.*

A former partner in my firm, Paul R., often talked about the need to address entrepreneurs' "fear of the dark issues." By this he meant all the concerns they had about working with investors, all the problems that might come up after we invested, all the things that both sides knew might go wrong with any growing company. He wanted to convince them that, whatever fortune might bring on the business side, we as investors would react in an honorable and predictable way.

Fear of the dark, of course, is a common bane of childhood as well. It's really just one expression of a larger fear of the world's unknowns, which remains potent even after kids have outgrown their night-lights. Childhood (at least before adolescence) is supposed to be a carefree time, but that's unrealistic. Nowadays, in particular, when children know so much about all the sad and evil things out there, how carefree can a small, weak, powerless person really feel? Still, the more secure we can make our kids in their *immediate* environment, the better the foundation we'll be giving them for the day they have to go out into that big, bad world.

Like Paul R. with his entrepreneurs, we must show our children that their parents and homes function according to established rules. Obviously, we must leave room for flexibility and creativity, but only within the larger structures we have erected. We dads must demonstrate three kinds of stability: stability in *ourselves*, in our *marriages*, and in our *families*.

In *ourselves*, we should try to keep a relatively even keel—at least as far as the kids can tell. We don't have to become Stepford Dads, robotically repeating the same words whenever a situation recurs, but we should try to have somewhat predictable reactions when our kids please us, disappoint us, intrigue us, or infuriate us. If we play it cool the first time our toddlers spill juice on purpose or our teenagers miss curfew, but explode the second time, they'll have no way of knowing how serious a no-no they've really committed. Much more gravely, though, what will it tell them about our predictability as parents? about our general reliability? about other people's predictability, since they don't know how typical we are? And what about consistency as a virtue in their own approach to life?

We all have frustrations at work, and there's nothing wrong with telling our families about them. But that doesn't mean we can let them affect how we *treat* our families. We'll never make our kids' fear of the dark go away, but the least we can do is prevent them from fearing dark, unknown, unpredictable places inside their own fathers. As Eldridge Cleaver said in a different context, you're either part of the solution or part of the problem. If our children never know whether the Daddy coming home from work will be Happy Daddy who hugs them or Angry Daddy who slams the study door without saying hello, it's only a small step to wondering whether Daddy is coming home at all, and from that to hoping he doesn't. No business dad can be happy all the time, but we can at least let our kids see us dealing with problems and frustrations constructively.

We must insulate our relationships with younger kids, especially, whose impressions of us and the world are still being formed. Younger kids, moreover, believe that everything they observe is somehow related to them. If they see us in a foul mood, they naturally attribute that to something they did, some failure or shortcoming of theirs, rather than to a bad day at work or a final-round upset of our favorite team. If we repeatedly snap at them or pound the table at the smallest provocation, it could cause them needless anguish and self-doubt. They're exquisitely sensitive, of course, so they may detect an ill humor even if we try not to show it. If so, we should attempt to explain what really caused it, so they don't blame themselves or consider us arbitrary in our moods.

Ancient navigators needed a lodestar as a reference point. The lodestar, usually the North Star, never varied its position in the night sky. Our children, who must sketch their own personal maps of the world, need us as stable reference points by which to explore the rest of their universe. They need to know that they can always come back to us, that they can always bounce concepts off us and get a consistent set of responses. If we zigzag wildly from one constellation to the next, the map they draw will look more like abstract art than like reality.

Stability in our *marriages*, the second type, assures our kids that their homes are going to last. They need to see their parents happy together—working out problems in a constructive way, giving each other compliments, being thoughtful of each other, making each other laugh, and treating each other with respect. Many fathers are reluctant to indulge in what as teenagers they used to call PDAs (public displays of affection)—hugging their wives in front of the children. One reason may be that they are embarrassed; another may be that children don't want those embraces to go on too long, lest they feel left out (or grossed out, depending on their ages). With all the Oedipus and Electra complexes kids go through, you'll be lucky if you can count to three before any hug is interrupted by a frantic play for attention.

Try not to let it annoy you. As the old joke goes, "Oedipus, Shmoedipus, as long as he loves his mother!" And don't rub it in that a couple means only two. But hugs should send the message that there's a lot of love around them—the kind of love unlikely to be dispersed by some unknown whim or out-of-the-blue caprice. (Leila, as early as her sixteenth month, would make happy kissing sounds when she saw Julie and me hugging.) Long after their Oedipal alarms have sounded (or their teenage mortification has swung into play), that message remains, bearing with it an ambient glow of confidence.

As the third and last kind of stability, kids need to know that the rules by which their whole *family* works will not change with the weather. That security depends on consistency in discipline and sibling management, as well as a strong family culture. Every family, like every business, has its own culture. Some are haphazard, while others are carefully planned. The best cultures (at home and work) appear to result from a mixture of planning and natural evolution.

Stability does *not* require a static environment, which is neither possible nor advisable. Rather, stability means that, when the environment does change, you're there to explain it and help to deal with it. When you're going through a rough week at the office and don't have time or energy to play as much as usual, make sure your kids understand why; when you decide to "reengineer" your marital division of labor, try to minimize the ensuing disruption; and when you decide to tinker with a family institution, be prepared to discuss it openly.

Those are the four elements of LASS. They're a little like the four elements of all creation identified in ancient times: water, air, fire, and earth. Love is the water children need to thrive, acceptance the air without which their growth suffocates, self-esteem the fire that ignites their explosive change and progress, and stability the earth upon which they can always keep a firm footing. Depending on their temperaments and your family circumstances, the right mixture for each child may vary, but all four elements should be present.

Giving our kids the LASS they need can be exhausting (look up LASSitude and you'll see that the dictionary agrees), but it's our greatest single responsibility as fathers. Just as no living things could exist without water, air, fire, and earth, no children can achieve their potential long-term happiness without love, acceptance, self-esteem, and stability.

Intellectual Capital

Education is a key to great happiness, a key bestowed by parents upon their children. Part of its value is commercial, of course. In our information-based economy, it keeps getting tougher to earn a good living without an education to match. Harvard's president Derek Bok once said, "If you think education is expensive, try ignorance." One of our greatest responsibilities as fathers is giving our children the tools to provide for themselves. We may not always be able to finance their every need, for one thing. But even if we could, they can't thrive without the stimulation and fulfillment that come from making their own way in the world.

But education should not be viewed as merely a crass investment in productive human capital: it plays a crucial part in building what I call *consumptive* capital. To wit, not only does knowledge equip people to earn more, but also it gives them a fuller appreciation of the richness of life, so that they *get more happiness whatever their income*. The best things in life, they say, are free—but some are locked in mystery for those without the keys of understanding. Children who never learn the beauty of an elegant equation, the magic of a sonnet, the music of a foreign language, the oaken soundness of a syllogism, or the regal sweep of history—such children, whatever their future incomes, are doomed to endure lives of fewer, flatter pleasures.

Please note that I am not focusing on grades here. I'm not urging you to put academic achievement above all else, so you can have designer children to accessorize your own success. As a mentor, you must focus on what *really* counts. To see what I mean, try this thought experiment. If people acquired their kids through the classifieds, how would your want ad read? Like this? "Wanted: Child. Must be tall, handsome, A-average, gifted athlete, class president." Or like this? "Wanted: Child. Should be kind, loving, curious, honest, and respectful, have a positive personality, and use talents to the fullest." Not a tough choice, I hope. Albert Einstein, no intellectual slouch, wrote this warning, which is useful to businesspeople and parents alike: "We should be careful not to make the intellect our god; it has, of course, powerful muscles, but no personality."

Make sure your kids understand that you value them for who and what they are, not primarily for what they accomplish. When you criticize their grades or correct their homework mistakes, make it constructive. Don't forget to separate the criticism from any denigration of their worth as children and human beings. Love the children you have, rather than the children you want. If you follow this rule, by the way, they're much more likely to *become* the kind of kids you'd want, at least in the important ways.

Focusing too much on your kids' grades, moreover, can make you oblivious to major progress in other areas, such as street smarts and emotional intelligence. In the corporate world, information is too often confused with knowledge, and knowledge with wisdom. Let's not make the same mistake at home. I believe Mark Twain once said, "I tried never to let my schooling get in the way of my education." There's a defensive reason to avoid putting too much emphasis on grades, as well: doing so essentially hands your kids a weapon to use against you. The more you seem to care about academics (or any other area of specific performance), the more likely it is that some perverse fit of pique will drive them to underachieve for the wrong reasons.

All that being said, no business dad wants to send his kids out into the world without giving them the best possible shot at success. To build intellectual capital in our children, we must instill *intellectual curiosity*, make sure they keep *active minds*, participate in *home instruction*, supply *academic encouragement*, maintain *links between home and school*, teach the right *homework habits*, and give them *freedom to roam*.

Intellectual curiosity makes kids interested in the "why" of whatever they observe. Children who are interested in most things tend to be interesting themselves; by the same token, children who are bored by most things often become relatively boring. Boredom is a deliberate choice. It kills the urge to learn. It sucks time away from playing and thinking and asking and tinkering. If kids say they're bored, give them chores to pass the time and they'll soon be cured of the habit. In fact, I try never to utter the word "bored" at home. When I read stories aloud and a character says, "I'm bored," I cheerfully censor it to read, "I'm looking for something to do." Childhood is too precious to waste in ennui.

At my firm's annual strategy session a few years ago, our founder gave a talk on the key lessons he had learned in nearly thirty years of venture capital. First on his list was the importance of intellectual curiosity. Every news article, he told us, every exposition booth, every business plan, every research report contains something of interest—if only we keep our eyes open. I have observed him carefully since then. At sixtysomething, he still makes a point of learning every day—to satisfy both his curiosity and his need for an investment edge.

The secret to learning, both within and outside business (is *any* information irrelevant to business?), is the ability to be surprised. It's a classic virtuous cycle: the more interested you are in life, the more you learn; the more you learn, the more you know; the more you know, the more often you are surprised by anomalies, things that somehow don't fit what you know; the more interest you have in getting to the bottom of those anomalies, the more you learn; and so on. If *you* have this capacity for surprise, surely you will want to pass it on to your kids. In them it will be called a sense of wonder, which has two connected meanings: a potential for wondering *at* new things, and a potential for wondering *about* new things.

How can you bestow upon your children this sense of wonder? For most kids it comes naturally. Parents just need to find their own ways to nurture it, to shield it like a flame from the gales of modern culture. Tell your kids about the things that most excite you, the things you take joy in, the things that surprise you. If your adult life has for some reason dulled your own sense of wonder, their own natural capacity for amazement may spread, a wonderful gift from them to you.

Those questions! Questions and kids go together like charts and consultants. Questions teach kids about the world, but they also teach you about your kids: what they're learning, what they're thinking, what they care about. No matter what the topic, your children's questions are gold, and so should be valued accordingly. Listen to any sincere queries ("Are you a banana-head?" doesn't qualify) with your full attention, and give clear, serious, rewarding answers. Aside from getting their curiosity satisfied, having their questions treated with respect will motivate your kids to ask even more.

If you don't know the answer, admit it but say, "Let's look it up together!" That simple response shows that not knowing is okay; that honesty matters more than looking smart; that knowledge is important; that they can actively collect knowledge; and that you care enough to help them. Not bad, for five little words! Whatever you do, don't make up answers. Sooner or later they'll find out, and they'll feel both foolish and betrayed.

Active minds, the second requirement for building intellectual capital, stand in bright contrast to the learned passivity found in too many Americans today. We are, in a way, victims of our own commercial success. Just as business has grown more efficient at providing food and clothing for consumers, it also has exploited new technologies to keep us informed and entertained. Our grandparents were less constantly amused and updated than we are, but the lack of pervasive electronic media forced them to inform and entertain *themselves*, which carried its own benefits. Not only could they not turn on the information at the click of a switch, but getting their media in print form required use of their memories and imaginations. Memory and imagination, like muscles or brand names, atrophy with disuse.

If those qualities become vestigial appendages in our children because all their stimulation is fed to them electronically, they fall victim to "media-ocrity." A kid with a remote grafted to his hand resembles a lab monkey who gets food whenever it presses a lever. Take away the lever or the clicker, put the monkey in the wild or the kid in the real world, and they're unable to fend for themselves. It's sad, really. Richard Riley, the U.S. secretary of education, warns, "The teenager who is perpetually glued to the tube is well on his way to having a very dull mind and a very dull—and perhaps risky—future."

Television does carry legitimate benefits, such as education or family fun, when used judiciously. For better or for worse, it is part of our culture, and it wouldn't do to isolate kids completely. Sometimes, when you really need to keep the kids occupied, TV may be the only choice. Some videos may also help you promote the right values. Banning TV altogether, finally, would endow it with the charm of the taboo, so the best policy is containment rather than eradication.

If you don't want your kids growing into couch potatoes, don't let them start out as Tater Tots; establish the right habits early. Limit TV to one hour a day or less, and try to steer them away from the most mindless shows. TV can be hard to limit, what with peer pressure, multiple kids' favorite shows, and its seductive convenience. If you must, buy one of those TV allowance boxes that let you define daily limits for each family member. We know one smart family that has chosen to let the kids tape the hot evening show while they're doing their homework, then watch it at breakfast the next morning. The kids are staying current with their peers, but they're still living their lives.

You know how, when you bring home a new computer, you get to pick all the default settings? Early childhood is your chance to set the "default setting" for what your kids will do with their free time. Rather than automatically switching on the tube, this default activity should be picking up a book or bouncing a ball or building a skyscraper. Have the guts to say no to TV, and find caretakers and other parents who feel the same. In today's society, it can take extreme measures to avoid raising a tube boob.

The third requirement for intellectual capital, **home instruction,** is usually not the same as home schooling. Home schooling is certainly an option (one chosen for almost two million American children each year), but most parents elect to outsource their kids' schooling. Sending your kids to school, however, doesn't mean abdicating your responsibility as their mentor. By reading to them and showing them how much *you* enjoy learning you will expose them to the wealth of human knowledge (without forcing it) and will both prepare them for schooling and supplement their schooling once it begins. *Teaching is like charity: it begins at home.*

The fourth requirement for intellectual capital, **academic encouragement,** is all about motivation. Kids may be able to reach their academic destinations by rowing, but the journey will be faster and more pleasant if you blow a little wind in their sails.

Some dads view criticism as a way of expressing their love, particularly if their own fathers felt the same way. Because their fathers (or bosses) always held them to impossibly high standards, these men now apply the same standards to themselves—and if it's good enough for them, it's good enough for Junior. It's a variant of that old slogan, "When you care enough to send the very best." These dads, with all good intentions, want to show they care enough to demand the very best. Constructive criticism has its place, obviously: kids need to be corrected and reminded of their potential, and without occasional criticism your compliments will lose credibility. Criticism is so much more potent than praise, however, that too much of it could constitute an overdose. Heavy doses of criticism may toughen your kids, yes, but solid confidence (tempered with the appropriate humility) ultimately equips them better to face new challenges.

At work, bosses can be demanding, can push workers to perform beyond their limits, can accept nothing but the best. Those workers, however, are adults, presumably with some independent basis for self-esteem and motivation. (Personally, I've observed that few employees who receive only criticism end up staying long.) At home, however, we are dealing with *children*, who do not have their own families somewhere else, and who therefore look to us for validation. If we withhold that validation when our kids strive mightily but fall even a little short, they will soon wonder whether striving at all is worth the trouble.

In the spirit of giving your kids the right attitude toward learning (and toward themselves), try to get in the habit of applauding effort. Effort, after all, can be encouraged, whereas talent is innate. There's a big difference between "not good enough" and "great— can you do even better?" When they show you their drawings, don't say, "This horse has six legs. What is he, some kind of bug?" When you read their English homework, keep your criticism constructive, and save it until you've also seen clear, *specific* things to praise: What characters! What dialogue! Now, just one or two things about this punctuation . . .

Specific praise always motivates kids better than general approval. It gives them something to hang their hats on. Detailed compliments carry both the ring of truth and the ring of true love.

If you really want your kids to succeed, give them all the support you can. The academic arena is stressful enough for your pint-size gladiators without your making it more so. Make their playing field smoother, with empathy, trust, and kind words—not rockier, with complaints, comparisons, and criticisms. Encouragement means giving your kids courage, which in turn means strength of heart. In this world of continuous assessment and competition, you can be sure they'll need it.

The fifth requirement for intellectual capital, **links between home and school**, recognizes that school has much to contribute that you, no matter how sterling your intentions, cannot match. School lets your kids practice their social skills, and it demonstrates (or should) that the world has impersonal rules, rules that apply to all without fear or favor. The academic skills your kids pick up there are important, of course, but so are the lessons they learn about things like the costs and benefits of conformity. Robert Fulghum wasn't kidding when he wrote *All I Really Need to Know I Learned in Kindergarten.* The nonintellectual parts of their schooling will affect your kids' success at least as much as the intellectual.

The keys to maximizing the good that school can do are picking the right school or school system, staying in close touch with your kids' doings there, and keeping your kids feeling positive about school. To pick the right school, it helps to give academic quality plenty of weight when deciding which school district to live in. If you can't relocate and have doubts about the public schools, consider making private school a financial priority. As a business dad, you know that there are times in every enterprise when quality is the overriding concern.

As for staying in touch with your kids' school lives, attend PTA meetings when possible, spend as much time as you can volunteering at the school, and get to know your kids' teachers. Needless to say, it is also crucial to maintain regular communication with your kids. (During my own childhood, my mother took me to our favorite ice-cream parlor each semester to discuss my report card. If I'd done well, it sweetened the congratulations; if I'd done poorly, it cushioned the discomfort of my mother's gentle inquisition.) Most important, make sure that your kids trust you enough to confide any problems before they get too serious.

Keeping your kids positive on school, finally, should be easier if you've picked the right school. Resistance is inevitable from time to time but should be short-lived. It's a mistake, however, to try overcoming that resistance with bribery: that reinforces the idea that school is somehow bad. Presumably they'll be hooked on school's rich environment before too long, but in the meantime they must understand they have no choice. If they show a stubborn aversion to school, there may be hidden reasons (teacher problems, for example, or bullies), which you will need to coax out of them and address.

The next requirement for intellectual capital, **homework habits,** overlaps somewhat with keeping your kids motivated about learning and positive about school, but it requires special strategies as well. Make sure that they have the raw materials they need to do a high-quality job—the right work space, good reference works in print or electronic form, and enough time. You may also need to set limits on their extracurriculars and after-school jobs: they can be positive in moderation, but overdoing them can negatively affect your teenagers' homework, family time, or sleep.

Help your kids remember and organize their homework responsibilities, but don't nag them. That only turns homework into a power issue and transforms you from ally into policeman. Let the teacher be the heavy, not you—you've got enough heavy lifting to do in other areas. You may even want to show common cause and a good example by doing your own homework (from the office) in parallel to theirs.

Assist your kids all you (and they) want, but only as guide and cheerleader. In addition to making sure they complete their homework, you will also be involving yourself in the fine details of their lives, which in turn encourages intimacy and openness in other areas. Don't *do* their homework for them, of course: just show interest and give hints. Leaving the actual work up to them ensures that they absorb the subject matter and practice their general learning skills, but that's only part of the story. As a bonus, it teaches them to handle responsibility and feel pride in their own achievements. I know a wealthy manufacturer who robbed his daughter of those benefits by telling her many homework answers when she was young and hiring college students to research and write her papers once she reached high school. He believed he was giving her a boost up the ladder of success, but in fact he was only greasing the rungs.

The final requirement for intellectual capital, **freedom to roam,** requires vigilance against long-term thinking—of the wrong kind. If you limit your children's learning to fit the narrow type of lifestyle or training or job you envision for them, you may well end up cheating them of true happiness. Victor P., a venture capitalist I've known for many years, languished in medical school for four years to please his surgeon father, only to decide he was never meant to practice. He ended up spending two more years to get an M.B.A. Think of the tuition and opportunity costs of those four years of medical school.

In fact, most dads have to start relaxing their expectations about two decades *before* their kids are old enough for graduate school. Preschool may be a heady time when all things seem possible, but reality begins setting in when grade school starts. New vistas do open as kids learn to read and to interact better, but it also gradually becomes apparent where their greatest gifts do *not* lie. Now is the time for disappointed dads to get through the mourning period for the hopes they used to have for their kids, which might have included prodigious academic or athletic prowess. Once dads have worked through that process, they can get down to the serious work of helping their kids build on whatever strengths *have* become apparent. Again, love the child you have, not the child you wished for.

It's a little like venture investing. Once our companies have entered the marketplace, it's tough for us backers to change them much. The management team is almost entirely in place, and replacing it would be difficult and costly. The most we can offer is advice, contacts, information, additional financing, moral suasion, and strategic thinking. If possible, we try to keep companies out of unhealthy relationships and away from destructive ideas.

Similarly, fathers of school-age children can't change significantly their kids' personalities or fundamental attitudes. They must instead focus on providing whatever support they can to help the kids consolidate their values and life skills in preparation for adolescence. That support includes not only positive actions such as teaching and coaching, but also negative ones such as keeping them away from the wrong types of friends.

Work to correct your kids' intellectual weaknesses, of course, but don't neglect their strengths. Indulge their intellectual passions, and they will learn life skills far more important than the subject matter itself. Even if you disagree with their choices, better for them to be fully engaged in a "mistake" than halfheartedly pursuing the "right thing." You may not share their passion to be the world's foremost archeologist, but that doesn't mean it's wrong. Your children are not you, so it's unrealistic to imagine that they should or will reproduce your precise mix of intellectual interests and career goals.

Ironically, even if your kids don't share your interests, it still behooves *you* to share theirs. Consider it a mind-extending opportunity. If they do share your interests, life will be simpler for you, but don't let those common interests constitute your entire relationship. If you do, you'll end up talking mostly along the surface and missing the deeper currents in their lives.

During grade school, I developed an enthusiasm for chess.

Neither of my parents had much interest in the game, and it wasn't easy for them to schlep me around to clubs and tournaments, but they knew how much I enjoyed playing. On weekends, they would sometimes drop me off at a local Unitarian church that hosted informal competitions. As the crowning sacrifice, they would even let me walk them through the evening's game once I got home, reliving my mistakes and epiphanies. So, do I still play? Only now and then, but the strategic and competitive skills I learned during those lazy weekends have stayed with me, as has the pleasure of knowing my parents cared about something simply because I did.

Don't presume that you know your kids or the world they'll be entering so perfectly that you can predict the best future for them. Take a lesson from Leonard Bernstein's father, who was often criticized for not having encouraged the legendary composer and conductor's talents more during childhood. "How was I to know," the man would protest, "that he would grow up to be Leonard Bernstein?"

As a college senior, I began casting about for career plans. Depression-era child that he was, my dad thought having some professional degree would give me extra job security. He believed I should go to law school, since I clearly wasn't cut out for medicine or dentistry. "With a law degree, you can always hang out your shingle," he would say. Nonetheless, I ended up opting for business, departing from family tradition—and he backed me in that decision despite his misgivings.

He even gave me a handsome briefcase, a gift to him that he'd never used, as a token of moral support. It had his initials engraved on it, so, slightly embarrassed to own a hand-me-down, I had them embossed over. To this day, though, even after fifteen years (and counting) of hard use, I recall that monogram and why it's there, under the extra embossing. Whenever I open that battered case, so tested and true, I can still envision the solid "L.S.H." as clearly as if it had never been covered. Sometimes I pause and smile as I remember the history we share, my everyday workmate and I, and the imprints my father left on both of us.

Adding Values

Intellectual capital is certainly important for any growing child, but it's useless or even dangerous if that child lacks the values to go with it. Theodore Roosevelt wrote, "To educate a person in mind and not in morals is to educate a menace to society." Children are basically born savages, with all the selfishness and altruism, all the baseness and nobility, all the violence and gentleness that that implies. Just as companies send their employees both obvious and subtle messages about what kind of behavior is encouraged or unacceptable, parents must do the same with their children. Without your active indoctrination, your kids will learn their moral systems from television and their most persuasive peers, and those moral systems will become more ingrained as they age. Without you as a guide, they risk growing up with self-interest as their only moral compass—a wavering, ignoble, and inconsistent one at best.

The same hard truth applies for companies: without strong and appropriate values, any enterprise is likely to fail, regardless of its intellectual capital. In Roy Disney's words, "It's not hard to make decisions when you know what your values are." In 1998, Geoffrey Colvin wrote in *Fortune*:

> The fact is that for most of us, most of the time, infotech will not catapult us ahead of the competition in any reliable way. . . . For sustainable competitive advantage, you have to look elsewhere. Where? The answer I'm hearing from executives around the world and in all sorts of industries is: in the distinctly human elements of business—culture, character, leadership. . . . Culture is what people do when no one is telling them what to do.

Culture, character, leadership. It's hard to build good character in your children without a good family culture, or a good culture without good leadership. The Conflict Resolution chapter covers family culture and the enforcement of good behavior, but how are your kids to know what good character is in the first place? They're not born knowing it, that's for sure. What are the best ways to educate them?

Rights and Wrongs

Start with empathy. To my way of thinking, it's hard for kids to understand *any* interpersonal ethics before they master empathy. Rabbi Hillel, when challenged to recite the holy scripture while standing on one foot, said, "What is hateful to you, do not do to your neighbor. That is the whole Torah. The rest is commentary."

Empathy is the foundation of the Golden Rule: do unto others as you would have others do unto you. Cynics may joke that in business the Golden Rule goes, "He who has the gold makes the rules," but the true twenty-four-karat version still applies in both commerce and family. It's all about fairness and consideration, about understanding other people and how your actions affect them. Companies show empathy (and good business sense) when they treat their customers with respect, or when they enhance their employees' work lives. Children can practice it on a small scale by deciding not to kick a classmate because they themselves wouldn't want to be kicked, or on a larger scale by picking up litter because they know people like seeing clean sidewalks. Empathy may motivate them to comfort a friend, or to make the world a tiny bit better.

To teach empathy, lead your children through a thousand hypotheticals. "How would you feel if . . . ?" should be your mantra until you are satisfied that they understand it. If you are an empathic parent, you will serve as a natural example to them anyway. You can strengthen your example even further if they see you being empathic to third parties, perhaps through some kind of community service. I don't mean writing a check to charity, but actually rolling up your sleeves and helping people who need help. If you encourage them to participate alongside you, not only will they develop a deeper empathy for those outside the family, but also they will find a new source of meaning in their lives. *A sense of meaning is one of the greatest gifts parents can bestow upon children.* On top of that, you'll find a fun, fulfilling activity to pursue together.

Once your kids have learned empathy, you can use it as a tool for teaching just about every other virtue. And empathy toward *you*, if you explain yourself well, will also make discipline an easier process. It's really no different from the role-playing games featured in many corporate training programs, where employees take the parts of the customer or the team leader. Once your kids know how to imagine themselves in other people's shoes, they'll begin to put their best foot forward.

Self-control comes next. Without self-control, your empathic kids might feel others' pain, but not restrain themselves from continuing to cause it. Self-control enables nearly every virtue, including those that don't directly affect other people. Leaving aside interpersonal transgressions committed by the empathy-challenged, "victimless sins" such as substance abuse are less likely to happen when people think ahead. In most cases, self-control means delaying gratification to get some greater pleasure (or avoid some greater pain) in the future.

As a business dad, you may actually be able to make a special contribution here, namely, by carefully explaining your job. Business, after all, is all about choosing between short-term benefits and long-term rewards, about making decisions in the context of the big picture. The better your children understand what you do and how and why, the greater their exposure to disciplined decision making. Get them involved at least vicariously in the life of your business (see Dual Titles for tips), and you'll be preparing them solidly for the business of life.

Responsibility. Imbuing in your children a sense of responsibility serves many purposes: it helps them function better, makes them more reliable, increases the incentive for self-control, and boosts their self-esteem with each job well done. It prepares them for life and grounds them in reality. A saying that applies equally to employees and to children is: To get their feet on the ground, put some responsibility on their shoulders.

Before our children can really profit from responsibility, though, we must teach them a healthy enjoyment of work and a respect for the value of all work. Like any marketing challenge, it's all in the positioning. Many parents give their kids spoken or tacit messages that work is a necessary evil, inherently less fun than play or passive entertainment. That is a big mistake, for at least two reasons.

First, effort supplies some of the meaning in every human life, so we short-change our kids if we position work as meaningless except for the money or grades it generates. The quality of their work, any work, should be a source of pride to them, as Martin Luther King Jr. wrote: "If a man is to be called a street sweeper, he should sweep streets even as Michelangelo painted, or Beethoven composed music, or Shakespeare wrote poetry. He should sweep streets so well that all the hosts of heaven and earth will pause to say, here lived a great street sweeper who did his job well." Read your children those words from time to time, teach them to take pride in whatever work they do, and they'll be happier for the rest of their lives.

Second, work does not in fact *have* to be any less fun than play—especially in today's America, where technology has reduced work's tedium dramatically. To quote that respected authority Mary Poppins, "In every job that must be done, there is an element of fun. You find the fun, and snap! The job's a game." It's all a matter of attitude. Children who never find that element of fun treat schoolwork as drudgery, not an exciting challenge. Not surprisingly, they often grow up as either clock watchers, whose hearts are never in their jobs, or masochists, with "no pain, no gain" as their only rationale for work. Life is too precious to waste half our waking hours just waiting for the other half.

The best way for your kids to learn responsibility is to practice it. Let your kids help you set the table or carry in groceries, for example, and absolutely get them in the habit of cleaning up after themselves (it will limit the messes they make in the first place.) Position chores not as annoying necessities, but as opportunities to be part of the family team. Chances are that younger kids will feel honored; if not, don't offer them candy or other bribes, which only confirm that work is somehow bad. Instead, help them find that "spoonful of sugar" *within* the jobs themselves. Even if all this "help" ends up making extra work for you, their pride as contributing family members will make it worthwhile. For older kids, having to pitch in may help keep them connected with the family as they enter adolescence. The less housework you have to do yourself, moreover, the more time you'll have to spend with them (and with your wife).

My father certainly believed in household teamwork, more than I would have liked at times. When our lawn disappeared each fall under more leaves than I could have imagined possible, he would hand me a rake and assign me a sizeable area to clear. I grumbled, but it was good outdoor work, and it did save him time. It also taught me the value of diligence, because he wouldn't let me put that cursed rake down until the job was done to his specifications. And as I look back, that time spent by my father's side, working toward a common goal, doesn't seem so bad after all.

Accentuate the positive. Given that we want to pass on the values that will make our kids happiest in the long term, it would be folly to leave out the power of positive thinking. As Abe Lincoln said: "Most folks are about as happy as they make up their minds to be."

In business and life, things work out best for those who make the best of the way things work out. Train your kids to turn stumbling blocks into stepping stones, to find a solution for every problem instead of vice versa. Children who've learned positive thinking as a key value not only are happier than otherwise, but also are more pleasant to be around—both for you (which makes your life better) and for others (which makes your kids' lives better). About that, I'm positive.

Manners are morals. In business, a dose of rudeness can stop any deal in its tracks. No matter how much financial sense it makes, people are often reluctant to deal with partners who show bad manners. Rudeness betrays a lack of judgment, of self-control, of self-awareness, and of respect for others. On top of all that, it's annoying. Who would have thought such superficial things as manners could be so important?

Parents often teach etiquette as a social nicety, as a way of demonstrating you've been properly brought up, but as no more rooted in human reality than are arbitrary customs such as black tie or fish forks. That is wrong, for two reasons. First, it teaches your kids that "please" and "thank you" are nothing more than empty passwords, like some kind of secret handshake to get what they want. If they believe that, they will learn those conventions for the sake of form, but their hearts won't be in it.

More importantly, though, a dry, cynical approach to etiquette misses the whole point of manners. Yes, politeness is a convention that has accreted slowly over centuries, and some of its older en-crustations now seem quaint. But if you scratch any of the common conventions, you will find a deeper moral purpose not far under the surface. What are "please" and "thank you," other than words to ac-knowledge that someone's doing something nice and that you ap-preciate it? What is "How are you?" but a way to say you care about someone? Why is boasting of your own good fortune, or exulting at another's misfortune, taboo if not to preserve others' feelings (and avoid making enemies)? What about "excuse me" and "I'm sorry" and being a "good winner"?

As Julie and I have struggled to teach our own children civilized behavior, it's grown clear that it all comes down to feelings, to em-pathy for others. Niceties evolved for a reason, namely that people must be "nice" to live in civilized proximity without degenerating into animal conflict. Rejecting manners means rejecting one's own humanity.

It's all in the timing. Values are so fundamental, so pervasive in all that we do, that they cannot be absorbed all at once, but only in many small doses spread out over time. Values cannot be lectured into your children. Rather, "teachable moments" tend to sneak up without warning during the most humdrum activities. If you're not looking for them, you might miss them.

Relaxed, one-on-one instruction works better than any formal public approach in both business and child rearing. Focusing on teachable moments also lets you teach with specific, concrete ex-amples. At work, teachable moments with your subordinates might include the end of an unsuccessful client pitch or a fit of bad be-havior by a colleague; at home, they might include an encounter with a difficult schoolmate or a discussion of dinnertime duties. It all depends on what lesson the occasion offers, whether you think your kids need the lesson, and how receptive you judge their mood to be.

Timing also determines how you should seize these teaching opportunities. Like any job of persuasion, instruction in values is best achieved with a hard sell at some times, and with a soft sell at others. Businesspeople have made a science of both. There's no more successful example of a soft sell than General Motors' Saturn dealerships, where the salespeople barely speak unless spoken to. As for hard selling, I've heard that the largest high-growth corporation in the tight San Diego labor market poaches other companies' best employees in the following way: When you go to interview, they ask you to bring along your latest pay stub. The hiring officer takes your pay stub, lays it facedown without even looking at it, and promises you a 30-percent raise just for switching companies. You then hear that you'll get a six-thousand-dollar up-front bonus if you call your old employer to give notice then and there, two thousand dollars more if you give less than one week's notice, and two thousand dollars more if you give no notice at all! Now that's what you call a hard sell.

Depending on the situation, the difficulty of the moral lesson, your kids' mood, and your relationship with them, it may pay at times for you to take the Saturn approach, and at times to be as relentless as any headhunter (either the Silicon Valley or the Borneo variety).

Take a tip from Madison Avenue. Since you're selling values to your kids, so to speak, you might as well borrow a few techniques from the geniuses of advertising, the people Vance Packard called "the hidden persuaders." One of their standard tactics is to present to the audience a role model who uses the product being peddled. To Packard's generation, for example, it might have been the Hathaway man or the Marlboro cowboy. With your children, it can be anyone you like—assuming you're in the habit of telling them stories. It might be heroes from history like Paul Revere or Harriet Tubman, or it could be storybook characters like Robin Hood.

When Benjamin was three, I made up a knight of the Round Table named Sir Gallant, who embodied every knightly virtue. He never lied, whined, broke a promise, or acted selfishly, but he always won against great odds. Gallant, his horse Gallop, and his sword Slicer starred in tale after bedtime tale, each with its own "sponsoring" virtue. Because Gallant had such exciting adventures, he represented a glamorous role model.

Walk your talk. It's no use supplying your kids with role models from history and fairy tales if you don't also present yourself as a real-life, here-and-now figure who embodies the struggle for every value you teach. "Do as I say, not as I do," whether a spoken or unspoken admonition, both weakens your teaching of virtue and exemplifies a serious vice: hypocrisy. They say the apple doesn't fall far from the tree, and this is especially true if the tree is rotten.

When CEOs are trying to promote cost-consciousness among employees, does it work if they retain their limos and private jets? Fathers are under even more scrutiny, and so must be even more careful to live by their words. In today's cynical society, some men no longer feel comfortable acting like Boy Scouts, even in front of their children. If you fit into this category, please forget what's cool—for your kids' sake. Personify love, honor, compassion, cooperation, reliability, and self-discipline. Admit your mistakes. Get what you want without violence or threats. Treat women with respect. Dress warmly enough when you go out. Share.

And, for selfish reasons if no other, treat your own parents like royalty.

Let's hear it for censorship! Families are not democracies, nor does the First Amendment apply within them. Bad ideas can be dangerous even for adults (remember Jonestown?), so parents are well within their rights to guard their kids carefully from bad influences. That may present a paradox for businessmen, who tend to favor free trade, but John Stuart Mill's "free marketplace of ideas" was never meant to apply to children, at least not young ones. Parental censorship is not about *blocking* harmful ideas such as gratuitous sex and violence—it is just about *delaying* them until the kids are stronger.

The next few paragraphs discuss what I might call negative censorship, blocking out bad ideas from schools, other children, and television. There is also such a thing as positive censorship, how-ever: exposing your children to ideas you think will help them. Clas-sic children's books are full of such ideas, if only you know where to look and how to reinforce them with your own teaching. You don't even need predigested anthologies like William J. Bennett's *Book of Virtues*, although they certainly can't hurt. Try *Androcles and the Lion* to explain the value of kindness, for example, *The Little Engine that Could* for perseverance, *The Secret Garden* as an antidote to selfish-ness, or *Charlie and the Chocolate Factory* to teach obedience. That be-nign propaganda effort may sound clumsy and vaguely Soviet in concept, but it works. (Even the Soviet Union's Ministry of Infor-mation was effective in its time.)

Does your kids' school make the grade? In Greek myth, Sisy-phus was a cruel king condemned in the afterlife to keep rolling a huge boulder up a hill, only to have it tumble down every time it neared the top. That is what teaching values will seem like if you pick a school whose values don't fit with yours. Every day, lessons learned in school will contradict what you've been teaching, and you'll never reach the summit of that hill. If you were outsourcing part of an important business function, you'd make sure your sub-contractor shared your core values. What household function is more important than your children's moral education?

Take a long walk from peers who fall short. If you're like most executives, you wouldn't want your employees associating with businesspeople of dubious ethics. As the saying goes, lie down with dogs, and you'll get up with fleas. The same principle applies even more to your impressionable children.

Peer pressure can undermine much of the hard work you've put in to teaching your kids values. It's a necessary evil: you've got to ex-pose your kids to it so they can get inoculated while they're young. Still, there are ways to make sure they build immunity rather than succumbing. You can monitor the groups your kids join, and try to observe your children with their friends as much as possible.

Another protective strategy is to coordinate with the peers' par-ents when possible, so as to set benchmarks for acceptable behavior.

Or you can fight peer with peer: find counterexamples to the bad apples in your kids' classroom. You can train your children to stand up for themselves, so they won't get railroaded into acting against their better judgment. The more practice they get in saying "no" to peers *before* adolescence, the better! Finally, when all else fails, assist your kids in finding new friends, for example, by helping them join activity groups at school or in the larger community.

Limit the opposition's airtime. The American Psychological Association estimates that the average American child, who watches twenty-seven hours of TV a week (!), will observe no fewer than eight thousand murders and one hundred thousand other acts of violence *before high school!* Even sitcoms, supposedly benign, strive for cheap laughs and a fast pace by showcasing only superficial interactions rife with rudeness, put-downs, and sexual innuendo. Is it any wonder that our society's lowest common denominator falls lower and lower? To combat this enemy influence within your home, it makes sense to limit your kids' overall consumption of television, censor the shows they watch, and rebut what you overhear television teaching.

"We answer to a higher authority." Selling values without any religious tradition is a little like selling products without a brand name: you may not need it, but it sure helps. (Sometimes religion and brand names even coincide, as with Quaker Oats or Hebrew National Hot Dogs, whose slogan begins this paragraph.)

Religion takes many forms and serves many purposes. It may be private or organized, tradition-bound or free-form, stern or forgiving. At its best, religion can provide an ethical framework, a cushion against loss, a sense of community, and a reassuring continuity. For older kids, youth groups formed in church or temple can also provide a wholesome setting for peer interactions.

Even many atheists have a hard time sustaining robust value systems without some belief, conscious or not, in *something* larger than themselves. Businesspeople often point to the bottom line as their guide, but the *long-term* bottom line requires ethical conduct in any enterprise, including life. Can we derive our moral code, the code we teach our children, from utilitarian considerations alone? I'm a business dad, not a theologian, but to me right and wrong do not seem reducible to calculations of profit and pleasure. Edwin H. Land, the brilliant inventor behind Polaroid, once said, "The bottom line is in heaven."

Don't give up. It may at times be tempting to yield in the struggle to raise moral kids—either because it's going so well that you think momentum alone will let them coast, or because it's going so poorly that nothing you do seems to help. But kids can never coast, because they're always encountering new choices and new moral challenges. As for the "hopeless cases," you never know when all those values you've been sowing in the fertile soil of their minds will finally take root and blossom forth. Kids hear and remember everything you say, and the vehemence with which they protest against it often correlates directly with how true they know it is. Over time, the truth will win out.

I know whereof I speak. For most of my grade school years, I myself was in many ways a problem child. My parents persevered, however, and something finally clicked around the time I entered high school. I became, inexplicably and miraculously, not much worse than the average teenager. Friends of theirs, who had witnessed my early incorrigibility, were amazed to meet me in my twenties and find me unincarcerated, relatively content, and apparently functioning. I still don't know what did it, but I'm convinced it would never have happened if my parents had simply thrown up their hands and surrendered.

Kids form values slowly and by their own methods, no matter what inputs we give them. Their minds move in mysterious ways, more complex than any black box rising from Silicon Valley like the monolith in *2001: A Space Odyssey*. They may drive us crazy by dyeing their hair fuchsia or seeking out repulsive music, but those are merely style differences, frustrating though they might be. Inner character, values, and actions are what really count, and in those, committed parents can *always* make a difference.

The Finance Committee

Money is central to your life as a businessman. You've had plenty of opportunities to learn and to develop values about money. It is incumbent upon you, especially as a business dad, to pass your knowledge and values on to your children.

According to an old French proverb, "A father is a banker provided by nature." Children begin to cost money before they're born, with prices per ounce comparable to those of truffles or caviar. They start asking for money almost as soon as they understand what it is, and they don't stop until they've got jobs of their own (or maybe ever)! They learn how to get it, but do they learn how to keep it and use it? Given the importance of money in most lives, it never ceases to amaze me how economically illiterate so many Americans are. We're businessmen, so we should be used to discussing money, right? If you can talk frankly about sex with your kids, you should certainly be able to speak dollars and cents.

Your kids' economic curriculum should include three levels of complexity: *being intelligent consumers, household finance*, and *business and economics*.

To be **intelligent consumers,** your kids must first understand the true value of money—not only how much it can buy, but how much it costs to earn. Money cannot buy happiness, but can be (and too often is) bought at the price *of* happiness. They must realize that money doesn't spring from nowhere, doesn't grow on trees, isn't available at the teller machine for anyone who wanders by. Their reflexive eagerness to spend it may be tempered once they know that it's finite, and that someone they love has to work to earn more.

Money is a limited resource, so children need to learn to make choices in spending. Let them see you say no—not just to them, but to yourself as well. In the supermarket, take time to do comparison shopping, getting the most value for your budget. Let them hear you *choose* not to buy the latest electronic doodad, and let them hear your reasons: because you can't afford it, because you plan to spend the money on other things, because you want to save more money first, because you prefer to wait until the price comes down, or simply because it would be an obscene self-indulgence in a world where people are starving. If you're thinking about buying a new car, include them in the process, so they know there are some models that are simply too expensive. It's important to serve as a good example: too many executives feel pressured to buy beyond their means, spending money they haven't yet earned, to buy things they don't need, to impress people they don't even like.

When Benjamin was four, I took him to a museum exhibit on diamonds. They were so beautiful and alluring that he asked on the way home whether we could buy some. It certainly opened his eyes to learn that one of those bright shiny objects could cost more than the contents of our entire apartment! (The term "bright shiny objects" is used in a different context by Arnold K., a seasoned Massachusetts CEO, who told me he writes memos warning his staff to execute their young company's core business plan without getting distracted by "BSOs"—enticing, uncharted sidelines. Arnold has succeeded by working with, rather than ignoring, his scarcity of resources. By contrast, I sometimes wonder whether entrepreneurs who overspend would be more prudent if they had been kept on fixed allowances as children.)

When you are explaining the value of money, it also helps to distinguish between things that money can buy and things that it cannot. Spending money on things does not automatically make them valuable, and the best things in life are, in fact, free. Birthday or holiday cards, for example, can be made instead of bought—they'll be more meaningful for both giver and receiver. Be very, very careful when using money to reward your kids for good behavior, or withholding it as punishment (at least until they are teenagers). It would be a pity if they learned to equate money with love, much though their future employers might want them to. Adults who overspend and undersave often do so because they attach too much importance to material possessions, and to having them sooner rather than later.

Similarly, don't make the mistake of spending money for your kids as a substitute for spending time with them. If you do, they'll come to rely on material acquisition, rather than human interaction or inner resources, to keep their spirits up. If you've succeeded in business, don't let your affluence distort their outlooks, focusing them either too much or too little on standard of living as it affects standard of life. One useful remedy is to involve them in community service, so that they can practice a little selflessness and learn something about the lives of those less fortunate.

In combating materialism, as in so many endeavors, you will find yourself competing with television as your children's teacher. According to a 1998 article in *Business Week*, the average American child sees twenty thousand TV ads each year, and advertisers spend $1.5 billion on kid-targeted media alone.

One unfortunate consequence of ads is that they expose our children early to the need for skepticism. I know of one little girl who lost interest in Snoopy, dismissing him as "the insurance dog," after he became a shill for MetLife. In our weekly trips to the supermarket, Benjamin learned early to scorn the dozens of cartoon animals beckoning from the fronts of cereal boxes. Each critter wanted us to buy his wares, but they couldn't *all* be right, so we couldn't believe any of them. "That silly tiger. He wants us to buy his cereal, but are we going to do what he tells us? No!" Ads also use peer pressure as a lever, since your kids' classmates are exposed to the same commercials. Here, as in other areas, you must teach your kids to walk to their own drummer's beat — not the Energizer bunny's.

To illustrate the value of money more clearly, consider letting your children earn at least part of their allowance with household chores once they get older. If they overspend their allowance, let them earn more the first time or two, but after that let them live with the consequences.

Get them a piggy bank and eventually a bank account, so that they learn to salt away for tomorrow's urgent desire whatever cash they don't need to spend today. (Alternatively, they can buy shares of a favorite stock, such as Disney or Mattel.) As they mature, you can get more sophisticated, moving from weekly to monthly allowances, paying them for major extra work, or matching whatever they save each year.

In some cases, requiring your kids to earn their allowances may teach them financial lessons even more sophisticated than you intended. There's a great story about George Lucas, the creative and business genius behind such films as *Star Wars* and *Raiders of the Lost Ark*. When George was eleven, growing up in Modesto, California, his father made George mow the lawn for each week's allowance. That was okay in principle, but in practice George found the family's old manual mower too big and ungainly for a boy his age and size. He pleaded with his father for a different job, but George Sr. wanted to build his son's character. He did, but in unexpected ways. Without telling Dad, George Jr. saved thirty-five dollars out of his allowance, borrowed twenty-five dollars from Mom (repaid out of future allowances), and *bought himself a gas-powered mower!* His father was angry at first, but later realized that his son had the makings of a tycoon.

The next level of complexity, **household finance,** means educating your kids about the general state of your family's economy. The principle is the same as for a CEO who keeps her division heads up to date about her whole company's finances, so that they all know the parent's investment constraints and return requirements. The better your children understand what the household can and cannot afford, the more realistic their own expectations will be.

Neil S., a successful San Diego entrepreneur, has a twelve-year-old son who was worried during a recent golf game about losing too many balls. "Dad," he asked, "can we afford to buy more?" Neil wasn't sure how much to tell him, but decided in the end to be completely frank. They are a relatively privileged family, he said, lucky enough to live in a beautiful suburb and afford good schools, frequent vacations, and plenty of golf balls. But with that privilege, he added, comes responsibility—responsibility to make life a little better for others as well. They ended up having a good conversation about what makes a good life and what gives life meaning—and all because Neil was not afraid to tell the truth about money.

Home economics, as they used to call it in high school, is something like a game, and making a real game of it is a great way to get older kids familiar with household finance. For example, you might let them know the budget on your next trip to the supermarket, and make a challenge out of buying what the household needs within that budget. Let them conduct the whole transaction, from estimating the budget to carrying the money, choosing the groceries, and dealing with the cashier.

The third level of complexity, **business and economics,** is really a must for the children of any self-respecting business dad. Young people, and others outside of business, have shockingly little understanding of what we really do. As a result, they tend to view our activities with some mixture of ennui, contempt, and suspicion. Once your kids understand how responsible individuals and households make their financial decisions, they should learn more about where that money comes from, and what happens to it after it's spent or saved. If they want to understand modern society or function adequately therein, then they must, as Deep Throat told Woodward and Bernstein in *All the President's Men,* "follow the money."

Explain the miracle of modern capitalism to your children with concrete examples they'll find relevant, like a potato farm or ice-cream factory. When you pass a store that's gone out of business, you can explain that people must not have wanted the store's goods enough to pay for its upkeep and profit. Point out newspaper articles about businesses succeeding or failing because of bigger trends. When your kids are ready, give basic descriptions of the time value of money, the law of supply and demand, and other foundations of business. Before they leave high school, there's no reason a bright-enough child can't understand equity (in both senses of the word), fixed income, and other ways of investing in companies and countries. That may sound like a lot, but it's just the fundamentals of how our economy works.

Encourage your children to think entrepreneurially, so that they can have the experience of running their own small businesses. Lemonade stands work wonders in this regard, as do lawn-mowing and baby-sitting services. If you act as your kids' consultant, supplier, and even customer, they'll learn important lessons for life as well as for business.

The World Wide Web has a wealth of resources for older kids who want to learn about business and investing. Point them to sites like www.younginvestor.com (general information and games), www.mainxchange.com (an engaging stock-market game), www .moneyopolis.org (math and finance for middle schoolers), and www .gazillionaire.com (a space-age business simulation).

Conflict Resolution

DISCIPLINE AND THE BUSINESS DAD

Quality Control

Discipline is easily the most vexatious topic for many business dads. At work, after all, we have a whole range of monetary threats and rewards with which to motivate people. At the extreme, if we can't fire them ourselves, we have access to people who can. Our businesses depend on cohesive, coordinated action, and we put rules and structure in place accordingly.

At home, rules are even more important for safety and success, but how can we enforce them when monetary threats are meaningless? Novelist Peter de Vries wrote, "There are times when parenthood seems nothing but feeding the mouth that bites you." Below the surface, however, successful discipline at home is not really that different from in the workplace. They both depend on a combination of the right *philosophy*, maintaining *authority*, and a range of established *tools and techniques*.

Philosophy
The right philosophy requires clear definitions. Many fathers confuse discipline with punishment, whereas in fact punishment is just

one of discipline's tools. Punishment, without a larger purpose, is done *to* a child; discipline is done *for* a child. Discipline should be centered around teaching, as its roots in the word "disciple" indicate. *The ultimate goal of discipline is to teach self-discipline*, which your children will need in order to function as adults. Children who act correctly only from fear of punishment have not yet learned self-discipline, and so could lack their own internal resources (also known as a "conscience") once they escape your reach.

Just as your job is to teach, your kids have *everything* in life to learn. Nature has made them inquisitive, instinctive experts in the scientific method. They have a hypothesis, they test it, and then they revise and retest, over and over. You and your wife, you lucky people, will be the subjects of most of their early experiments, particularly those focusing on issues of power and free will. Your children will test you constantly, to see just how far they can push you before you push back. You know those thousands of people who claim they've been abducted by small alien beings, only to have bizarre and uncomfortable experiments conducted on them without their consent? That's how I feel sometimes, without even leaving the planet!

What these small beings learn from their experiments, however, is up to you. They are such quick studies that it is easy for them to absorb the wrong lessons in discipline from a few thoughtless responses on your part—damage that will require extra work to undo. Discipline, like all the best teaching, should not be too personal (driven by a desire to get back at your kids, for example) or too arbitrary (determined ad hoc, based on your mood, perhaps, with no discernible system). Just as the same rules of grammar or physics or math apply to all students, so discipline should have the same aura of integrity and uniformity. Not only should it apply equally to all the kids in your household, but also it should be applicable by any of the adults—whoever happens to be around when it's called for.

When I say discipline should not be too personal, I also mean that it should reflect on behaviors, not individuals. Criticize what your kids *do*, in other words, not what they *are*. If you label them as no-goods, you may find that the effect on their self-esteem makes it a self-fulfilling prophecy. If you appear to reject *them* as well as their actions, you might as well be throwing out the baby with the bath water. Draw a distinction between who they are and what they do, then tell them you'll always love who they are, which is part of the reason you want to bring what they do up to a worthy standard. Reassuring them that you still love and accept them lets them focus on improving their behavior instead of defending it.

Discipline is not about stoking your ego, about propping up your image as "no pushover," about "not letting them get away with anything." Obviously, one goal is for your kids to respect and obey you, but any father (or employer) who disciplines while thinking "I'll show them who's boss!" is probably going to lose rather than gain respect. Power struggles have no winner in the long run: they may result in surrender, but not agreement. Discipline means channeling your kids' spirit, not breaking it. Making kids your "disciples" means getting them to internalize your rules, to become vessels of your ideas, which they in turn will pass on to their children. Discipline, when done right, is really not that different from enlightened management.

Discipline is a process, not an event. It doesn't end when you scold kids and send them to their rooms. That may let them know they've made a mistake, but the next step is also crucial — to help them to do better in the future. The most effective discipline, like the most effective medicine or crime-fighting or assembly-line quality control, is discipline that *stops problems from happening* rather than addresses them once they've already happened.

But children need guidance, and guidance is impossible without limits—reasonable and consistent ones, but limits nonetheless. Children take a long time to become more than bundles of impulses, but they know enough to be scared by the power of their impulses if left unchecked. Young children especially are like live wires, and to avoid short-circuiting they need the insulation provided by limits. That old saying, "Be careful what you wish for, or you might get it," applies most of all to children, who might wish fervently for freedom and power but would desperately hate actually having them in abundance.

Children's tendency to spin out of control is like a force of nature, which parents must constantly work to keep at bay. So don't let guilt over your job's hours or some other fatherly shortcoming drive you to deny your kids limits, because that would be the worst deprivation of all. And they should be limits *you* feel comfortable with, not the ones "all the other kids" allegedly have.

This discussion of philosophy may seem a long way from business, but the fact is that home and office management present us with many of the same disciplinary challenges. *Executives who bully their staffs into submission, who make every issue personal or a power play, who focus on short-term at the expense of long-term results, who overstress punishment or understress prevention, will fail just as surely as they would in fathering.* However, changing kids' behavior is tougher—which is why business dads will be well served in home discipline if they calmly remember what has worked for them at the office.

Authority

Once you have a workable philosophy, another success factor for discipline is maintaining authority. Authority is important in both office and home—at least, if you want anyone to listen to you. Without authority at work, you're an empty suit who can exercise control through fear or not at all. Without authority at home, your status as father loses its natural potency, and you are forced into playing the role of ogre or wimp.

When it comes to discipline, there are basically three kinds of dad (or boss): the dictatorial, the indulgent, and the authoritative. For the dictatorial dad, fatherhood represents a constant power struggle, which he can win only by breaking his children's wills and keeping them in submission. For the indulgent dad, fatherhood is a popularity contest, which he can win only by maintaining high approval ratings from the peanut gallery. (I believe that indulgent dads typically worry that being too strict will make their kids hate them, whereas indulgent moms worry that strictness will somehow damage their kids.) The authoritative dad exercises true leadership, by virtue of the authority vested in him by nature, and maintained through comprehensive, continuous effort.

Authority: Use It or Lose It

• **Know your beat.** "Community policing" is all the rage in law enforcement these days. It turns out that citizens trust police better if the officers know the neighborhood—understand its personalities, follow its problems and tensions. Similarly, the better you know your children, the more clearly you'll explain the rules, the more effective you'll make your system of punishments and rewards, and the more appropriately you'll develop expectations. You won't squander your authority by asking them to do too much for their age, their level of development, or the time of day. Just as workers resent being managed by strangers, children who can legitimately claim "My parents don't understand me!" (they all say it, but only some are right) will have less respect for parental authority.

Read the books for parents on child development, and keep track of the behavioral norms set by your children's peers. If you gauge your style of authority to your kids' ages and personalities, then at each stage you will be laying the foundation of trust and credibility for the next. It serves no purpose to punish a toddler, for example, for squirming: it's in their nature. Adjusting your expectations by age means that you don't make unrealistic demands on your kids, or at least you give them extra coaching when they need it.

• **Take tantrums in stride.** I think we would all agree that fewer tantrums are better (in the office as well as at home), and certainly prevention is the best policy. With toddlers you can still use distraction, just as a CEO might hope a big acquisition will draw shareholders' attention away from poor underlying performance. Rather than tell toddlers they have to stop doing one thing, for example, you can tell them it is time to begin another. It is also helpful to keep them fed and napped so they have some control over their own actions.

No matter how artful, though, all parents must deal with tantrums from time to time. You're the adult, remember, so you can't fight tantrum with tantrum. You can't stop it or shout it down, so the best course is to contain it. Remove yourself emotionally from the situation (could this be the origin of the term "tantric yoga"?) and re-move your children physically if necessary. Your primary responsi-bility is to keep kids and their surroundings safe from their wild motions and emotions, but your next thought should be about what lessons they take away from the episode.

Tantrums can offer children three lessons. First, you still love them, and you will always provide comfort in times of distress. Sec-ond, they have gained nothing from this tantrum—neither victory in the original dispute, nor any placating treat in place of victory. If you sense that this tantrum was due not to lack of sleep or food but to sheer orneriness, you may choose to say the tantrum *cost* your children something, preferably with some logical connection to the tantrum. ("That tantrum disturbed the other people and made us leave the restaurant. We can't take you to any more restaurants until you've shown you can control yourself better.") Third, you yourself typically do *not* have tantrums, but are a relatively predictable pres-ence no matter what your children do.

• **Mean what you say.** At the office, your colleagues know that you mean what you say—so you need to say it only once. At dinner, by contrast, when your kids are tilting dangerously far back in their chairs, they know just how many times you'll tell them to stop be-fore they really *have* to. It will save you untold aggravation, in this and many similar situations, if you consistently set that number at one or two. Having to tell your kids something five or six times is simply not sustainable. You're probably angry and yelling by then, which means they end up listening only when you yell, which means you're forced to yell more often, and so forth in a spiral that sends your authority plummeting and your blood pressure soaring. If you mean business only when you're yelling, you won't get much busi-ness done, and none of it pleasantly.

To avoid that cycle, you should make an explicit or implicit threat by the second warning, which they know you will carry out if they disobey again. After the first few incidents, they will learn to be-lieve you when you tell them, "If you don't, I'll . . ." Children should be trained to trust their parents' threats just as completely as they trust their promises. It makes life simpler for everyone.

In the same spirit, your children should learn to accept refusals of their requests. Once you've said, "The answer is no," that answer must be completely, immovably final. Kids have long memories and believe (correctly, in most cases) that exceptions *disprove* the rule. If you go back on a firm "no" even a few times, they'll treat every "no" as a challenge, seeking to surmount it "because it is there." Instead of trying to climb that mountain, they should learn to walk around it and get on with their lives.

• **Keep the initiative.** When new industries are born, which happens these days with stunning regularity, the initial market entrant has what consultants call "the first mover advantage." That company establishes the standards, picks the best partners, and generally sets the pace. Once in the lead, it can be very hard to dislodge. By the same token, it's always helpful to stay at least one step ahead of your kids. Don't make a move without thinking how they might counter, and what your likely response might be. You're the grown-up, so you should be the one in control.

• **Pull rank when necessary.** A certain amount of reasoning and explanation can prevent your orders from seeming arbitrary and so can preserve your authority, but the original source of that authority is your position as father. Fathers are large, fathers are competent, fathers earn money the household needs, and, last but not least, without fathers children would not even exist. (The word "authority" comes from "author" in the sense of creator.) Whenever, therefore, your kids happen to find your explanations insufficient (or whenever you don't have time or energy for explanation), gently remind them who is boss. If not overplayed, "Because I said so!" can always be your trump card.

If they complain that it's not fair, remind them that you were once a child, and that they will one day be adults who choose their own rules and enforce them with their own children. Yes, they may know kids whose parents let them run wild, but that just means the parents are falling down on the job. Explain that you hold yourself to the highest standards in both your paid and unpaid jobs, and that you expect them to try their best as well. Remember, you can never be their friend as long as they're children, but you *can* be something even better—their father.

• **Consistency is king.** Say you've had a rough day. Your secretary called in sick, your boss had one of his little episodes, and you ran into a competitor coming out of your number one account's offices. (He gave you a big smile.) You're tired when you arrive home at the end of the day, and you're not thinking clearly. Your kids are jumping on the sofa, and they hold their breath when they see you walk in, because they know they're breaking the rules. Instead of rousting them posthaste, the way you usually would, you ignore them and walk into the kitchen to greet your wife. You just don't have the energy.

Your behavior is understandable, but what does it tell them? That rules can safely be broken? That you don't really care about rules? That your authority is a sometime thing? How about all the above? Consider this as an alternative: "I hope I'm not seeing you jumping on the sofa, because I'm tired and in no mood for rule breaking!" Even if it takes more energy, it's much simpler for everyone if you just stick to the rules.

Not that you should be a slave to consistency. As Emerson said, "A *foolish* consistency is the hobgoblin of little minds." (Italics mine.) Some flexibility can actually preserve your authority, but only when circumstances warrant it and you explain the reason clearly. Suppose you're trying to encourage your three-year-old to walk to the bus stop, but he keeps asking to ride the whole way on your shoulders. You want him to get used to walking distances, so you keep saying no, but then you see the bus coming. You don't want to miss the bus, so you pick him up and walk faster. If you don't explain why, he'll think that nagging works. But if you do explain it, you've remained *logically* consistent—which is what counts, because kids are amazingly astute logicians when it comes to getting what they want.

• **Double-team it.** At work, coordinating with your teammates can make the difference between kudos and chaos. When it comes to discipline at home, your major teammate is your wife. You both will become more effective by setting and implementing disciplinary policies together. Don't try to claim a monopoly on authority in any one area or to walk away from your responsibilities in another. Each of you will be with the kids at different times, so each of you should be authoritative on every aspect of discipline. Like any chain, the boundaries parents set up to guide their children are only as strong as their weakest link. Don't be that weak link. (And don't even consider simplifying things by leaving *all* the discipline to Mom, who will think you're behaving less like a weak link than like a missing link.)

Sharing authority requires coordination, but not the kind of coordination we sometimes do with colleagues in negotiations, where one of us takes the "good cop" role while the other plays "bad cop." Business dads who decide to let Mom play the heavy because their own schedules are too full to be anything but Mr. Nice Guy are undercutting their wives, which in turn means undercutting the whole idea of discipline.

A 1998 *New York* magazine article quoted an investment banker, who makes more than a million dollars a year but who travels twenty-two weekends a year, whose absences have damaged both household discipline and his marriage. "You're not quite clear what the rules are anymore. Your son misbehaves or he does something you think is amusing, and your wife goes, 'He's forbidden to do that.' It creates these conflicts."

• **Never waste a good failure.** Harvard Business School has made the case study its primary instructional tool. Case studies are the next best thing to practical experience, and they give large classes a common point of reference. Similarly, at home, opportunity knocks with each mistake your children make: every wrong move has real-world consequences, and so should be viewed as a concrete teaching aid. Think positively. Use their errors as chances to help them understand exactly what went wrong, and how they can improve in the future. That is far preferable to wasting your children's mistakes by either turning a blind eye or showing nothing but annoyance. A little bit of constructive criticism, enabled by and demonstrating understanding, goes a long way.

• **Be the strong, sensitive type.** Never let an articulate subordinate (or child) pull the wool over your eyes with excuses, but do at least acknowledge extenuating circumstances. Child raising is filled with shades of gray, so a sense of nuance can help you preserve and extend your authority. Understand the circumstances under which a rule was broken, and it may help you to moderate your response. Prefaces like, "I know you're upset about your test this morning, but that doesn't give you any excuse to smear butter on your brother," or, "I know you don't think you've been getting enough attention, but interrupting is rude," will give your enforcement more weight, since your kids will feel you've got their number.

Judicious use of empathy can make your power more palatable at home and at work. Just as you can remind subordinates that you were in their position once, you can also reminisce about your own childhood experiences: frustrations you felt, mistakes you made, things you learned. That should convince your kids that their problems are not unique (offsetting a universal misconception among the young), that you might actually understand them, and that you have in some sense paid your dues. It works especially well with younger kids, since older kids find it hard to believe that you ever could have had anything in common with them.

• **Open systems win.** In business, openness usually wins the day, whether in operating systems and data networking protocols, or in financial and human-resource processes of decision making. Employees buy into management's decisions more fully if they understand what went into them, and even more if they had a genuine chance to contribute their own input.

Similarly, it pays to tell kids why you are applying the discipline you are, so that your rules and punishments don't seem to be emerging from a black box. If you're stymied about how to correct a repeated offense, you might even consider saying, "Look, we've got a problem here. This behavior is not acceptable. I don't like having to keep punishing you for it. Is there a better way you can think of to make sure you stop?" It can't hurt, and you might even learn something.

• **Control yourself.** Bosses who fly off the handle at the slightest provocation often face mutiny—not only because they make unreasonable demands and show little respect for their subordinates, but also because they've proven they can't even control *themselves*. Nowadays, there are consultants who specialize in reducing outbursts of rage within the corporate world. (The Anger Institute in Chicago charges one thousand dollars per seminar.)

But does it make sense to keep your head at work, only to lose it with people you love? Remember, your kids will respect your authority more if you show you've learned to obey your own rules. You may have all kinds of reasons to blow up, to "lose it," to "go ballistic." You may have had a tough day at the office. You may be experiencing tension with your wife. You may be in a public place, and therefore embarrassed at your kids' misbehavior. But these are all extraneous causes that do not justify an explosion, so your authority will be compromised as a result. How can you expect your children to control their behavior, if they see it's too hard for *you* to control yours?

Because children can be so provoking, you need your self-control—your ability to think before you speak—*most* when they have lost theirs. When things begin to get out of hand, you need to marshal all your cool precisely to make up for their lack of it. What techniques work best for you in office confrontations? Use them here, where acting like an adult matters even more. Count to ten, step back, make a joke, hum a tune, whatever. Figure out what's *really* making you mad, and separate it from your kids' behavior. Talk things over with your wife.

You don't need to act roughly, or even to shout, if your kids have learned other signals that they're in trouble with you. Neil S., the San Diego entrepreneur I mentioned earlier, practiced this at work before bringing it home to deal with his son. "I've learned in business that you should always be up and breezy," he told me. "When there's a problem and you want to make a point, don't yell—lower your voice. It's like at home, when I say in a quiet tone, 'Son, let's talk.'"

Get angry when the situation warrants, but do it in a controlled way, not by losing your temper. Channel your anger, use it, control it; don't let it control you. You're human, so some things make you angry, and it's important for children to see the real-life results of their actions. But frequent abuse of power, at home or at the office, can produce defiance, resentment, lying, passive resistance, and other unproductive reactions.

• **Apologies won't kill you.** Different companies have different cultures. Some are relatively open about admitting mistakes, either internally or publicly. Others demand "best face forward" at all times. If you admit you goofed, it's like falling on your sword.

Because openness is so important within families, fathering requires the more honest approach. If, despite all efforts at self-control, you do lose your temper at a slight infraction, or if you punish your kids for something it turns out they didn't do or didn't intend, don't be afraid to apologize. If you're clearly in the wrong, admitting it won't diminish, but will actually strengthen, your authority. As the saying goes, "it takes a big man to admit he's wrong." Don't bluster like Sam Goldwyn, who insisted, "I am willing to admit that I may not always be right, but I am never wrong." Base your power not on always insisting you *are* right, but on always doing your best to *become* right.

• **Pick your battles.** Leaders know they have a certain amount of capital, which cannot be squandered on minor issues. Focus on what you *can* change, and on what you *must* change, such as safety issues or basic social functioning. If you don't recognize what is not feasible, you'll be banging your head against a wall. Even Teddy Roosevelt, never one to give up, recognized that he'd found his match in his strong-willed daughter Alice. When a visitor once objected to her lack of decorum, he replied, "I can be President of the United States, or I can control Alice. I cannot possibly do both."

If you find fault with everything your kids do, it wastes your emotional energy, it doesn't do wonders for their self-esteem, and it draws attention away from the rules that really matter. If every remark is either a command or a criticism, your kids actually may act out more. As the acid test for what's worth investing your authority capital to correct, ask yourself, "Will it matter in a year?" Matter-of-factly point out the other lapses in passing, rather than amplifying them into showstoppers. Occasionally they may escalate, in which case you'll step in quickly and forcefully, but you can't run your life (or your children's lives) with zero-tolerance policies.

• **Is "authority over teenagers" a contradiction in terms?** Have you ever lived through a hostile takeover? If so, you know that the employees of the company that's been taken over are no picnic for the acquirer to manage. Often, they were competitors of the acquirer, they didn't sign on to work for the acquirer, and they represent a nightmare for the transition managers. It's nothing personal against the managers, but the target's employees often want no part of the acquirer, its culture, or its mission. If you don't cut them a little slack, you will have such terrible morale problems that you could ruin both companies and defeat the whole purpose of the transaction.

Teenagers' attitudes toward their parents tend to be similarly unwarm and unfuzzy—which is odd, considering that *they're* the ones who've done the takeover: the hostile takeover of your children's bodies. It's like that chronicle of the epic battle for RJR Nabisco, *Barbarians at the Gate*, except that here the barbarians are *inside* the gates, eating vast amounts of your food, and playing loud music with words you should be glad you don't understand.

Those barbarians will cause you no end of trouble. (Look in the *American Heritage Dictionary*, and one definition of "teen" is "*Obsolete*. Injury; misery; affliction; grief." Coincidence?) Teenagers want all the responsibility they can worm out of you, but their hormone-warped judgment actually makes them less worthy of it than the average ten-year-old. It's frightening, because they now are capable of inflicting deadly harm on themselves or others. In this age of AIDS, addiction, and killer posses, parents can't afford to let their teenagers run wild. If you think the British merchant bank Barings should have kept a tighter rein on Nick Leeson before that maturity-challenged currency trader caused a venerable institution to implode, look to your own family and the potentially fatal attractions you must guard against. And don't think your high achievements make your household immune: a late-eighties study by Medstat Systems (based on insurance claims coming out of big corporations with group coverage) showed that 15 percent of nonexecutives' kids received outpatient treatment for drug or psychiatric problems each year, whereas the figure for executives' children was a stunning 36 percent.

Teenagers are at roughly the same stage in their lives as the companies described by Geoffrey Moore in his bestseller *Crossing the Chasm*. It *is* possible for your authority to survive the leap to teendom—but only given sufficient planning and preparation. It's when adolescence hits that all the investments you've made in your children really pay off, and you find that the goodwill you've accumulated over the years actually means something on the balance sheet. The closeness you've maintained, the authority you've built up, and the values and self-control you've cultivated in your kids can make the difference between crossing the chasm and tumbling into it.

Tools and Techniques

The third major success factor for discipline is the proper use of well-established tools and techniques. These do not include nagging, bribes, contempt, disgust, hoping, begging, or other parental follies. They include only sane, sound, sensible measures, many of which can be found in Management 101 at any business school.

Use these tools and techniques judiciously. Some will simply be wrong for the occasion, for your particular kids, or for your own personality. Luckily, there are quite a few to choose from, accumulated over time from the experiences of many parents.

Disciplinary Actions

• **Expect to repeat yourself.** In business, we're taught to avoid redundancy. With kids, however, rules take a while to sink in. Ogden Nash wrote,

> Children aren't happy with nothing to ignore,
> And that's what parents were created for.

Children do eventually pay attention if you are persistent, but it takes them a long time to learn good habits, and a longer time to break bad ones. "How many times do I have to tell them to pipe down when we're in a restaurant?" you may wonder in exasperation. The answer, unfortunately, is until they don't need reminding. Tell them only once or twice per visit, though, and warn them on the second telling that they'll be in trouble on the third. Be prepared to start all over again next time, and the next time, until they can tell themselves. You may want to do it preemptively, before you even walk into the restaurant. "And I know you'll be using your inside voice, right?" You don't need to let them forget before you remind them.

Constant repetition may strike you as a dull, assembly-line part of discipline, but it's a normal part of the job—and it's even less fun for them than it is for you. Kids dislike being told over and over what to do—so much, in fact, that it may actually goad them into doing it without being told! After all, just think back to all the things your own parents kept harping on till it drove you crazy. You swore they were wasting their time, but gradually those rules took root, like little seeds that finally found cracks in the sidewalk where they could germinate. To prove it, how often do you hear yourself saying *those very same things* nowadays, without even thinking about it?

• **Socrates again.** Just as questions can be among the most useful ways of conveying information at the office, they are terrific for teaching discipline at home. "What is the way we act when . . . ?" often works better than "I've told you not to . . ." It works better because it forces your kids to listen, not tune you out, and makes them think through the issue. But don't let them off the hook if they *do* try to tune you out. Insist on a straight answer. Words that come out of their own mouths will stay with them longer than words that come out of yours.

Make sure your questions are not rhetorical or overly general, such as "Why in the world won't you . . . ?" or "How many times have I told you not to . . . ?" Those questions clearly cannot be answered, which could reduce your children's inclination to respond to more specific questions as well. Moreover, rhetorical questions have a way of raising the emotional temperature in a discussion, which can distract children from what you're trying to teach them.

• **Make it relevant.** When businesses are selling a new product, they strive to show how that product can make consumers' lives better. In convincing your kids that rules are *not* arbitrary tools of parental oppression, you can always point out how your kids are achieving (or can achieve) better living through self-discipline. Not only does it help them get along better with *you*, but it gives them better relationships with their peers and teachers.

In some ways, the most valuable lesson may be that those benefits do not stop with childhood: the same rules you're teaching them apply to adults also, which is a major reason for learning them in the first place. Help them understand that you are only enforcing the rules that you *yourself* must live by if you are to succeed in life. If they're skeptical, devise hypotheticals to prove your point. "Suppose a policeman stopped me for speeding. Should I admit my mistake and pay the fine, or should I cry and say he's wrong and a smelly dumbhead? What would happen if I did that?" It puts the matter in a whole different light.

• **Sorry's not enough.** Apologizing is a two-way street. If you're willing to apologize for your own mistakes, you should certainly require your older kids to say they're sorry before forgiving them. (Younger kids may not *feel* sorry for what they've done, so by forcing them to apologize you are rubbing their nose in it and also teaching them to say things they don't mean. Part of your job is to raise them so that they learn as soon as possible to feel remorse for hurting others, and to apologize sincerely for it.)

Simply mouthing an apology, though, should not be sufficient. Your kids must appear as if they mean it, and explain in their own words what they're apologizing *for*, which serves an added educational purpose. Another part of apologizing, often, is saying they won't do it again, but true repentance means following through on that promise and *changing their behavior*. Federal Express's "absolutely, positively" overnight claim would be meaningless if the company failed to back it up with performance, and you should apply the same standard to your kids' apologies. Saying "sorry" never absolves anyone, but if they actually change their behavior, your primary goal in discipline has been achieved.

• **Attention as currency.** Why is attention something that gets *paid?* Because it has value. Advertisers, for example, spend several hundred billion dollars a year just to attract our attention. If it's valuable for someone who wants only to sell us deodorant, imagine how much more it counts for our children, in whose lives we are central figures. That is why they are constantly bidding for our attention, even if that means misbehaving. Well, as they say on Wall Street, you don't have to hit that bid.

If your kids are acting out just to get attention, even if it's negative attention, the surest way to encourage them is to grant their wish. Set limits when you need to, but you should not feel forced to react—unless their behavior involves direct disobedience, disrespect, danger, pain, or property damage. And when you do react, it can be with a time-out during which you are not particularly responsive. Lavish them with attention when they're behaving *well*, even at times when they're not explicitly requesting it. If the only attention you give them occurs when you're scolding, then of course they'll misbehave to get it.

• **Swift, sharp shocks.** Businesses both enforce and reinforce their most serious rules by taking instant action when employees break them. At home also, when it comes to discipline, there's no time like the present. If your kids do something wrong, don't twiddle your thumbs and let the moment pass. It doesn't matter if you're in a store, or halfway through your dinner, or in the middle of a bedtime story. They must learn that any significant transgression will receive an immediate response (including time-out or punishment if appropriate). Young children have short attention spans, so instant reaction is essential to communicate any cause and effect relationship. Also, children have selective memories, so they may dispute what really happened if you punish them later. (With older children, you can simply warn them of punishments to be discussed later.)

As an extra benefit, swift reprimand lets you get the annoyance out of your system, so it doesn't linger to poison your mood or emerge later in some more virulent, possibly inappropriate form.

Your displeasure should be like a summer squall that subsides as quickly as it appears.

• **Issue approval ratings.** Punishments don't always have to be tangible. Because kids crave approval as much as any modern politician, your compliments are major rewards, and your active disapproval is actually a form of punishment. In some ways, the old "hairy eyeball" is the purest kind of punishment, more painful than many kinds of deprivation and more clearly connected to the misdeed being punished.

I have referred to kids previously as "customers" of your parenting, but that relationship works both ways: they have obligations to you as well. They owe you obedience, respect, and honesty, among other things, if you've lived up to your duties as a dad. Like any good customer, you should notify them when they fail to deliver. Unlike major corporations, they don't need J.D. Power to measure customer satisfaction: all they need is a word or two from you.

• **Deterrence, not revenge.** If done correctly, punishments are unpleasant enough to linger in the memory, yet not so odious that kids block them out. The goal, remember, is to influence future behavior. For punishments to act as effective deterrents, they must be memorable—and closely connected to the original misbehavior. Kids are talented at recalling the connection between a misdeed and a punishment, but only if you make it perfectly clear at the time (for instance by taking away a toy they've thrown). Punishment should focus them on their mistake, not distract them from it.

On occasion, you may find yourself getting so angry that you punish your kids with a little extra harshness in order to get back at them. If you feel like this frequently, however, you may want to talk it over with your wife, with their teacher, or with someone else whose judgment you trust. It's not good for you, for them, or for the relationship between you.

• **Punish gradually.** Business dads can use their incentive-setting experience in fine-tuning disciplinary measures. Heavy-handed punishments, not finely tuned to the severity of the offense, can create resentment and a determination to keep misbehaving. Far better, then, to develop a system of escalating penalties that can be applied in a consistent way. The first time in a day that your kids disobey you, for example, could be met with a warning; the second time, with five minutes less computer play before bed; the third time, with another ten minutes less; and so forth. Thus they will have stronger and stronger incentives to shape up, returning the relationship between you to equilibrium.

It's much better to be clear about such a system beforehand, so that you don't risk getting into a battle of wills, where kids keep acting worse *in retaliation* for your increasing their punishments. That destructive kind of escalation fails at changing their behavior, and it may cause you to impose penalties too harsh to sustain. If computer play is a nightly treat, for example, depriving kids of it for a month may be tough to follow through on. Giving too harsh a punishment is a mistake, but going back on a punishment is even worse. Any punishment should also have a defined time period, so that your kids don't have anything to gain by begging for it to end, and so that you can end it without seeming weak or inconstant.

• **Discipline by objective.** Most business dads have heard of "management by objective," in which employees sign onto certain quarterly or annual goals and are judged by how fully they achieve those goals. The key is picking realistic goals that fit the corporation's needs. You can apply the same technique to discipline by getting specific about what you want from your children and what will happen if they do it or don't do it. Focus on what really matters to you, and you can measure your *own* performance as a teacher of self-discipline by seeing how well you meet those goals.

When you're trying to focus young kids on specific issues, you may want to set up daily or weekly goals, perhaps with charts on which they earn a gold star (or dinosaur sticker, if they prefer) for every day of sticking to a particular good habit. If they earn six stars in a week, for example, they might get some special treat. Once they have made lasting progress on that habit (not grabbing toys, for example), you can move them on to another one if needed. Older kids may not need charts but can also respond to a sustained focus on one behavior if promised a reward for improved performance.

• **Discipline has its rewards.** An anecdote about Dwight D.

Eisenhower has him holding up a string and saying, "Pull it, and it will follow wherever you wish. Push it, and it will go nowhere." Leaders throughout history have known the power of rewards, and discipline is nothing if not an exercise in leadership.

Most businesses use rewards more often than punishments, as I mentioned before. You've seen many Employee of the Month awards, but have you ever seen one for Stupid Mistake of the Month? The same policy works at home. Punishments may be more powerful than rewards, but that's a reason to use them less, not more.

To be effective, positive incentives do not need to be as systematic as the weekly sticker charts mentioned above. Often the most influential rewards, as any management textbook will confirm, are those that arrive unpredictably (one business mom I know says her B-school textbooks gave her the idea): "You've been behaving so well, I feel like doing something you'll enjoy!" It might be a toy, or a special outing, or just a word of praise, but knowing that their good behavior produced those random acts of kindness will encourage your kids to behave well more often. Don't make such rewards a regular quid pro quo, since they might begin to be regarded as entitlements or bribes (which imply the rules themselves have no intrinsic value), but do make them frequent. In addition to providing more powerful incentives than most punishments, rewards also help your kids feel loved and valued.

• **Make discipline consequential.** Punishment and reward can provide powerful incentives, but they lose potency if overused. One of their greatest strengths, that they come from you, is also their greatest weakness, because your kids' reactions to them can get tangled up in their current feelings about you. It often provides a welcome relief, therefore, to let the natural course of human events provide the incentives, both positive and negative. That time-honored technique is called consequences.

For example, suppose your son is playing recklessly with his ice-cream cone. If you tell him you're going to throw it in the garbage unless he stops, he will (with some justification) think you're being unduly harsh. But if you tell him that it might fall on the sidewalk, he'll be more likely to pay attention. He might find fault with *you*, after all, but he can't blame gravity. It's even better if you can express consequences positively—not that something bad will happen if kids misbehave, but that something good will happen if they behave. Try to demonstrate a direct cause and effect, without emphasizing your own role in the matter.

As an example of positive consequences, let me tell you about a problem we had with Benjamin's bedtimes. Close to his fourth birthday, shortly after Leila was born, he started calling for us after lights out, or even coming into our room, over and over. We ordered, we cajoled, but the boy simply would not go to sleep; he kept popping up in (or out of) his bed like a jack-in-the-box. The minutes would turn into hours, and only dire threats of punishment or his own exhaustion would finally force him to stay quiet and fall asleep. We understood he felt deprived of our attention by the new arrival, but that wasn't helping any of us to get more sleep. How could we get him down, without resorting to knockout drops?

We started by introducing a new treat: playtime in the morning. He had often felt rushed while getting ready for nursery school. We told him we would wake him earlier, so he'd have time to play before leaving the house—*if* he limited himself to only two calls after lights out. We explained that time does not stretch like a rubber band. People's bodies need a certain amount of sleep (note the invocation of a natural law), so if he wanted playtime in the morning, he would simply have to get to sleep earlier. In the following months, we occasionally had to resort to negative consequences (two minutes less playtime for each extra call, for instance), but overall we've had no recurrence of bedtime problems.

For consequences to work, they must connect to some verity of physics (touching a hot stove will burn) or society (the librarian will ask us to leave if we make noise) or human nature (friends don't invite obnoxious guests back). In marginal cases, the human nature involved could even be yours. If you always get angry when your children track mud into the house, for example, you might remind them as they go out, "Remember to wipe your feet when you get back. You know what always happens when you don't." In addition, the consequence you identify must be something that really matters to your particular kids, so you've got to know them pretty well. Finally, the connection must be direct enough for your kids to understand.

Consequences are a great teaching tool, because they work even when you're not around. Children learn that they have the power to choose good or bad actions, and that life will tend to respond in kind. If you explain that *all* people, grown-ups and children alike, face the same kinds of choices and consequences, they will gradually stop bemoaning the unfairness of it all—and buckle down to making the right decisions.

• **Why not spank?** Spanking is an important and controversial issue for today's parents. Go to any parenting Web site, open any parenting book, and you will be barraged with opinions on one side or the other. Here is my own opinion, for what it's worth.

When kids misbehave seriously or repeatedly, it's tempting to give them a swat or two—sometimes to reassert our power or to deter them, sometimes just to get out our own frustration. Bear in mind, though, that discipline is not for your benefit, but for theirs. In previous generations, spanking and other forms of corporal punishment were seen as a necessary part of the disciplinary arsenal. Some parents still see it as a worthwhile way to guard their children's future well-being. Nowadays, however, many people (myself included) believe spanking is an ineffective and destructive way to punish.

For such an extreme punishment, spanking can be curiously impotent. It's over so quickly that it may give kids the impression of absolution, almost as if they have paid the debt for their wrongdoing through their pain. It doesn't give them time or incentive to think about what they've done wrong: all they're focused on is getting through this humiliating and painful experience with some shreds of pride and dignity intact. You may leave an impression on their behinds, but not on their minds. They're also quite likely to think you're being unreasonable, which automatically invalidates your criticisms of their behavior.

Over time, spanking puts a distance between you and your kids, lessening their trust in you and making it harder to know them. Ask yourself: Do you want your relationships with your kids to be based on fear? Should the people who are supposed to love your kids be hurting them? Should the people who are supposed to teach them self-control be losing theirs?

Corporal punishment often doesn't work for older kids, who may try to hit you back. More troubling, it sends the message that might makes right, and that disputes can be settled with violence. You should be setting examples of nonviolent problem solving. For some children, spanking is especially counterproductive: whacking an overaggressive boy can be like trying to extinguish a fire with gasoline. Do you want your kids learning to hit when they are angry? Studies show that kids who get hit at home are more likely to be aggressive with their peers.

If you're not sure where you stand on these issues, talk them over with people you trust—starting with your wife. If your children seem impossible to discipline in any other way, perhaps you can grow to understand them better by talking with their teachers, guidance counselors, or others who know them. In the meantime, if you feel yourself losing control, if your anger is overwhelming, if you think you might end up hitting your children, don't get mad—get help.

The Negotiating Table

With the growth of teams in the workplace, negotiation is increasingly substituting for formal authority as a means of getting our colleagues to do what we want. On a larger scale, companies frequently find themselves locked in negotiations with their customers, suppliers, and even competitors, as every one of those relationships assumes new dimensions. Customers are often seen as partners nowadays, suppliers as strategic resources, and even competitors as allies within certain limited spheres. Even before those trends took effect, though, negotiation was a key business skill, and people have long recognized that it was equally important in other areas of life. Even the classic text on techniques of negotiating, Roger Fisher and William Ury's *Getting to Yes*, acknowledges that on its first page:

> Everyone negotiates something every day . . . You nego-tiate with your spouse about where to go to dinner and with your child about what time the lights go out. Negotiation is a basic means of getting what you want from others. It is back-and-forth communication designed to reach an agree-ment when you and the other side have some interests that are shared and others that are opposed.

That last sentence surely describes the typical conflict between father and child. It is therefore not surprising that negotiation is a powerful force for good in child raising. Not only does it offer a relatively constructive way to get kids to do what you want, but it gives them practice in important life skills such as problem solving, promise keeping, and follow-through. Negotiating is a good habit to develop early on, because the problems you need to negotiate will get progressively more complex, and it's important to build a foun-dation of trust and mutual respect on the simpler stuff.

Getting to "Yes, Dad"

• **Information rules.** Success in negotiation, as Fisher and Ury make clear, depends on exchange of information. The skillful nego-tiator focuses on interests, not positions, and on problems, not people. He neither accepts nor rejects the other side's position, nor takes the trouble to defend against ad hominem attacks on his own. Instead, he recasts attacks on himself as attacks on the problem, part of what Fisher and Ury call "negotiation jujitsu."

Focusing on problems and interests requires the fullest possible knowledge of *why* the other side is demanding what it is, as well as what lies behind one's own positions. Seeing the other side's point of view is easier at work, where the other side is relatively articulate and adult (most of the time), and where there's usually less emotion involved. Good fathers, therefore, must exercise even more empathy in negotiations with their children than they do in business. As the old saying goes, "No matter how thin you slice it, there are always two sides." Even in negotiations where you can't give way very much, just the process of being listened to and understood may make your kids feel better about the outcome.

It helps if the other side understands your position as well. At home you have more influence on this variable than you do at the office. If you've taught your kids to listen carefully, then simply explaining your interests may make your position more acceptable. When Benjamin was becoming toilet trained, for example, he was still not yet fully weaned from the bottle. No matter what pressure we exerted on him, he adamantly resisted giving up his bedtime nip. I eventually tried negotiation, but it was only when I explained the problem in terms he could understand that he made headway. "Benjamin, you want to keep having your bottle at night, but you're also proud not to be wearing diapers any more. If you have a lot to drink just before bed, you'll have to either wear a diaper or get your bed wet. What should we do?" He thought a moment, then proposed his own compromise: he would have his bottle one more night, and then give it up. It was his own solution, and so it let him feel in control of a major change.

There are, of course, limits to explaining your side in a negotiation. Sometimes kids ask why rhetorically, or in hopes of changing your mind; sometimes they already know the answer; sometimes the answer is too complex; and sometimes it's an answer you know they won't like, which will only provoke more argument. (Why should they hurry up and come with you to the doctor? So they're not late for getting their shots.)

Those information principles apply to just about any kind of bargaining. When I am negotiating a deal with entrepreneurs who would like us to invest in their company, my opinion about its true value (supported by extensive due diligence) is only one ingredient. I try to explain our priorities: the kind of return rates our limited partners require, the kind of multiple on investment we expect, our concerns over risks in the company. I also try to inform them about the kind of value we can add as investors, such as assistance in recruiting, sales, strategy, and additional fund-raising. Finally, I do my best to find out what is driving *their* decision: how quickly they need the money, how much they have already sunk into the company, what the last-round valuation was, and how many other investors are speaking with them now. All this information affects the outcome of the negotiations just as much as does the "fair" value of the company.

• **Who's got the power?** Sometimes kids are not willing to negotiate. They pursue what game theorists call a "beggar thy neighbor" strategy, refusing to cooperate despite all blandishments and threats. The key to stopping that behavior quickly is not to let them win, that is, not to let them get anything better than your last offer. Game theory, which in recent years has become less theoretical as it's been applied to things like tariff negotiations, predicts that no intelligent party withholds cooperation for long if it has less power than the other side and if the other side consistently follows a tit-for-tat strategy of punishing intransigence.

In Fisher and Ury's phrase, everyone decides whether or not to negotiate based on their BATNA: best alternative to a negotiated agreement. Through consistency and meaning what you say, you must convince your children that negotiation will always produce a better result than confrontation.

Knowing how your kids feel about their BATNA will, of course, make you a more powerful negotiator. No agreement, at home or elsewhere, occurs unless it is by some measure good for both parties. In business, you've got to know what alternatives the other side can find in the marketplace. If you offer too much, you're wasting money; if you offer too little, you lose the deal. Samuel Goldwyn, for example, knew the market for actors as well as anyone, so when a certain performer said he'd join MGM but was asking fifteen hundred dollars a week, Goldwyn was in a position to snap back, "You're not asking fifteen hundred a week. You're asking twelve, and I'm giving you a thousand!"

As an adult, you've inherently got much more power than your kids. Negotiations routinely occur, however, even between parties whose levels of strength diverge widely. You shouldn't be ashamed to negotiate: it's no reflection on your manhood. Negotiation is simply an alternative to force—a civilizing touch to make your life easier, and a skill your children will need. If negotiations fail, force is always there, and you're the one who has it.

• **Reward negotiation.** Okay, you're the adult. You've got the power. Once that is established, however, be careful about how deeply you rub it in. If you insist on "winning" every negotiation, you may end up pushing too far. Even the most reasonable kids, if they start to feel boxed in, may find their adrenaline pumping and their dander up. They suddenly feel they have something to prove, which leads to nowhere good.

If your kids ask for three more pages of reading before lights out, and you offer one, you can feel proud if they come back with two. Tell them you're glad they're learning to compromise, and at least give the offer due consideration. Kids should feel rewarded, not penalized, for negotiating. It's an important life skill, and it's certainly preferable to whining, nagging, or defiance.

By definition, a successful negotiation means that both sides have gotten at least some token benefit. Failed negotiations, by contrast, lead to only temporary resolutions, because one side has not bought in. The artful negotiator knows how to leave a little something on the table, to let the other side keep its pride whatever the power imbalance. In business, sometimes a very good deal is wiser to negotiate than a great one; otherwise, the other side may feel so taken advantage of that they will refuse to do another deal (or perhaps even to honor this one).

• **Know when to negotiate.** Negotiation, whether in business or at home, is all about leverage. Our power as dads gives us natural leverage over our small opponents, but timing can either magnify or diminish that leverage. In assessing our power, children focus on our ability to grant or withhold something they desire *in the near term*. Giving them necessities like food and love is of course nonnegotiable, but nonessentials such as toys or treats can make effective bargaining chips. If your kids like to watch their daily allotment of

TV during breakfast, for example, should you let them do so before they get dressed? Not if they are prone to dawdling rather than dressing. Negotiation is one tool for managing difficult dressers, and your negotiating leverage is much higher *before* you've allowed them their TV time than after.

• **Know when *not* to negotiate.** Once you've uttered a definite no you cannot allow yourself to be budged, even by the most reasonable-sounding Kissinger wanna-be. If you cave, you promote the idea that the last word is in fact only a prelude to the fun of negotiation, an idea that will end up undermining your authority and wasting your time. You've got a job and a household to run, after all, and can't take time out for endless negotiation. Your kids must learn that some things are not negotiable, and that adults decide what those things are. "You don't ask, you don't get" may be a strategy that's enriched many a nervy business dad, but that doesn't mean it should be encouraged in the young.

• **Set the agenda.** Perhaps the most crucial phase of any negotiation occurs when the *scope* of the discussion is set. Before bargaining in earnest, both sides must understand the list of options. If they then find they can't settle on one option, they need to generate more or give up. In any negotiation, the greater power always resides with the side that establishes the options. At shareholder meetings, it's tough for dissident factions to get their proposals voted on, because management has such a firm grasp on the agenda. As a businessman or as a dad, you need to seize the same initiative in any negotiation. If you want to get your kids dressed for bed while you still have the leverage of a bedtime story, for example, offer them the choice between changing either before the story or halfway through, without even mentioning the possibility of doing it afterward.

Warning: kids pick up on this technique and may try to use it themselves. At age four, when I was reading him one book per bedtime, Benjamin once turned to me and said, "Daddy, we can read three books or four books. What's your choice?" (My choice was one, and I made clear that it was not negotiable.) Even after kids wise up to the power of agenda setting, however, it still works—as long as you're open about its being a parental prerogative.

• **Don't tolerate threats.** The ability to threaten confers power, and that ability is something we should never grant children. *You* can use threats as tools for negotiating, but that must remain an adult prerogative. If your children ever say things such as, "I'll just behave worse if you punish me!" it should set alarm bells ringing in your head. Such a threat, on whatever scale, constitutes a challenge to the entire social order of your home. Children *never* threaten adults. Once you've issued that warning, treat threats as misdemeanors in and of themselves.

• **Never open with your best offer.** For negotiation to prove rewarding for your children, you must leave yourself some room to improve your initial position. When there's no room, it is not a time to negotiate. Enter each discussion with a firm idea of your bottom line, though, and don't go beyond it unless your children introduce relevant new information or make a truly creative counteroffer. But just as you don't want to box them in, you don't want to leave yourself without options by extending your best offer too early.

As an example of keeping a better offer in reserve, consider this story about J.P. Morgan, who knew a thing or two about negotiating strategy. A certain ring took his fancy, so he asked the jeweler to send it over. The jeweler did so, along with an invoice for five thousand dollars. The next day, Morgan sent back the box, plus a note: "I like your ring, but not your price. Here is a check for four thousand dollars. If that price is acceptable to you, please return this sealed box unopened. If not, you may return the check and keep the box." The jeweler, thinking he could do better elsewhere, sent back the four-thousand-dollar check, opened the box, and found—a check for five thousand dollars!

• **Worry about *what* is right, not who.** Just as discipline should retain a certain coolness, no negotiation should ever be allowed to get too personal. Both sides come to the table with certain interests, and there exists somewhere an optimal solution. If extraneous emotions are permitted to interfere, however, the resolution is much less likely to please both sides. Show your emotions all you like *outside* of negotiations, and encourage your kids to do the same, but stay calm when there's an agreement at stake. Refrain from sarcasm, hurtful remarks, guilt trips, gratuitous chest-beating, and other emotional red herrings. When feelings get hurt, so does communication.

When you're negotiating, it's helpful to look forward, not back. Look for a prospective win-win solution, not a way to get even for something (spoken or unspoken) in the distant past. Try to avoid falling into patterns that have disrupted previous negotiations. The same caution holds true in business. Bill P., a San Francisco entrepreneur I know, was trying to ally strategically with a company he had cofounded, where the management team had worked closely with him for years before he left. "It's like trying to do a deal with family members," he remarked. "You're not just working the current opportunity—you also are partially working through the past."

• **Be creative.** As I have mentioned, no real resolution emerges from negotiation unless both sides feel they've gotten something. Resolutions are often easier at work, because the issues are somewhat less complicated by emotion. A certain amount of creativity, however, can unravel even the most Gordian of knots. You may be the one who finds the best solution most of the time, but you should encourage your kids to think laterally as well. That way, you're working on the problem together, and they're practicing the kind of interaction they will need in life. On those occasions when they come up with an appealing solution, embracing it will encourage them to continue being creative in the future.

As with the free market, the best solution occurs when both parties' happiness is maximized. That utilitarian philosophy works better in theory than in practice. With kids, though, it does make sense to take into account how *much* they really want something. Don't reward constant whining or insistence, but do factor their heartfelt desires into the flexibility of your negotiating stance and into the creativity you exert to escape a zero-sum trap.

• **Who's really on the other side of the table?** Once your kids are old enough to feel peer pressure, you may find that their negotiating positions are forced on them from outside. Whether or not they actually want to pierce their eyebrows, they may feel they have no real choice—unless, of course, you say no. Without ever saying it, they may be bargaining with you not on their own behalf, but rather on behalf of their peers. They may even be tacitly asking your help in negotiating *against* their peers. It's your job as dad to be the "bad cop" with them and for them, and to know them well enough to recognize those occasions when they happen. As final confirmation, they may surprise you with an unusually ready acceptance, maybe even a certain relief, when you say no. You'll know then that you've done the right thing, and that in their hearts they appreciate this "no" answer more than your last hundred "yes" answers.

Contract Enforcement

Even the most elegant negotiations are meaningless if either side is in the habit of reneging on its commitments. Without trust, there are few alternatives to constant surveillance backed up by force. Trust can affect quality of life on the national level: Francis Fukuyama's terrific book *Trust* documents the superior economic performance of countries where honesty and fair play are strong cultural and legal values. On a smaller scale, corporations that meet their commitments have happy, loyal customers, while businesspeople without that quality are doubted and double-checked by their own colleagues—not to mention their clients. Within companies, unreliability is also terribly inefficient, since people must waste time making sure their associates have actually done what was promised.

Within families, similarly, raising children is much harder if you don't teach them to become trustworthy. If you can't rely on their promise to do something at time x, you have to remember to be there at time x (or $x+1$) to tell them again and make certain that it happens. That requires them to acquiesce twice instead of once, it deprives them of any training in self-sufficiency, and it could render them untrustworthy or unreliable as adults. The indirect results are poor as well: you're forced to limit places they go and things they do without you, and your (along with others') mistrust of them is bound to affect their self-esteem, with viciously circular effects on their behavior.

Trust within the family entails more than just promise keeping, of course. It also requires you to teach your kids both moral and intellectual honesty. By moral honesty, I mean straight answers to direct questions. By intellectual honesty, I mean straight *thoughts*, undistorted by convenient assumptions or wishful thinking. By way of illustrating the latter, Abe Lincoln used to tell a riddle, which Warren Buffett has since repeated. Question: How many legs does a dog have, if we call a tail a leg? Answer: Four. Calling a tail a leg doesn't make it a leg. Whenever I'm tempted to make an investment based on unproven assumptions, that little riddle reminds me to press on with due diligence.

Moral honesty prevents your kids from trying to fool you; intellectual honesty prevents them from fooling themselves. Without both, your kids' future will be in jeopardy. Neither prospective spouses nor potential employers value the lies of the truth-impaired or the frankness of the self-deluded. How, then, can you raise kids to be honest with themselves and the world? Begin by recognizing the many reasons they may have to prevaricate:

- They may try to win your approval by improving on the truth.
- They may want to avoid punishment by covering up a misdeed.
- They may think they're making a joke, without giving you enough cues to get it.
- They may be indulging in wishful thinking.
- They may make a promise they have no intention of keeping, in order to avoid an unpleasant task.
- They may have convinced themselves of the lie before uttering it.
- They may want to prove they're smarter by fooling you.
- They may simply be taking after dear old dad.

Once you understand what is driving your children to lie, fool themselves, or break promises, you can take appropriate action. The suggestions below may help.

"I Cannot Tell a Lie"

• **Use examples.** Childhood literature and history are replete with examples of honesty and dishonesty. Remember Dr. Seuss's Horton? "I meant what I said, and I said what I meant. An elephant's faithful one hundred percent!" Or George Washington and the cherry tree? What about those who suffered from their falsehood, such as those other presidents, Richard Nixon and Bill Clinton? Or Pinocchio, with his long nose, or the boy who cried wolf, with his lost sheep? Those examples and counterexamples will give your children a standard of trustworthiness to live up to. Of course, you'll also have to live up to it yourself.

• **The Watergate principle.** When your kids admit to wrongdoing, you may want to show some extra lenience. But when they try to hide their responsibility, come down harder than usual. Make clear that you're punishing the obfuscation itself, which is probably more severe than the original mischief. It's the same principle that chased Nixon from office: the cover-up is even worse than the crime.

• **Appeal to their self-interest.** Are your children considering going back on a promise? Better explain quickly that they'll lose your trust by doing so, and so they won't be taken at their word again. If they promise to go to sleep quickly after you read them just one more story, but they end up rowdier than ever, remind them that you won't give them the same benefit of the doubt tomorrow night. If they break a promise to be home by curfew, don't let them go to next Saturday night's party. But after they've kept a promise, make a point of trusting the same pledge the next time, just to honor that track record. The more trustworthy they become, they'll learn, the more you trust them; and the more you trust them, the more you expand their privileges. If their word is golden, that gold will bring value to *them* more than to you or anyone else.

• **Make promise keeping easier.** Some promises are tough to keep, but those are the ones that mean the most. Explain to your kids that anyone can keep easy promises, like promises to do something fun, but it takes real honor and self-discipline to tackle a tough promise. But if you know your kids well, you should recognize when they're making an *impossible* promise (such as pledging not to ask for a single sweet tomorrow if you give them two today). In such cases, it's better not to accept it than to accept and have it broken.

When you think they might give up on a promise despite your encouragement, you sometimes may want to smooth their way a little, just to avoid the precedent of a broken promise. Preschool-age Benjamin, for example, was taking his dinner plate to the kitchen when three kidney beans fell off onto the floor. He promised to pick them up as soon as he'd had dessert. To give him practice at promise keeping, I agreed. When the time came, he was a little squeamish about picking those slimy things up with his fingers, so I handed him a spoon and said get to it. With his excuse removed, he had no real choice. Would it have been easier for me to pick those stupid beans up myself, not chase him to do it, and meanwhile not have to dodge them every time I walked back and forth to the kitchen? Sure. But in that case, would he have received a lesson on the importance of keeping his word? No.

• **Be honest with others.** Don't call in sick when you take kids fishing, or brag about the bundle you've saved by fudging your taxes. Your kids might take you at your word when you tell them to be honest, but be severely disillusioned if they catch you in the double dishonesty of lying and hypocrisy. If you feel a little embarrassed when they point out the inconsistency, listen to them and admit you were wrong. Excusing your lies by saying "everybody does it" would only undercut your lectures on morality even further.

You never know when everyday life will give you an opportunity to set the right example. A couple of years ago, I took Benjamin to the supermarket but forgot to take our big stroller, which I typically use for major grocery-shopping trips. (The place was only two blocks from home, so we usually just walked back and forth.) We bought a lot, so I asked the checkout people if I could borrow a shopping cart. When they looked hesitant, I promised to bring it right back. It was cold and rainy, so I ran all the way home with Ben riding in the seat. Recognizing a teachable moment, I was quite vocal when we got home about how awful it was outside, and how much I didn't want to go out again. Nonetheless, I said, a promise is always a promise, so out I went to return that cart.

• **Be honest with your kids.** The worst kind of lie is a lie to your children. If you make them a promise, that promise had better be kept, unless there's an act of God, a force majeure, or a clearly explained reason why not. If you make a promise you can't keep, your kids will lose respect for you, feel that you don't care about them and can't be trusted, suffer damage to their sense of security, and probably catch your bad habits. The Talmud says, "Never promise something to a child and not give it to him, because in that way he learns to lie." In business and at home, you'll always do better by delivering more than you promise, not less.

Being honest with your kids also means not sugarcoating the truth. Marketers have long known that you can disarm consumers' objections by acknowledging them as true. Once that's out of the way, they'll listen to your good points, appreciating your forthrightness all the while. That's why Avis had such a hit with "We're number two, so we try harder." Kids want the hard truth just as much, and they'll respect you for giving it to them. They'll also have the comfort of knowing that things really are okay when you're smiling. If you have a business trip coming up, for example, don't make believe it's not happening or that it's going to be shorter than it really is. Instead, come out with the truth, empathize with their reaction, and do whatever you can to make it better.

• **Be honest with yourself.** Let your kids "catch" you facing up to some hard truths about yourself, whether it's about your weight, your work, or your willpower. The more they see you being frank when it would be easier to fib, the faster they will learn the habit of intellectual honesty themselves.

Team Building

Families are supposed to work together as a team, not at cross purposes. When families were also small businesses, all members pitched in on the farming or the weaving or whatever kept the wolf from the door, and more adults from the extended family were around to provide child care. The modern family provides few life-or-death reasons for the youngest family members to work together, and extended families are often extended across the country nowadays. Together, these facts mean there can be less motivation to feel like part of a family team, and more reason for siblings to envy parental attention.

At the office, our colleagues sometimes butt heads, but we're all adults, we've chosen our jobs, and at least we share a profit motive. By contrast, kids show an innate ability to hate each other in the purest, most intimate way. That special rivalry, which makes intra-company feuds such as the Arthur Andersen/Andersen Consulting blow-up look positively gentle, also makes being a father of two or more a position as challenging as anything corporate America can offer — calling for the combined best qualities of King Solomon, Vince Lombardi, and Sam Walton.

It's not hard to understand why sibling rivalry can be so bitter. The two Andersen factions, after all, were fighting over mere money and bragging rights, whereas siblings are battling for their very identities as people, and for something more precious than gold — their parent's attention and love. In Springfield, Illinois, Abraham Lincoln's neighbor once heard a terrible ruckus in the street, and looked out to find Honest Abe standing helpless between his two bawling sons. "Whatever is the matter with the boys, Mr. Lincoln?" The future president shrugged. "Just what is the matter with the whole world. I've got three walnuts, and each wants two!"

Human nature is still nature. Any eldest child could at times identify wistfully with tiger sharks, which are *all* eldest children — because the first one to hatch immediately devours any nearby eggs. Yet human siblings can give each other a lot: when they're young, there's the fun and silliness and solidarity of having other kids around, and then later, the potential to be lifelong friends. Who else of their generation, after all, will ever know them as long as they've known each other? And who else will be there for them, come rain or come shine, once you're gone?

Of course, we don't have second, third, or eighth children just for their siblings; we ourselves have an ideal of a family life we want to live. But for many parents, ideals of family life become elusive goals. In the early years we're busy protecting the younger ones from the older, and the older's toys, block buildings, and artwork from the younger—and suddenly, when that stage is past, the kids are scattered to the four winds, at friends' houses, after-school activities, jobs, and the privacy (perhaps) of their rooms.

But wait—aren't issues of team building, territory, favoritism, and shared versus personal space part of any manager's daily job? No enterprise can succeed without teamwork, and your family is your most important enterprise. For a fascinating contrast between functional and dysfunctional teams, consider two car models launched in 1996: the Dodge Caravan and the new Ford Taurus. As recounted in *The Critical Path* by Brock Yates, Chrysler's cross-disciplinary team worked together brilliantly to make the $3-billion minivan project a huge success. Just as dramatically, Mary Walton's *Car: A Drama of the American Workplace* reveals how Ford's "martial" management style and conflicts within the design team contributed to the failure of the remodeled Taurus.

A business dad's experience can be a major contribution to building the family team. There are two mission-critical phases to focus on, expansion (when you are adding new family members) and ongoing maintenance.

You may remember how family expansion feels to the firstborn child if you yourself were one; if not, try this thought experiment. Imagine that you are the successful, lionized head of an entire corporate division, constantly receiving praise and affection from senior management and trade press alike. One day, senior management introduces to you a stranger, who they announce will henceforth be cohead of the division. They insist you did nothing wrong—in fact, you were doing such a great job that they wanted another division head just like you! Because you're more experienced, they're counting on you to show the newcomer the ropes, treat him nicely, and (for all you know) prepare him to take over completely. Now the trade press seems to be interested only in the stranger, while senior management shows him the same approval as you (to you, it seems greater). Everyone expects you to fawn over him, as if he's the greatest thing since Jack Welch. If you refuse, you're worried you won't look like a team player.

You're baffled, because the new guy is clearly incompetent, a fool. Well, if that's what they want, you'll dumb down to act like him. But that strategy just makes matters worse: management gets annoyed at you all the time, and the trade press clucks its collective tongue. So you change gear and start criticizing the newcomer, maybe even shoving and kicking him when you think no one's watching. You were here first, damn it, and you're not giving up without a fight. That resistance only makes them more protective toward the stranger, and you increasingly find yourself blocked from the inner circle. Given the trend lines, you fear it's only a matter of time before you are cut loose or, as the British so coolly say, "made redundant."

Sounds like a corporate nightmare, no? And yet this, and worse, is what every firstborn lives through. From the Eden of undivided parental attention, firstborns are flung into a pit of contention and self-doubt. In their lives, it really is a tragedy of biblical proportions, as if the first are suddenly made last, and the exalted made low.

Those feelings are inevitable, but any parent would want to allay them as much as possible, for the sakes of both children. Here are a few suggestions for doing so.

"OK, Daddy, Baby Go Back to Hospital Now!"

• **Minimize change.** The newborn's arrival is cataclysmic for any child, but you can mitigate the effects somewhat by maintaining a few strands of continuity. Keep up as many of your joint rituals as possible, whether that means Saturday dad-and-child walks or school-day breakfasts together. Be sure to take the baby off Mommy's hands as often as possible, both for your own bonding and to give her time for herself and the firstborn. If you extend yourselves this way, your firstborn will see that the world has not completely come to an end, and that there's still a special place available in your hearts. The most important thing about dealing with siblings is to make sure each child knows that there is some territory and some love earmarked just for him or her.

• **Maximize ownership.** A distant cousin of mine has never been close to his younger brother, a problem he attributes to being kept completely in the dark until mommy and baby came home from the hospital. That is no way to sell change. It's best to begin the process early, while the baby is still safely inside mommy—but not before you're pretty confident the birth will actually happen. Explain how the delivery will work, both medically (where the baby comes out) and logistically (where the firstborn will be staying). Don't over-sell the baby as a pure little bundle of joy, but give a balanced presentation of the pros and cons. If you begin building ownership about six months before B-day, your firstborn may actually refer to the newborn as "my baby" in alternation with "that stupid baby."

• **Let it out.** Another cousin of mine hated her sister until they were both practically adults, because their parents would never let her show any feeling for the baby but love. Firstborns never attain acceptance without being able to work through the intermediate stages of denial, anger, and rebellion. If you squash their expressions of those feelings, you will only delay or prevent their becoming loving siblings.

Once the baby is home, let your firstborn's natural fear and resentment flow out, as long as your vigilance allows no opportunity to act on them. You may be lulled into security by a lovey-dovey outward performance, but be assured that the bad stuff is still roiling inside. Keep in mind that it usually won't peak until six months out, when the baby has become more active and reality begins to set in. You may want to help organize the bad feelings and provide an outlet by asking about them directly, without loading the question in either direction. When we did so with Benjamin, he admitted resenting Leila terribly, saying in a small voice, "I thought I shouldn't say anything, so we could all have a nice time."

• **Make the baby a team challenge.** Most firstborns are miserable for a time, and misery loves company. They need reassurance that what they're feeling is not bad or unnatural, so it's okay to let them know that sometimes the baby annoys you, too. Yes, that crying can get awfully loud; yes, those diapers do smell; and yes, it's a shame how the baby sometimes monopolizes Mommy's attention. But you love the baby, and you can see lots of fun for everyone down the road. In the meantime, why not deal with some of those common problems together? If your firstborn can pitch in, after all, it will free up you and Mommy to spend more time with both children. Because kids love to be useful, give them tasks like bringing dirty bottles to the sink or fetching clean diapers to pack for an outing. By sharing your responsibilities, they will feel more closely connected with you, more integral to the family, and more understood in their own problems.

• **Lay off a little.** One reason firstborns hate the new arrivals is that they must suddenly be so careful about noise, roughness, and countless other issues. They feel barraged with "no's," "stop's," and "I told you not to's." So many of those are necessary for the baby's welfare that you may want to relax a bit in other areas of discipline— as long as basic safety and respect are maintained. Without a temporary respite, you may end up slowing both disciplinary progress and acceptance of the baby. Also, to prevent the firstborn from feeling singled out, you might even scold the baby gently if it pulls the elder's hair or swipes at someone's nose. If you do it in a normal voice, the baby certainly won't mind, and someone else will appreciate it.

Once your children have gotten used to the idea of being siblings, you still need to help maintain that relationship with a minimum of strife and stress. That requires two vital steps: working with your wife to establish a lasting team spirit, and training your children to function together as part of that team. There are entire books about these undertakings, but here are some business-dad perspectives.

Let's Hear It for the Home Team!

• **Look backward.** To cultivate feelings of family togetherness, it helps to have a rich soil of family history. Successful companies remember where they came from and make it part of the corporate culture. Hilton Hotels, to this day, leaves Conrad Hilton's autobiography in your night table drawer next to the Gideon Bible.

In the same spirit, take the time to flip through your wedding album whenever your kids can stand it, and tell all the stories you can remember about grandparents, great-grandparents, and your ancestors in the Old Country. Without even realizing it, you will be passing on the same lessons from adversity, the same examples of personalities, and the same philosophical views that you grew up with, and that underlie your hopes and dreams for your children. Tell them how your little family started and grew: how you and their mom met, what life was like before the kids, why you wanted to have them, how their deliveries went. You'll make your kids feel a part of something special, help them understand the "back story" behind the family drama, and give them a positive role model for romance and marriage.

• **Look forward.** For many years, Microsoft has been driven by Bill Gates's vision of "a computer on every desk and in every home." The words are engraved on a big plaque set into the ground at the corporate campus. Gates's vision of "The Road Ahead" has helped make Microsoft one of the country's most admired corporations. (Other characteristics have made it one of the most feared as well, but that's another story.)

Every enterprise, whether family-size or larger, needs a vision of what the future *should* look like. For that reason, you and your wife need to step back occasionally from the tumult of daily life in order to articulate for your family the goals toward which you should all be striving. What matters most to you, as individuals and as a group? Standard of living, time together, impact on the community? You don't need a formal mission statement to focus on what's important. Just try to define what kind of family you want to be. Don't be like most families—in Stephen Covey's words, overmanaged and underled.

To make your kids feel part of the family team, get them to buy into the family's goals, and remember that open systems always win in the end. What matters more to the family, a vacation home or greater financial security? community service or artistic activities? more time alone with one another or more time having friends over? Without reducing it to a vote, consider soliciting their input on these issues, so they can feel greater ownership. Just as companies prosper when the workers understand financial, safety, performance, and other figures—and get to have their say—families work best when the common welfare is both a shared priority and shared information.

• **Gimme an F, gimme an A, gimme an M-I-L-Y!** Did you know that there's an entire subsegment of our economy called the spirit industry? No, not the kind that comes in a bottle—the kind that comes from pom-poms and banners, megaphones and silly hats. If it works in athletics, why not at home? Your family may not need an actual chant to capture the same esprit de corps as your favorite college or professional team, but it sure can't hurt. Your family definitely needs cheerleading and coaching, which is where you and your wife come in. "The Smith family sticks together." "The Smiths aren't quitters." "Is that the way things are done in the Smith family?" "You hit your brother. How would you feel if another kid hit someone in the Smith family?"

You'll be interested to find that the warm glow your kids get from feeling they're in a special group also helps you to enforce family standards of behavior. Membership in the elite Smith team may begin automatically, but renewals must be continually earned by doing things the Smith way—both among siblings and otherwise.

• **Make time for the team.** Look at any effective team—military, athletic, business, political, or family—and you'll see a bunch of people who spend serious amounts of time together. Nearly every week of my professional career, I've attended a team meeting—whether among my industry group at Salomon, among the mayor's staff at City Hall, or at my current firm. In every case, we've discussed issues facing the whole team as well as the progress made by individual members, with the key understanding that the achievements of each member were also the team's business. Outside interruptions have been discouraged.

Similarly, once you and your family have decided that family cohesiveness is a goal worth striving toward, you must all rededicate yourselves to that goal every year, every month, every day. There will be many competing goals laying claims on your time, claims that have behind them the formal force of deadlines and appointments. To defend family time against each member's ever more structured schedule, you must all make a mutual commitment, your own promise that family, for some small slice of time each day or week, will come first.

What should this commitment involve, specifically? Different families have different needs, both in time allotment and in how the time is spent. However much time you take, though, and whatever you do with it, you will find that the very act of making and honoring that commitment strengthens your family. Honoring the commitment means being present not only in body but also in spirit. That means no TV and no phone calls for anyone.

Generally, the natural occasions for family time are meals: we all have to eat sometime, and food on the run is less satisfying. Eating together creates feelings of closeness. Why else would so much important business be done over lunch? Besides, the food that kids, or dads for that matter, fix for themselves is usually less nutritious than food the whole family shares. Some parents prefer to dine separately from the kids, since it's more civilized, but on most nights it's worth tolerating the occasional interruption or the noisy digression over who's kicking whom or who will or won't eat what. If you want your kids to be true companions, both to you and to each other, remember that the word "companions" means "those who break bread together." By having dinner with you and your wife, they may even learn table manners.

Nor are the benefits of shared family meals merely "warm and fuzzy." Studies from the University of Minnesota and the University of North Carolina, according to the *Wall Street Journal*, "found parents' presence at key times, especially at dinner, was associated with a reduced incidence of drug use, sex, and violence and emotional distress among teens." Viewed in that light, the "dinner meetings" you take as a family, besides being worthwhile and enjoyable, are extremely effective investments of time.

• **Tradition!** I mentioned vacation planning. My family always took vacations together, my parents gallantly claiming that they never understood friends who needed to take a vacation from their kids, beyond the occasional weekend getaway. We thought of ourselves as a traveling family, with new experiences always taking fiscal priority over new cars, TVs, and other objects. Those vacations gave us unbroken blocks of time together that also helped us know each other better through shared encounters with the unfamiliar.

Vince C., a successful technology consultant based in Texas, has two kids, now adults themselves. When they were growing up, he took them on a two-week cruise every winter, starting when the younger one was six. He likens the cloistered time they spent together to a corporate retreat, far from the daily interruptions of home and office. As an added benefit, he also got to observe them functioning in a circumscribed "polite society," a useful basis for future coaching on manners and people skills.

Vacations are one example of shared tradition. Others include religious observances, birthdays, and family holidays. Such traditions solidify a kid's identity as part of his family, strengthen his sense of security and stability, multiply his opportunities to communicate, and help the family to know each other as teammates should.

• **Work together.** You can't force team spirit, but it's a safe bet that your kids will never develop it if they're each in their own rooms all the time, doing their separate things. Give them tasks to achieve together, so they're forced to find ways to work in twos or threes. Those could be chores (one clears the dishes, while another washes and the third dries) or fun jobs such as planning and making a surprise for Mommy.

In some cases, you'll want to participate yourself, so as to keep the team formation on track; in others, you'll want to leave them to their own devices—since you want their relationship to exist independent of you. (You don't want to be Daddy Central, with the kids coming to you for everything. What if two of your subordinates came to you every time they needed help or information from each other? That wouldn't be allowed to last long.)

• **Play together.** For a complete relationship, your cubs should know what it's like not just to quarrel in the car or sit adjacent before the TV, but also to have genuine fun together. Think up games and hobbies that everyone can enjoy. That does not mean buying every box at Toys 'R' Us labeled FUN FOR THE WHOLE FAMILY!!! You could start with activities you love yourself, such as soccer or Scrabble, and the children may end up sharing your tastes. Because you'll all have different levels of ability, it may be prudent to stay away from competitive events and focus on "everyone wins" endeavors like hiking and fishing.

Eventually, you may well find that your kids begin to pursue those activities without your being involved at all. As important as family activities are, your children should have some things they enjoy just as siblings. One day, you know, you won't be there any more.

• **Give them a "starter network."** Having kids gives you a great reason to spend time with your own brothers and sisters, if you have any. Besides seeing you enjoy your own siblings, the children will get to know their cousins. Cousins are a treasure, the first small network your kids can enjoy outside the nuclear family. Cousins are often similar in age, so they offer much of the fun of siblings without the drawbacks, such as having to live together or fight for parental attention. Cousins are also part of the same bloodline. Seeing the extended clan may give your kids a clearer picture of the overall family culture and of the heritage you all share.

The magnificence of cousin networks, in fact, provides yet another reason to keep your kids from growing apart. The closer they remain, the more *their* kids will get to enjoy one another as cousins!

• **Don't compare teammates.** When we measure two siblings by each other, we hurt them both. The loser feels resentment and inferiority, which outweigh any competitive urge to improve, while the winner notices the resentment and also has cause to wonder when the tables might be turned. Everyone wants to be best at something. At some point, a child who always gets the short end of the stick will think, "If I can't be best at being the best, I'll be best at being the worst."

Even if you think you're being evenhanded in your comparisons, you may end up pegging your children into roles such as "the studious one" or "the outgoing one," which could entrap them, outlasting any actual tendencies. Better not to introduce the concept of better and worse at all, lest it spread (in their minds, anyway) from comparing who's better at clearing the table to comparing who's a better child. If your stated position is, "We love you both the same, but . . . ," your children simply may not buy it.

The one time you're forced to compare is when you're applying different rules to different siblings. Consistency in discipline is important, as we've already discussed, so you have to be very explicit in your reasoning. If an older child shows more responsibility or is stronger or needs less sleep, you have to say so. Even if you use objective standards, that can still sow dissension within the team. With luck, all your distinctions will either balance out or be offset by your general impartiality.

• **Teams share problems.** Sometimes kids make their own comparisons. One of your children may be having problems learning to walk, to read, or to throw a ball. Kids are always sizing each other up, so those differences will not be lost on any of them. They may tease each other, creating a destructive atmosphere. Good team leaders do not, however, play up such differences or allow their members to do so. If one kid starts to bother another about that lingering lisp or worrisome weight problem, put an end to it quickly. When appropriate, you might even enlist one kid's help in solving another's problem. Let the older teach the younger to read, or use all that excess energy and time to play ball—the extra practice is bound to help.

As a boy, I remember lagging in my bicycle riding. On those two skinny wheels, I was so nervous about crashing that I could barely move a few feet without keeling over. Rather than ribbing me over it, my older brother John took it on himself to drive the fear out of my head. He set me on the bike and began running backwards in front of me, yelling taunts and challenging me to catch him. Eventually, the taunts got so personal that I saw red, and I surged forward, forgetting all about the risk of falling. I never did catch him, but by our third circuit around the playground, I realized I now knew how to ride a bicycle.

• **Let them work it out.** In the office, nothing is more annoying than a pair of subordinates who can't get along and are always bringing their disputes to you for arbitration. They're grown-ups, aren't they? They should be able to work it out for themselves.

Your kids are *not* grown-ups—but you'd like them to be eventually. They should therefore see you as the court of last resort. Give them incentives to work out a negotiated settlement to each dispute, instead of resorting to the "litigation" of running to you. That will teach them problem-solving skills, self-reliance, and empathy, and it should ensure that they can get along once you're not around. In order to lay the groundwork for constructive rather than destructive sibling arguments, try to establish rules of order, and show them how you resolve disagreements with their mother. Each side must refrain from sarcasm and name calling, for example, and try not to interrupt. Focus on finding a way to satisfy everyone.

If you intervene every time your kids quarrel, they will never have a chance to practice those skills on each other. *They will also learn that quarreling is a fail-safe way to get your attention.* Unless one of them is hurting the other or refusing to engage in constructive discussion, you're better off staying out of it. To deter them from referring every dispute to you, act grumpy about getting the case. Try to get them to work it out, perhaps even give them hints, but step in only until you can step out. If they can't or won't settle it between themselves, don't come down too squarely on either side, or that side will be encouraged to litigate next time as well.

If one child tends to dominate, you will need to stay somewhat involved. And if the dispute clearly resulted from one side's bad behavior, it must of course be discouraged by the award of compensatory and perhaps punitive damages. Even in such cases, though, you may want to let consequences do the teaching for you.

• **Sharing should be voluntary**. Sharing is a virtue you want to teach, but can you teach it by forcing it? On the contrary, it's better to recognize your kids' property rights — as long as you enforce them equally. If each kid wants access to the others' goodies from time to time, then all will have the incentive to adopt a system of *voluntary* sharing, which is far preferable to your legislating and trying to police it. Only if all the kids feel that they are being treated fairly and protected from the others will they have a framework within which to form their own relationships.

• **Don't pick sides.** Executives need to make decisions based on the facts, not the personalities of the subordinates arguing each side. At home, likewise, sit in judgment when you must, but judge each case on the merits, not based on extraneous factors such as which child has annoyed you less over the past day or week. The only thing worse than playing favorites in a sibling dispute is doing it repeatedly, and the only thing even worse is choosing the same child each time.

If you feel your wife has been playing favorites, by the way, don't try to offset her by coming down on the other side. Two wrongs, as they say, do not make a right. Rather than form a second and opposing block, take your wife aside and discuss the need for impartiality. If you and she disagree for long, and you both feel strongly, something may be wrong. Seek outside counsel (grandparents, friends, teachers, therapist) to resolve the difference before you inflict it on the kids.

• **Fair doesn't mean equal.** Not every sibling issue can be resolved as neatly as halving a slice of cake (one divides, the other chooses). Sometimes, the best outcomes are unequal, either because the kids have different needs or because equality is not practical. Treat your kids uniquely, as individuals, not equally, as a matched set. If you give one a compliment, for example, don't feel you immediately need to even the balance by saying something nice about the other. Such tokenism only cheapens the value of both compliments. Instead, let the differences offset each other over time.

Would you give everyone in your department a promotion at the same time, so no one's feelings get hurt? Not if you want to motivate people.

Kids may not have CPAs, but they're keen accountants when it comes to who's one up. They'll keep closer track than you ever can, so it's best to treat them evenly — without going too far. It's not worth twisting yourself into contortions, leaning over backwards to be on both sides of every fence. Whatever you do, each kid will always think the other's grass is greener anyway! Isn't it better to work with them on tearing down the fence altogether?

• **First the bad, then the good.** Sibling rivalry is like methane. It may stink, but it's not actually dangerous when seeping out a little at a time. When it's kept pent up, though, it accumulates, the pressure mounting, until, one day when no one's watching, it explodes.

Not till the bad feelings between siblings come out can the good ones come in. As long as your children are divided by unspoken resentments, they will never be truly close. It is therefore a bad idea to stifle your kids' expression of rivalry by telling them that they're not being nice or that they're not being a good brother/sister. Provided that they're not being mean or doing something harmful, let that methane out.

• **No grudges allowed.** In business, where networking is a key skill, the smart professional avoids making enemies. We never know whom we might need on our side, after all, in the constantly shifting sands of the New Economy. Why should we teach our children to act any differently in their family lives?

Even in the happiest of families, anger happens. It happens between children and parents, and it certainly happens between siblings. But just as you should not let your own anger linger in your mind and sour your relationships with your kids, you should not let them hold long-standing grudges against one another.

If you don't teach your kids either to work through their anger or to let it go, it will stay to haunt your whole family. In Julie's extended family, there are two brothers, once quite close, who have refused to speak to each other for forty years. That may be an extreme example, but many families have suffered from long-standing feuds. They may not be explicit: the feuders may with effort act civilly at family gatherings, but there is no family closeness between them.

Often, feuds begin with some real or imagined grievance, which is neither corrected nor forgiven. The next time either party acts at all imperfectly, it's interpreted in light of previous events, that is, in the least favorable way. Soon a pattern is set, and it becomes impossible for either side to escape its typecasting in the other's eyes. The natural incentive to resolve the differences shrinks as the gap widens, and both resign themselves to effectively losing a family member. They may even try to explain it away by saying they've somehow grown apart.

It's sad, especially because it doesn't have to be that way. It's never too soon to teach your children the art of forgiveness, which goes hand in hand with the art of apology. If one child never learns to forgive, openly and genuinely, there'll never be anything for the others to gain by apologizing. You must encourage them all to voice their grievances and to respond respectfully when siblings voice theirs.

If there's any silver lining to the cloud of sibling rivalry, it's the practice it affords in the crucial skills of expressing anger, and seeking and granting forgiveness. Without those skills, your kids will ultimately get along with no one — not with each other, not with colleagues, and not with anyone else who has feelings. They won't even get along with themselves, since any flowering of positive feeling will get choked by ever-sprouting weeds of discontent and resentment. Teaching your children the art of forgiveness will therefore help them to be happier over the long term.

Funny Business

Remember the movie *Big*? Tom Hanks played a boy, magically transformed into a man, who managed to thrive in the corporate world.

He enchanted his boss with his sense of humor and childlike playfulness, and could probably have become CEO if he hadn't preferred to go back and get big the normal way.

The film was true to life in one respect: a sense of humor and playful creativity really can help us in our business lives. John Cleese's success as a training consultant following his Monty Python role, the continuing media fascination with what Steve Jobs calls his "insanely great" innovations, and the spread of concepts like "out of the box" thinking all serve to demonstrate that a little craziness can go a long way. Now, if it helps us with big people at work, imagine how much more it can improve our performance with the small ones at home!

In the office, people without creativity and humor can muddle along, though they are less productive and engaged; in a family, such a deficiency can be much worse, producing boredom and stress. There's a lot of psychobabble these days about the inner child, but the most successful adults do still have some of the child in them (they're child*like*, not child*ish*). Their own kids, moreover, love feeling that at least a little part of their parents is like them.

We dads are lucky, because we're typically bigger and stronger than our wives, so we have more physical options for clowning around. Men also mature less quickly than women, for better or for worse, and arguably many get away with maturing *less* as well. How often do you hear some successful businessman admiringly called "really just a big kid"? More often per capita, I'll wager, than for their female counterparts. Whether we're less mature or not, we're often less inhibited, so we have unique talents for playing in public. As long as we're not embarrassing the kids, that kind of display is valuable, because it tells the kids we care more about having fun with them than we do about the opinions of strangers.

Besides physical clowning, of course, there are many other delicious styles of humor, some of which you may have performed since you could talk, and others of which may not come naturally at all. There's exaggeration humor ("I'm so hungry I could eat an elephant!"), scary humor ("I'm so hungry I could eat—a boy!"), music humor, surprise humor, noise humor, fantasy humor, rhyming humor, puns, opposites, and many more. The more of those modes you have in your repertoire, the more likely you are to have a joke for any occasion.

Having fun with your kids is all very well, but what's in it for you? A lot more than laughs, actually.

- You'll be apt to spend more time with them, since that time is more enjoyable for everyone concerned.
- You'll feel better about your work as a father, both because you like it more and because you're more competent at it (as ever, these two go together).
- You'll get to know your kids better, because each of you will tend to reveal more in a spirit of fun and games than you might if all were solemn talks. John Cleese tells businesspeople that "there is all the difference in the world between being serious and being solemn."
- The kids will trust you more as a result of that extra bonding.
- You'll teach your kids to approach life's adversities with their own sense of humor. If they stub their toes or bump themselves three times in one evening, they should be able to laugh and say, "This just isn't my night!" instead of burrowing into a funk.
- You may find that humor sparks innovation in them—creative solutions to family problems or their own. John Cleese believes that laughter actually has a physiological effect on people's thought processes, opening them up to new ideas.
- You'll be able to establish a groundwork for applications of humor to other challenges, such as discipline.
- Because humor gives you another way of tackling challenges, it saves you stress, makes you tougher, and lengthens your life. *He who laughs, lasts.*

Humor also has many specific applications, such as getting your kids' attention, cheering them up, defusing tension, or making a point without being hurtful. Those are not that different from the ways we use humor in business. Humor can also be a weapon, of course, but don't use it against your kids (by laughing *at* them) or teach them to use it against others. If your jokes are good-humored, not insulting, they are unsurpassed as brighteners of mood, both yours and your children's. Unless your kids are in midtantrum, a good guffaw is bound to make them smile through their tears (or their snarls). Science bears that out, since laughter has been shown to stimulate the brain's production of endorphins, those mood-altering drugs that induce feelings of well-being, balance, flexibility, and perspective.

Perhaps the most practical application of humor is as a lubricator, taking the friction out of daily interactions with your kids. Kids often resist doing what they're told—sometimes because they don't want to, and sometimes because you *do* want them to. In such situations, nothing greases the skids like an impromptu game or a joke. I'm often amazed at the power of humor to persuade. My theory is that kids, besides being distracted by humor and put in a better mood, are more willing to please you, since you've taken the trouble to amuse them and treat them like people instead of cogs in the family machine. Or, it could be that humor removes the bone of contention from the spotlight, allowing them to yield without losing face. Whatever the reason, a simple jape can melt the most solidly frozen opposition. Here are a few bedtime samples, each one tested in action by yours truly.

- Instead of carrying them up to bed kicking and crying, try challenging them to chase you upstairs.
- If they resist getting into their pajamas, see if they can do it while being held upside down. (This is the kind of roughhousing dads excel at.)
- If they don't want their teeth brushed, make the toothbrush talk. Have it insist that it can count every tooth in their mouths. It will count every tooth correctly (while brushing it) until the last one, which will suddenly be number eighty-nine.
- When they're lonely and don't want you to leave their bedside, use a funny voice and pretend it's coming from their favorite snuggle animal. Start a conversation that leads to a good long

snuggle for the animal, courtesy of its owner—lights out, tucked in, head on pillow, and mission accomplished.

It's sad that some dads stifle their own natural sense of humor or creativity when they're around the kids. They want to be seen as serious, the disciplinarians in the household. Unfortunately, this is really only *self*-seriousness—which tends to backfire, with kids taking their dads *less* seriously than if they just acted normally. Remember the father in *Peter Pan*, who said virtually nothing to his kids but "a little less noise, there"? He didn't seem to know how to have fun at all. No wonder the children had doubts about wanting to grow up!

Yes, fathering is a big responsibility that should be taken seriously, but that's not the same as taking *oneself* seriously. The rules may be important, but they can be enforced with a bit of humor without making them seem laughable. Those grim dads are nothing but stressed-out straight men, without kids who enjoy them or humor to leaven their own lives. All they're buying themselves for their earnestness is resistance, stress, and shortened life expectancies. So, if you've ever felt the urge to do comedy, fatherhood is the golden opportunity you've been waiting for.

So, go ahead—put the "loco" back *in loco parentis!*

Dual Titles

HOW SMART DADS WIN AT WORK

A Zero-Sum Game?

Brian T. is a wildly successful investment banker who, at the age of thirty-five, is running the combined media and telecommunications group of one of Wall Street's largest firms. He also has four kids, ages one to six years. He freely admits that he's concerned about his future as a father, because the demands of his job seem to increase, not decrease, as he rockets upward. "It's a case of constantly receding goals. If you're conscientious, you never really feel you've done the job right. And of course the capable ones get all the work."

The dilemma facing any man who wants to succeed as both businessman and father is one of dual titles and, it seems, *dueling* titles. In today's economy, we're like salmon leaping upstream, knowing that, if we pause for an instant, we'll be swept away like flotsam. The difference is that the salmon are hurtling over those waterfalls for the noble purpose of begetting the next generation, whereas we're just trying to earn a buck. With the constant threat and extra burden of downsizing, we may be earning a bit more, but we're paying for it dearly—we and our families. Worst of all, in a cruel trick of timing, our most severe period of career testing typically coincides with our prime child-rearing years.

Nor does labor-saving technology generally solve the problem. No matter how swiftly PCs, faxes, cell phones, palm-top computers, wireless modems, and the rest increase our productivity, expectations rise to keep pace. Spreadsheets that *can* be run overnight must extend to countless permutations, people who *can* be reached will be reached, and E-mails that *can* be read demand replies. That is the unspoken reality behind a recent AT&T ad. There's a picture of a man in his undershirt, pecking awkwardly at a laptop with an infant draped across his shoulder. The word "micro-manager" is scrawled across the photo, and underneath we read: "Just baby and you. Till urgent E-mail makes three. No problem. Pull down marketing plan from London office. Scope out competition's offer online. E-mail revisions worldwide. With Internet access from AT&T WorldNet® Service, put every little detail to bed. Except maybe one." The ad tries to strike a warm family chord, but it really shows how technology can force us to put work ahead of family. Technology may help us salmon swim faster, but it also makes the current *flow* faster, so we must keep accelerating just to move upstream. And if we try to leave the rushing river altogether, we risk getting trapped in some stagnant backwater, gasping for oxygen.

In 1996, the recruiting firm Robert Half International surveyed one thousand men and women, of whom fully two-thirds reported that they would take a cut in hours and pay to spend more time with their families. Unfortunately, most jobs do not offer that choice. In too many corporations, personal commitment is still measured by "face time," even though time is our most precious commodity at home. Dallying at work to meet such misguided requirements is like being forced to swap gold for silver, ounce for ounce—day in and day out, year after year.

Some may dream of leaving those uneven trades behind to become their own bosses. Entrepreneurs' greater freedom is no cure-all, however: now, instead of working to earn a paycheck, they slave to meet payroll. Instead of answering to one or two bosses, they must treat every customer as a boss. Instead of worrying about one family, they in some sense have two depending on them. Instead of having to find a new job, the penalty for failure may be losing their equity, their homes, and their dreams.

Even the least hidebound employers, who give their people the most entrepreneurial opportunities, can introduce new types of stress. Mike S., for example, is a twenty-five-year veteran of IBM, with two grown kids raised by an at-home wife. Now a senior executive in the Global Services division, he has seen the culture change dramatically since Lou Gerstner's ascension. He reports that face time is now irrelevant in assessing employees, who instead are measured by how fully they've achieved their goals for the year, and through 360-degree evaluations from every colleague they've worked with.

In a sense, though, being held to concrete goals instead of just showing up for the requisite hours can actually raise the bar. "There are so many strong incentives to perform that there's a lot of stress. I see a lot of younger people get pretty fragile pretty quick." Mike also remembers when every employee could carry vacation over from year to year, and part of his job as manager was to "kick people in the shins to make 'em take vacation." Now the new leadership has decided that they're "grown-ups, so it's use it or lose it." He's convinced that people are taking less vacation now that he's not there to remind them it's okay. "It's easy to get caught up in things."

Note: lest we feel too sorry for ourselves, we should not forget that there are workers less fortunate, families working three or four jobs just to make ends meet, who would love to have our problems. Business dads do not have it easy, but others have it even harder. That being said, we still owe it to ourselves and to our families to make the best of the time and opportunities we've been given.

Men, of course, are hardly the only ones to face such problems. Women have faced them for considerably longer, since before the days when Gloria Steinem complained, "I have yet to hear a man ask for advice on how to combine marriage and a career." But balancing work and life is no longer a "woman's issue," either at home or at the office. According to James Levine and Todd Pittinsky's book *Work-*

ing Fathers, company surveys about work-family conflict are answered similarly by men and women, with the same percentages calling the level of conflict "high," and with men identifying childcare concerns as one of their greatest causes of stress at work. Similarly, a 1997 *Business Week* survey found that 46.2 percent of male managers said their company asked too much at the expense of family, versus 44.0 percent for female managers.

Men also face some special challenges of their own: just as society still assumes women will give priority to being lead parent, it expects men to prove their ambition and drive. Many men have internalized those expectations. Craig Byquist, a manufacturing engineering manager for Hewlett-Packard, told *Business Week*, "There's a self-imposed pressure, when you get into an environment like HP's and you're surrounded by overachievers. You want to be successful, and you want the company to be successful." That combination of pressures pushes many of us to clock *mucho* macho hours at the office.

The ever-expanding demands of work can really squeeze a dad's home life. It leaves him the choice between cutting back his emotional investment at home ("I gave at the office") or trying to cram just as much involvement into fewer hours ("Two more minutes of catch, then I'm scheduled to bond with your brother"). Even when he's home, there's always more office work to catch up on, not to mention the possibility of urgent calls, faxes, pages, or E-mails. At-home work may be the worst kind of all. The kids might understand why he has to go to the office to do his job, and they might think about him less while he's gone. But when he's home and *still* won't be with them, it sends a definite message about his priorities.

Many men work hard to succeed in the office *and* at home, but the constant feeling that somehow their best is never good enough burns out too many sooner or later. David W., a New York investment banker and father, told me, "No matter how hard you try, there's always more." It's hard to reverse burnout once it sets in, because performance deteriorates in both settings, so the tradeoffs only get harsher. As matters get grimmer, frustration rises and may goad men into lashing out at their colleagues or, even worse, at their eight-year-olds, which hurts the harried dads' self-images even more. For such men, something's got to give, or they end up fried to a crisp.

But all is not lost. The conflict between office and family may never go away, but, like so many of life's profound challenges, it can be addressed with certain adjustments in outlook. When time and energy are *rationed*, it requires *rationality* to make the most of them. Business dads, in other words, can benefit from a little practical philosophy. This is not a theoretical exercise, but *a way for men of action to make their actions count for more.*

If you ask yourself the following seven questions, work and home can become at least friendly competitors, and can even enrich each other at times—a concept that consultants now call "co-opetition." Everyone will answer these questions differently, but almost anyone can benefit from asking them.

1. Can you have it all? Wouldn't it be great if we each had a Superdad within us—some amazing paragon who could combine the perfect executive, the perfect father, the perfect husband, and the perfect citizen in one shining package? We would spend all our days shuttling from boardroom to town-hall meeting to volunteer fire department, and divide all our nights between sharing candlelit dinners with our wives, perusing the latest *Foreign Affairs*, and tucking our adoring, perfectly behaved children into bed.

Well, it's always nice to have an ideal. But unrealistic dreams present their own dangers. If we business dads hold ourselves to that standard of perfection, we are bound to become disappointed and frustrated. We may even feel so guilty that we turn bitter and defensive when our families ask more of us, which will only widen the gap between reality and ideal. Just as many would-be Supermoms have discovered, it's much healthier to face up to our obstacles than to wish them away.

Bill F. is a widely respected columnist, consultant, and investor based in Pennsylvania. He has two sons and considers himself a good father, though "not the nurturing type." I've had many chances to see him at work, feeding realism like spinach to talented but overly optimistic management teams, and his approach to work-family issues is no different. "If you think you can have it all, you're fooling yourself. Make priorities. To be a good father, you've got to cap your ambition—give 80 percent to work, but not that last 20 percent. And give up hobbies. Don't spend all Saturday playing golf and all Sunday watching football." Bill has not recently been accused of living in a dream world.

2. Are you climbing the right ladder? A day has only twenty-four hours, and we have too many things we'd like to do during those hours. On the other hand, great lives, like great buildings, can be created by making the most of our materials. Just as the best architects throughout history have invented cantilevers and buttresses to counteract the force of gravity, the best business dads go beyond the obvious to engineer new ways of reconciling job with family—even if that means finding or inventing a new kind of job.

People change over the years, as do their needs, and the career that made sense for you once may no longer do so. If you're not happy with the path you've chosen, choose again. No one can be truly successful if he doesn't feel satisfied with his job. If you don't love what you do, it will make life harder for both you and your family. As the saying goes, "Find a job you really enjoy and you'll add five days to every week of your life."

At least once or twice a year, take stock of your life. Imagine you could wipe the slate clean and start over—because you can. Don't be shy about talking it over with your wife, who knows you so well. You may even, once or twice in your life, want to retain a career counselor. Do you have the right job within your company, the job that best suits your needs, and promises to do so in the future? Are you at the right company, or should you switch? If there's a problem, maybe it's not just with the company but with the industry—are you a restaurant owner trapped in a marketing manager's career? Is it worth retraining to get into a faster-growing or more exciting industry? Who knows, you may even find you're in the wrong sector—academics or government may fit you and your family best.

If you have the right job, but it *still* impinges too much on family, maybe you should change it in a different way—reengineer it. Reemphasize certain parts, such as devoting more time to original thought and less to paperwork, or more to quality control and less to sheer volume. The better you do your job, the more you'll like it, and the sooner you'll succeed by financial measures as well. You may even find that your increasing seniority gives you more power over your own schedule and workload. *You can change your job without leaving it.*

Reengineering can be especially useful for business dads with long commutes. You probably already use your commute to get work done, but have you considered shortening the commute by using flextime to avoid rush-hour traffic? What about trying to get home early every third or fourth night? You could consider taking occasional vacation days at home, just for a break in the routine. And if your long commute continues to be a major problem, perhaps some economies would help you afford a house closer to work.

In addition to reengineering your job, consider new ways of managing the life into which your job fits, so that your overall stress decreases (see the Time Management sections later in this chapter). Your work isn't the only part of life subject to change, after all: the idea is to reexamine your family life as well, so that your two lives coexist with less friction. If you keep diligently readjusting so that you perform optimally in both lives—given the limits of space, time, and personal finance—you may find that, within your world of possibilities, you actually *can* have it all—more or less.

3. What does money cost? I am not referring here to interest rates, which determine the financial cost of money. What I mean instead is the *human* cost of money—the penalties you and your family pay for you to earn that extra bonus, or to keep that fast-track job. When businesspeople decide which ladders to climb, one criterion they use is the size of the paychecks at each rung along the way. But there are tradeoffs here, and we're better off making them consciously (if at all) than blindly. If the extra money you earn buys your family a fancier kitchen, but you're not there for meals with them, is it worth it? If it buys the family a bigger lawn, but you're not there to run and play with them, is it worth it? If it buys them a swimming pool, but you're not there to teach them swimming, is it worth it?

The major single fallacy to which business dads fall victim is that we are somehow better fathers the more money we earn. In fact, once you get above very basic needs such as food, clothing, and shelter, the absolute level of your household income matters much less than its reliability (given children's need for stability).

Assuming some minimum level of income and stability, I don't believe a family's wealth necessarily increases its children's long-term happiness. In fact, richer businesspeople can more easily afford to bribe their kids with money and gifts in lieu of the real essentials, such as parental time. That bribery is a classic example of the trade-off between short-term and long-term happiness. Buying Junior the entire Mutant Power Pandas collector set (among a million other toys) may score you some momentary points, but the hours you sacrifice to work for that standard of living can never be replaced.

There is hidden truth in this eighties joke about the two bond traders. One says, "Hey, I got a Porsche for my wife!" To which the other replies, "Good trade!" Too much attention to getting and spending can interfere with knowing and loving.

In business, success is measured by money, but *what you take home matters much less than what you bring to home.* In fact, the dangers can increase, not decrease, as people climb the income ladder. The more money the really wealthy have, the more time it takes just to manage that wealth, and the more their limitless opportunities for epicurean excess in Paris and laid-back luxury in the Bahamas can blind them to the treasures of family in their own home. They don't have time for simple things like putting up shelves, sweeping the porch, washing the car, and teaching their kids to drive. Your kids need you, not your bank account. You've heard that money can't buy happiness: for kids, money alone can't even *rent* happiness for long.

It's a shame, really, that many men feel like failures as fathers (and husbands) if their income doesn't grow rapidly. It makes them feel less competent with the kids and drives them to work insane hours — which, combined, can make them fail at *real* fathering. They're also setting themselves up for a double downfall if they lose their jobs (it happens), because they've defined themselves so much by their work that they lack the safety net of a genuinely close family. You'd think that they would have learned in business school about the benefits of diversification, but instead they let that uncontrollable variable called "career" define their self-worth not only as businessmen but also as dads. Many portfolio managers like investments with low beta, that is, low correlation with price movements in the overall market. Family well-being *should* have a naturally low beta in relation to the marketplace of work, but too many business dads strip away that protection by linking the two artificially.

Do your supposed financial needs constantly push family to the back burner? Sooner or later, it will boil over. But money has other human costs. If it keeps you locked into a career you don't love, for example, and your heart is not in your work, you'll never be a true success however large your bank balance. But if you find a job you really adore, you've often got a better chance of striking it rich in the end—and still knowing your kids when you do.

Try taking that clean slate again, and ask yourself these questions. How much money do you and your family really need? How badly do you need it? Why do you need it—for subsistence, for social standing, for a chance to improve your future earnings, for your kids' education, for a sense of accomplishment, for kicks? How much difference in your life does each extra dollar really make? Is the difference greater when you earn it, or when you spend it?

Money is never simple. Even if you are lucky enough to have a job you love that pays well, you can still blow it by spending too much. Saving for your family's future is prudent, of course, but the money you put away also buys you freedom. If you should one day decide that it makes sense to change careers, those savings may buy you the time or confidence or flexibility you need to get your new work life off the ground. If you've spent every cent you earned on the latest PC or the fanciest wallpaper, you could find yourself in a splendidly decorated prison.

Too many business dads, feeling something lacking in their lives, assume that working just a little harder will earn them enough money to solve all their problems. But that materialism itself is the real problem, not any lack of cash or the luxuries cash buys. *If they're not happy with what they have, what makes them imagine they'll be any happier with more of the same?* When given the choice between "your money or your life," without even thinking, they choose the former. In the most extreme cases, they end up spending their hard-earned loot on the best that money can buy—the best child psychologists, the best marriage counselors, the best divorce lawyers.

You may remember the story of Midas, legendary king of Phrygia, whose wish the god Dionysus once granted: to turn everything he touched into gold. Midas was ecstatic at first, turning his chair, his table, and everything else within reach into solid gold. His enthusiasm dimmed when he got hungry—the food turned metallic before he could swallow it. The worst part, though, happened when his young daughter came rushing up to him. In his arms before he could stop her, she turned into a statue—beautiful and pure gold, but dead. It was only once he'd learned his lesson—that wealth is meaningless without love and humanity—that Dionysus relented and turned everything back.

4. Why are you working so hard? Of course, you may feel you're logging all those hours for the challenge as much as the money. It's wonderful to love what you do, but how much can you love a job that monopolizes your time, causing your kids to grow up without you? Why did you have them in the first place—to give your wife some company? Think hard: maybe it's not actually love of the work that's driving you, but competitive colleagues (declare a mental truce), marital stress (don't flee what's wrong at home, fix it), unhappiness with your kids (talk about circularity!), or sheer perfectionism (get over it).

Or, finally, perhaps you're simply overinvested in your job. You're not in it for the money, although money may be a handy way to keep score. It's just that you see yourself as the ultimate tax strategist (or taxi fleet owner, or taxidermist), and you've got to kill yourself to keep that identity alive. *Being overinvested, however, implies that your portfolio is insufficiently diversified.* If you neglect your family in favor of your career, then all your ego eggs are riding in one basket—and a flimsy one at that, in this age of downsizing.

Maybe you'd be better off choosing a job that does not require such rabid dedication, a job that does not demand the senior role in your life, subordinating all family bonds to its demands. As any debt specialist will tell you, bonds lose their quality once they're subordinated. You may think your family bonds are still strong enough to provide high yields, but at some point the risks you take may downgrade them into junk, in which case your family may lose interest.

5. What does family cost? Everyone knows that raising kids is expensive, but I'm not referring to direct costs like cribs and braces. It's opportunity costs I have in mind, the activities we give up to participate in raising our kids. Is the tradeoff really as dire as the head of the investment bank Deutsche Morgan Grenfell recently described it? "Dinner at home," he warned his troops, "is a wasted marketing opportunity."

Clearly, there are some committed dads whose careers do take hits in the solar plexus as a result. Perhaps they work at a place like DMG, where the boss explicitly disapproves of split allegiances, and so threatens them for spending time with their kids. Or maybe their employer offers the wrong kind of daddy track, which seems family friendly in the short run but leads to second-class status in the long run, with limited room for career advancement. Or they may feel forced into the wrong kind of "downshifting," not only to a lower income but also to work they find less challenging.

Those kinds of career damage are lamentable, all the more so because they are far from the only choices available. We can, in fact, change our work lives to make room for commitment to our kids— *without* suffering penalties and *without* shunting onto the wrong kind of daddy track or doing the wrong kind of downshifting. All we need is a job that gives us *control.* By that I mean control over how and where we spend our hours, but not necessarily shorter hours.

Jobs that offer more control are typically more interesting too.

The New Economy is full of them. They let you come as close as humanly possible to the mythical Superdad: faster than a speeding toddler, more powerful than your corporate rivals, able to leap tall deadlines in a single executive decision. If your job does not meet that description, then change your job. Change it from within, without moving desks, or change it externally, even if that means moving halfway across the country. Whatever high-control job you're qualified for, "upshifting" to it could be the best business *and* family decision you'll ever make.

For example, having your own consulting firm is often more lucrative, interesting, and flexible work than holding out for the gold watch. Being an entrepreneur may give you more control than working for one. Mischa Weisz, CEO of TNS Smart Network, has had that experience, as he described in a 1998 issue of *Forbes*.

> When I became a single dad, I knew I couldn't do the 9-to-5 thing. I started my business so that I could be with the kids. I have a traditional office, but most of the time I work at home.
>
> My business exists because of my family. I don't think I would have started my own business if I hadn't become a single parent. I would have been stuck in the same old cube for my entire life. Now, if my daughter is in a play, I can be there. I don't have to ask permission from anyone.

I just heard that Brian T., the investment banker with four kids whom I described earlier, has quit his job and joined a prestigious private-equity investing firm. And on a personal note, venture capital gives me more control over when and where I travel, and whether I do my late-night work at home or at the office, than investment banking ever did. Salomon was a great place, but it's not a total coincidence that I left there three months after our first child's appearance on this earth.

One more example, from a 1998 *Wall Street Journal* article profiling an executive, John Sites Jr., who made the leap to a higher-control job:

When he quit one of Wall Street's top-paid jobs at Bear Stearns in 1995, some observers thought Mr. Sites had lost a power struggle. He said simply that he wanted more time with family. Three years later, he's . . . a partner at Daystar Partners, a bond firm near his Connecticut home.

And he is spending more time with his family. Though he works 8:30 A.M. to 5:30 P.M., he is free of his former 2½-hour commute and the administrative burdens of his former job. Also, his work no longer keeps him chained to global market trends. He often goes home for lunch or picks up his kids, ages five and seven, at school. "They used to see me mostly in the dark. They knew me by my silhouette" at bedtime, he says. Now, they are part of his day-to-day life.

For Mr. Sites, resigning "to spend more time with family" was, in a broader sense, a way to reorder his priorities in life. He now carves out several hours a week for charitable and religious pursuits. "Changing your lifestyle frees you up to do what you want to do, as opposed to what you have to do."

Putting it another way, business dads in the New Economy have no need to choose among off-the-rack career choices. In this age of customization, wouldn't you rather design your own options? Apply the same creativity and ingenuity to your own career that any worthwhile job demands of you each day. Why settle for the wrong kind of daddy track, when the New Economy lets you lay your own fast track even as you're rolling along? The cost to your career of family commitment can shrink considerably if you think creatively—even if circumstances prevent you from leaving your current position. In fact, to the extent the conundrum forces you to think laterally, your career may even benefit.

6. How many people are you? In the movie *Multiplicity*, Michael Keaton played a construction executive who felt so overwhelmed with his responsibilities as an executive, husband, and father that he was shortchanging them all. In desperation, he had a clone made to take over his work responsibilities, and then another to do household chores, and then one of the clones made a clone, and things really got out of hand. He finally realized that he had to take responsibility for his own life (including Andie MacDowell, of course), and the clones rode off together into the sunset. Moral of the story: a man's got to do what a man's got to do—singular, not plural.

Much though we harried business dads might dream of cloning ourselves, it's probably just as well that we can't. We have one life to live, so we shouldn't try to live it as two people. Is the business part of us so different from the family part? Bill Clinton may have mastered compartmentalizing, but is that really the best way? So many business dads feel compelled to split into two: tough at work but mellow at home, or controlled at work but natural at home, or absorbed at work but restless at home. The problem is, we're not really built that way. The feelings we try to restrict to one environment bleed over into the other. If we don't recognize that, the tensions between the two are bound to increase.

It's better to take an integrated approach to our lives, finding the common ground between work and home. That philosophy requires what the consultants call process re-engineering: instead of dividing ourselves into *com*partments the way corporations used to divide themselves into *de*partments, with little or no internal communication, we should focus on the *processes* in our lives, whether they belong to office or home.

The whole thrust of this book, that business and fathering require many of the same skills, is a recognition of how similar many processes are between the two. There's no "dad" part of you to handle the processes at home, while the "business" part takes responsibility at the office. Instead of thinking like two men, Homo corporatus and Homo domesticus, let's stay true to our nature as Homo sapiens.

7. Who needs you more *right now?* Consider, if you will, the 1995 Nike Air Max. A pair cost about twenty U.S. dollars to make in China, and they sold well in the United States at several times that amount, but in Japan they have become a cult classic. In certain colors, they can fetch as much as two thousand dollars on the Ginza! Or consider the amazing popularity in France of Jerry Lewis. In each case, the very same commodity has widely differing values in different places, all through the hidden logic of supply and demand.

It's the same with your time and energy. When the office is in a genuine crunch period, it needs you desperately, and you may be forced to miss a baseball game or ballet recital. But opposite extremes occur as well. Take the case of David Williams, offensive tackle for the Houston Oilers, who in 1993 missed a game in order to be with his wife for the birth of their first child. His father said, "He's proved to me he's a real man," but his coach fined him eleven thousand dollars for letting down the team. What would you have done if you were Williams? And if you were Bob Young, the coach? Hint: the Oilers play plenty of games every year, but your first child is born exactly once.

Most situations fall into the big gray area between those two extremes. In 1995, Ross Garber and a partner founded the Internet software company Vignette just a week after the birth of Garber's first child. He told *Forbes* recently, "I knew there'd never be this window of opportunity again." In the company's first year, he flew more than one hundred thousand miles, which he admits took a serious toll on his marriage. Fortunately, the relationship was strong enough to repair itself, the company succeeded, and now he's worth many millions. But what if it hadn't all worked out? Many entrepreneurs are less lucky both in business and in love, abandoning their families to leap headlong through windows of opportunity that turn out to be painted on brick.

Genuine work emergencies do happen, but too many business dads let one blur into the next, treating the intervening merely busy periods with the same level of urgency. For those dads, standing up their children becomes a regular event, and the reasons begin fading into pale excuses. It makes them feel good to think their work is important, and they believe the kids will benefit from their economic success, so they treat more and more office tasks as if they can't wait. The children, meanwhile, apparently *can* wait, so they wait and wait and wait, even though Dad's presence may at times have ten times the value for them that it does for his company.

Tony Prophet, the well-named CEO of AlliedSignal Power Systems, does whatever he can to avoid that syndrome with his two young children, as he recently showed in *Forbes*.

> I was going to go on a trip to Asia—it would have been my seventh trip to Asia in seven months. You could see it was wearing on my kids. When the tears started flowing, I asked my subordinate to go.
>
> A lot of executives have a savior complex. We think nothing happens if we are not there. It's a superman complex. You have to have a superteam perspective rather than a superman complex.

How many executives do you know who think they're indispensable to the company when really the company could muddle through without their killer hours? Jim McCann, the CEO of 1-800-FLOWERS, warns against that mistake in his book *Stop and Sell the Roses*. "Workaholics are people who are basically insecure: they secretly feel that they are not really up to snuff. They believe that unless they are running around plugging up imaginary holes in the dike, the whole dam will burst and drown them in their own fundamental worthlessness. . . . If you worry all the time, you will inevitably screw up. No one can stand that much tension and still maintain efficiency."

For guys who need to be needed, it's ironic how often workaholics underestimate their true importance to their children. Don't let that happen to you. The better you know your kids, the more clearly you'll recognize when you can really "add value" in their lives.

For example, Frank P. is the president and chief operating officer of a $3-billion technology company in southern California. I met with him in an effort to recruit him as CEO of an exciting young company in our portfolio. As we were driving to the airport, I mentioned I was working on this book. He smiled. "We've got three daughters. The youngest one just started college. When I was twenty-three, my wife told me I could never succeed in business if I was going to be a good father. I told her, I'm going to prove you wrong. And I did. It's just a matter of balance. I can go see the basketball game at three or four, then go back to the office—there's nothing wrong with that. The key is, if things aren't going 100 percent perfect at work, I don't let it drive me crazy."

Coming through when your kids need you can change how you plan your next minutes, hours, or even years. Bruce Entin, a VP at chip maker LSI Logic, told *Business Week* that he'd once refused a transfer and promotion because he didn't want to disrupt his kids' lives by moving the family. That "was where I came up with the philosophy that I'm going to be a father longer than I'll be a working man."

I am on the board of an East Coast company that recently recruited a new CEO. One of our prime candidates, a brilliant marketer from California, wouldn't even interview with us, because joining would mean either uprooting his family or commuting cross-country. He told us his three children were still at an age "where they think I'm a god," and they needed him more than we did. Our chairman nodded sagely and remarked, "As those of us with older children know, you go from 'god' to 'jerk' in about eighteen months."

It's all about the marginal value of your time. For each incremental minute you're tempted to stay longer in the office or in your weekend study, ask yourself whether that minute could more profitably be spent with your kids. Which has slid further down the slippery slope of diminishing returns, our time at work or our personal time? We give so much more time to work than to our families that it's reasonable to suppose it's the former. (One of our portfolio companies offered a high-ranking executive a slight raise to take *shorter* hours, because that executive was brilliant for certain responsibilities but *counterproductive* the rest of the time.) If you face the choice between a futile, waste-of-time meeting and your kid's soccer game, you don't have to view the soccer game as crucial to give it higher priority.

It's a classic problem of resource allocation, with the ideal solution being "Pareto optimality," the state described by economist Vilfredo Pareto in which every resource is devoted to its best and highest use. You are a key resource to your kids (maybe more than you think) and to your company (maybe less than you think), so you owe it to both to be "resourceful" and allocate yourself in a sane, balanced way.

I could write another paragraph here, describing the art of allocation more fully. But if you'll excuse me, I think I'll go spend some time with my kids instead.

Staking Your Claim

The previous section proposed reengineering our jobs so that they conflict less with our family lives. Some of this reengineering may require only individual decisions, such as how much work to do after the kids' bedtime, but the rest relies on changes in corporate policy. For any of a number of reasons, many business dads do not have the flexibility of being able to change jobs, or even to reengineer their current jobs unilaterally. At some point, therefore, it may become necessary to speak up for what we and our children need.

Unfortunately, many managers are even less sympathetic to working dads than they are to working moms. Fatherhood rarely gets priority as a workplace classification for men, with issues such as race, class, and personality taking precedence in the minds of most managers. Even parent-oriented programs are subtly targeted to women. Ellen Bankert, director of the Center for Work and Family, acknowledged to *Business Week* that, when it comes to fathers' needs, "even work-life champions don't think about that." I think it's about time that society's conception of "working parents" be expanded to include fathers, don't you?

We have only ourselves to blame for being misunderstood. Most business dads were brought up believing that real men don't feel stress, or, if they do, they certainly don't talk about it. We won't admit it when we're lost on the freeway, let alone in life. Our managers, many of whom are also men, do not consider themselves mind readers, and so figure that quiet workers must mean contented workers. It's only anonymously that we feel free to speak, in hallway conversations or surveys. But speak up openly? Never.

Even when we're offered opportunities for direct improvement, as with companywide flextime programs, we shrink away, assuming that it's okay only for women to take advantage of them. We are often perceived, with some justification, as making career choices based mostly on factors other than family. Deborah Holmes, director of retention at Ernst & Young, has told the *Wall Street Journal*, "Men and women are equally passionate about wanting life outside work, but men don't vote as much with their feet."

Given this history, it can be tough for business dads to ask for family-friendly policies such as flexible hours, to get weekends away from the office, or just to take an afternoon off to watch a soccer game. Here are a few thoughts that may be helpful, or at least encouraging.

If You Don't Ask, You Don't Get!

The times, they are a-changing. Luckily, most workplaces are evolving in the right direction—impelled not by concern for our fathering but by the hard reality of a tight market for skilled labor. (This is one side benefit of the loosened bonds of loyalty between employers and employees.) In addition, computing and communications technology is making options such as flextime and telecommuting much more practical. Those two factors are already combining to usher in a new era of enlightened management in some highly competitive white-collar industries, such as advertising and software. Laurel Cutler, vice chairman of ad agency Foote Cone & Belding, was quoted in a 1998 *Wall Street Journal* article in a way that indicates she "gets it."

I wish I had known sooner that if you miss a child's play or performance or sporting event, you will have forgotten a year later the work emergency that caused you to miss it. But the child won't have forgotten that you weren't there. I learned it, but not in time for my own kids. I was a very good boss in this respect, though. By the time I had a number of young parents working for me, I would tell them, "It's more important to be there for your child."

Perhaps the most progressive industry so far is accounting. The major firms are engaged in a veritable arms race of family-friendly policies, competing to win and retain the most talented parents. Part-timers can now make partner, and pay is determined by performance rather than hours. The firms say they're acting out of alarm at how many capable women they were losing, but CPA dads are benefiting as well. The chairman of Ernst & Young has hired an alumna of Catalyst and the Work/Family Institute, reporting directly to him, to implement family-friendly policies.

As part of my research, I asked Ernst & Young if they could put me in touch with an employee who has benefited from their flexible work arrangements. Don Robinson is a consultant in the Denver office, helping clients implement large software projects. A father of three, he speaks enthusiastically of the culture at E&Y, which he calls one of the major reasons he joined in 1996. He hasn't seen another firm quite like E&Y, which mandates a "counselor" for all employees to make sure they keep balance between work and home life, becoming neither burned out nor underutilized.

"Every position I've had before, I was expected to be in a building or at a customer site for a particular length of time. At E&Y, they gave me a cell phone, a laptop, and a credit card, and that's my office." Don can work wherever he wants, as long as he gets the job done—and "hoteling" lets the firm provide a workplace for eighty consultants in Denver with only thirty physical offices. The consultants are often on-site with clients, but E&Y sells clients only a forty-five-hour work week for each consultant on a project, letting Don spend three days at home with his family each week, and work only four days on the road. Don values those three days, even if he spends one working from home. "My children are too important to let them raise themselves."

Another accounting firm, Deloitte & Touche, rank fourteenth on *Fortune*'s 1998 list of the hundred best companies to work for. Its human resources people tell employees with new kids that "they can work fewer hours and still make partner." J. Michael Cook, the CEO, recently expressed views that might have been anathema to his predecessors:

> I wish that over the years I had had more control over my time and more opportunities to be involved in family things. I wish I'd understood the importance of that Thursday afternoon soccer game. But it was a given that you dedicated yourself to your job. Flexibility was unheard of. One thing that we've tried to do culturally is to say to people, "Though client demands drive our days, we also have the flexibility of having multiple clients and the freedom to make our own schedules and to decide how and where to spend our time. Take advantage of that flexibility."

Encouragingly, such attitudes are also starting to expand beyond pure white-collar businesses. In the hospitality industry, for example, Marriott International has shown leadership from the top, and has even remembered that fathers are parents too. J.W. Marriott put it this way to *Forbes*.

> I have four children and eleven grandchildren. Parenthood is not a matter of balancing but of prioritizing. Fatherhood is job one, and I don't let anything stand in the way.
>
> We have a lot of women working for us, and they were telling us that they had lots of problems at home because they were not getting the right support from fathers. That's why we started the Fatherhood Project, offering our executives and our hourly employees effective fathering workshops, which help dads evaluate their relationships and become more involved in their children's lives.

Business dads, unite! Before speaking up to the policymakers, do your homework. Check out the work-family policies of other companies in your industry, especially as they apply to men. Next, start to build a base of support in your own company. How many of your fellow business dads could benefit from constructive changes in attitude and policy? Don't be ashamed to benefit from progress already made by and for women in your company. If you and the other dads devote to lobbying effectively together one-tenth of the energy you now waste trying to work around the system as individuals, you will be amazed at the improvements you are able to achieve.

Sound out fellow sufferers without seeming to bellyache. Approach men and women alike; if you make it just a dad issue, it will be too easy for the old double standards to prevail. First introduce the topic of kids into the conversation, instead of chatting about sports or the weather. Then drop a rueful comment about how the corporate retreat is scheduled for Father's Day weekend (I've actually known this to happen), or about how the boss seems to forget what it's like being a parent. Gently, wistfully, wonder what it would be like if attitudes changed one day. If your coworkers agree, ask whether that will ever happen before the old guard retires. A little more talk like that, and you will recognize kindred spirits soon enough. All it takes is opening up a little, and you may find you've got a movement on your hands. Once you've established critical mass, you can address the powers that be with more standing and authority—as long as you do it in a way that doesn't threaten them.

Argue enlightened self-interest. Don't imagine you can base your case on the social merits (can anyone even agree on what they are?) or on your employers' warmth and humanity. They may be made up of great people, but businesses are not charities. To get your bosses to make a change, you have to make it worth their while. We are operating in the marketplace, after all, not in some academic laboratory or policy wonk's imagination. To paraphrase Gertrude Stein, business is business is business.

Every company, every industry has different needs, and no reengineering can eliminate certain basic requirements of your job. No amount of wishing or lobbying or even legislation will change that fact, and we're fortunate that our government (usually) recognizes it and forbears from interfering too much. In countries such as Sweden, by contrast, half of all new fathers get to take *paid* six-week paternity leaves. Sounds swell, doesn't it? But compare Sweden's economic performance to America's, and our relative respect for market needs seems not so crazy.

Fortunately, there is now enough research to demonstrate that flexible work arrangements and other family-friendly policies, tailored to each company's needs and bought into by senior management, can help employer and employees alike. In 1996, the Ford Foundation released an extensive on-site analysis of multiple companies instituting such policies, which showed significant reductions in absenteeism and turnover, and improvements in morale. Productivity rose as well, partly because employers and coworkers could now plan for employee absences instead of having them occur informally and unexpectedly.

In 1997, Catalyst published a survey of two thousand *Fortune* 100 managers. Following the introduction of flextime, 92 percent reported improved morale, 78 percent believed that flextime "encourages employee retention," and about 50 percent perceived measurable gains in productivity. Research presented to the Conference Board in 1998 indicated that employees in companies offering higher flexibility experience significantly less work-family stress and are absent less than half as often as those in other companies.

If you and your colleagues let management know that the conflict between work and family is a major issue for you—and that anything management can do to alleviate that conflict will more than pay for itself through better morale, higher performance, more predictable attendance, and lower turnover—then accommodating you hard-working business dads (as well as business moms) should start to look like a pretty strategic move.

In the meantime . . . If your company is still not a candidate for work-family enlightenment, then you have no choice (if you stay there) but to make your own arrangements. In seeking flexible work arrangements, asking and getting both require a certain political skill. Vent your raw feelings of stress and frustration to your spouse and friends, not to your boss. If you sound too whiny, you could be written off as not only a malcontent but also a wimp. The trick is to couch the problem in the most reasonable, measured way possible, in order to maximize empathy with your position. Bosses are usually older, so it may help to jog their memory about what it's like to have younger children. Even if their kids grew up in a different era, when expectations on fathers were lower, bosses may now be grandparents, and their own children now may be in the same kind of work-family bind as you.

Don't position the problem as a conflict of generational values, though it may be—call it a logistical issue. It's tricky: bosses (male or female) have often gotten to where they are by making personal sacrifices or having different priorities from yours. If they think you're requesting special treatment, they could resent it. They could also worry that if they make an exception for you, "then everyone will want it."

Again, it will help if you convince them that their own interests lie in granting your request, because you will be objectively more productive (not just subjectively happier). It is understandable, although not necessarily fair, that more valued employees are more likely to get a yes. The better you are at your job, the more your boss will want to keep you happy; and the happier you are in you job, the better you will perform. As a shining example, Bill Woodburn, who heads General Electric's industrial diamonds business, turned down a promotion and transfer in 1996 because he felt it would disrupt his daughter's schooling. Instead of exploding or exhorting, CEO Jack Welch sent him one of his famous handwritten notes: "Bill, We like you for a lot of reasons—one of them is that you are a very special person. You proved it again this morning. Good for you and your lucky family. Make Diamonds a great business and keep your priorities straight. Jack."

Whether your company officially offers flexible work arrangements or not, any request should be thought out carefully beforehand. Be precise in your proposal, detailing why you need it, when you will not be working, what you will do to make up for it, and how you will coordinate with colleagues so that no balls get dropped.

(You'll need to get those colleagues' support first, of course.) It is equally important to follow through afterward, making sure that you deliver on your promises, that quality is not suffering, and that any extension of the arrangement is explicitly requested and granted, not just taken.

If you *are* allowed some special deal, please keep in mind that any suspicion of favoritism could cause resentment among your colleagues. It will help if you are open about what has happened, keep up your end of the deal, maintain professional quality, and encourage others to seek similar arrangements. Changing company culture that way helps everyone.

"Off the books" options. If reason and eloquence fail to produce reform, or if they're doomed to fail given the personalities involved, you may choose to switch jobs. The less drastic alternative, though, is simply to engage in a bit of guerrilla resistance. Some dads who choose to stay home with sick kids call in sick themselves, because they're embarrassed to reveal their priorities. The author James Levine recounts a vignette about two male lawyers facing each other in a deposition proceeding, each of whom has to pick up his kids from school but is ashamed to admit it. To avoid "coming out" as committed fathers, they each take the court reporter aside and beg her to announce that *she* has to finish up by five o'clock for family reasons!

More common (and ethical) than giving false excuses, though, is giving none at all. Instead of explaining why they must leave early, for example, many pragmatic business dads simply *take* the time they need, making up for the lost work when it's more convenient.

Those "off the books" actions may seem ignoble in comparison to a principled stand for full family rights, but this book means to describe the world as it is, not as it should be. Some business dads are already changing, such as Otto L., the North Carolina investment banker I was doing business with the other day. He excused himself early from a 5:40 P.M. phone call with a matter-of-fact, "Gotta scoot in a minute. My daughter's got a ballet recital." As more and more fathers become like Otto, it may become easier for every dad to find the flexibility he needs.

Baby's come home. Should you? Paternity leave is one of the toughest work-family issues. It's tough on your managers to lose you for a sustained period, and it's tough on *you* to incur their resentment and to take an unpaid leave—just when you have new financial responsibilities. If they don't see you as a "working parent," they'll wonder why you're taking the kind of leave "everyone" knows is meant for women. Never mind that the Family and Medical Leave Act of 1993 nowhere limits itself to moms. In that same year, Catalyst polled personnel directors and CEOs on how much paternity leave would be reasonable, and 63 percent answered none, leading some observers to describe it as career suicide. In practice, only 1 percent of eligible men take paternity leave.

Did I take it? No, reader, I did not. My company needed me, and I needed the income.

In truth, the press and politicians have made paternity leave more of a big deal than it really is: it's hardly the dividing line between good and bad fathers. That being said, even a one- or two-week leave can work wonders to set a healthy pattern for your future relationships with both baby and mother. If you can't take time off formally without unduly damaging your career or your bank balance, try doing it informally: use vacation days or sick days or half days. I essentially worked part-time for a week or two, and no one minded.

If you plan to use vacation days, you may want to start saving them up when you have an idea of the due date. In any case, give your colleagues reasonable notice, keep in close touch while you're gone, and be prepared to make cameo appearances for true emergencies. Clearly, your opportunities for vacation or flexible hours during this period depend on the nature of your company and industry. But if work grinds to a halt without you, or if this short-lived hiatus puts your job in jeopardy, then chances are you have problems at the office that go way beyond paternity leave.

Turnabout is fair play. Once you ascend to a position of authority yourself, you should try to create a culture where people feel safe at least to bring up family concerns. Even if they're not asking for change, they may still need it. As an employer, you may be interested to know that, in a 1998 Catalyst survey, 65 percent of men (and 72 percent of women) said "they would like the option to customize the pace of their career advancement, slowing it when family responsibilities are most pressing, without harming their chances for eventual success." Offering your employees such an option, if your industry dynamics permit it, would directly address the common problem of children needing us most just when our careers enter their make-or-break phases.

Beyond introducing family-friendly policies, by the way, you might even promote them actively to individuals you think could use them, thus setting the right cultural tone. If you "make change your friend," as the New Democrats liked to say, you'll attract better employees—and keep the ones you have happier, more productive, and less likely to take those constant headhunter calls. The cultural change you create within your own span of control could even spread throughout your whole company. Just hope it doesn't spread to your competitors!

Time Management: The Problem

Okay. You've done whatever you can to make your job family-friendly, either by working to change policy, by seeking special treatment, by taking action "off the books," or if necessary by changing workplaces. Your biggest challenge, however, can never be talked through, worked around, or moved away from—and that is the hard fact that each day has only twenty-four hours.

How often does it happen that you come home from the office, ready to take a break from the hectic, frenetic pace of work, only to find that you're under at least as much time pressure at home? First you've got to get through family dinner (assuming the meal's not waiting for you in the fridge), dealing with each kid's issues about what will and will not get eaten, and then you and your wife face the grueling logistical challenge of one or multiple bedtimes—perhaps with homework and baths factored in, not to mention some uncertainty about how long it will take the little darlings' eyes to actually close. By the time you're alone as adults, you're both ready for sleep yourself, and you've got just enough energy to catch up on each other's days for fifteen minutes before turning in — if you don't also have office work to do. Another glorious evening of family togetherness!

"Time is money," Ben Franklin said. This may be true in our work lives, but at home time has greater value by far. Dennis C., a successful San Diego software executive with seven children, once sent me a passionate E-mail calling Franklin's aphorism "one of the great lies of our time. Money can be earned, time cannot; money can be hoarded, time cannot; money can be used to make more money, time cannot; money can be passed down, time cannot; there are unlimited amounts of money, that is not true with time. We are only given so much time, and when our time allotment is up, that's it, your life is over."

Time's very importance, and the inevitable sense of scarcity, sometimes lead us to manage our family time in the most efficient, businesslike fashion — which only makes the problem worse. At the end of each evening or weekend, we feel drained, not renewed, precisely because we're trying to cram our messy family needs into an orderly, predictable schedule. Any deviation from that schedule creates stress, which exists only *because* of the schedule, and which itself does the family and us more harm than the delay that triggers it.

For some of us, our jobs are actually more free-flowing than our home lives, which can make it tempting to retreat into work as a calmer, saner place. A 1998 *Wall Street Journal* cartoon shows one business dad confiding to another over a desk, "After a weekend with family, it's good to have a little quality business time." It's always easy to justify spending less time with our kids — prospecting for one more big sale, keeping up with industry news, or just taking some time for our own needs. But business dads who yield to this temptation are tragically misusing the most precious resource our lives have to offer. Franklin also wrote, "Dost thou love life? Then do not squander time; for that's the stuff life is made of."

Kids know our time is valuable (it certainly feels valuable to them), and they're great time accountants when we spend it elsewhere. But they also take time for granted, since they themselves have so much. They can't understand the enormous pressure we're under to give "whatever it takes" at work. Younger kids think their parents are all-powerful, so any absence from home must be voluntary. They have not yet learned the ways of the world—which is part of what makes them so great to be with.

It is terribly inconvenient that our kids need us most just when our careers do, when we have those make-or-break five or ten years to create names for ourselves in business. Law firms sometimes address this conflict directly: I've heard several stories about female associates being counseled not to bear children until they make partner. Of course, once we've reached a certain level of success, the monetary stakes actually get higher, as revealed in a 1997 *Wall Street Journal* cartoon. A man is rushing out of his house, briefcase in hand, waving aside his son with the cry, "Later, Josh! These are Daddy's peak earning years." It seems as if business never gives us an opportune time to be a dad. Instead, we have to seize it.

William Gladstone said, "Justice delayed is justice denied," and I believe the same is true of fathering. Our kids change constantly and are only two, or four, or eight, once. Serious emotional problems can start early in childhood; if we wait until high school to address them, it's often too late. Business problems are often time-sensitive too, of course, but with kid problems it's not only the passage of time but also the *act* of delaying that makes them worse.

Just as there exists a "time value of money," so that a dollar today is worth more than one a year from now, there is also a "time value of parenting," whose effect is much more powerful. Children grow and change so quickly, so uncontrollably, and so unpredictably. Those protean shifts mean time with your kids is not interchangeable, today for tomorrow or tomorrow's tomorrow. And missing their changes, if done consistently, means missing their growing up.

That immediacy can be tough to fathom for intense, disciplined business dads. Our Yankee work ethic often drives us to put off today's pleasures until tomorrow, but what are we going to do, wait till our fortunes are made before we play or talk with our kids? Given the pace (and rate of acceleration) of today's economy, *it's pointless to pretend that we'll ever have more free time than we do this week, or month, or year.* If we wait until our retirements to spend time with our children, who knows if they'll still be alive, or at any rate alive and talking to us?

Then again, we can't even assume *we* will be alive long enough to retire. B.C. Forbes, Malcolm's father, wrote this cautionary tale:

> It isn't success if it costs you the companionship and chumminess and love of your children. Very often, busy, wealthy men of momentous affairs discover too late that they have sacrificed the finest thing in life, the affection of their family. . . . Frank L. Baker, prominent public utility executive, told a friend that he was going to give his young son an unusual Christmas present: "I am going to write my boy a letter telling him I am going to give him an hour of my time every day."
>
> Alas, Mr. Baker died two weeks later.

Work is always shooting tasks at us like an automatic pitching machine gone haywire, but our families can never be crossed off our "to do" lists. Recognizing that is a great first step, but not sufficient for effective time management. The more seriously we take our responsibilities, and the more we try to cram in, the more tenuous our quality control, as any assembly line worker could predict. "Mistakes are made," as the Reagan White House would have said. And the worse those mistakes make us feel about the job we're doing as executives or fathers, the higher the pressure climbs, and the more prone we are to making further mistakes.

Too many business dads feel they simply don't have the time they need to succeed in both commerce and fatherhood. It comes down to what the techies call "bandwidth," a data transmission term which in people means the capacity for processing, absorbing, and responding to information. We have only so many hours in a day, and the demands with which our bosses, customers, and colleagues bombard us compete with no less pressing ones from wives and children—not to mention our own needs.

Our challenge is always to use our bandwidth to greater effect.

It's hard, but it can be done. We must emulate the telecommunications industry, which has been vastly increasing the effective bandwidth of every strand it owns, from humble twisted-pair copper to the latest erbium-doped fiber optics. How has it done that? By reorganizing the data and changing the way it's processed, so that a forty-year-old wire which was long thought fit only for voice conversations can now transmit the movie *Titanic* in less time than it took the ship to sink.

Time Management Through Technology: Hype and Reality

It's easy enough to talk about managing *human* bandwidth, but far more difficult to do it. As befits a technical metaphor, the most common approach to maximizing our effective bandwidth is technology-based. Certainly, new advances in computing and communications are frequently hyped as time-savers. A 1998 ad for Compaq notebook computers, for example, showed an idyllic scene of a mom, notebook on lap, working in her sun-dappled living room while her daughter quietly does homework alongside. "You can make sacrifices for your career," reads the text. "You can make sacrifices for your family. Or you can choose not to make sacrifices."

Marketers seem to have jumped on this bandwagon en masse. In March 1998, for example, Hewlett-Packard began advertising its "e-business solutions" with full-page ads meant to look like clip-out coupons, reading as follows:

Save!

YOUR MARRIAGE

by spending more time at home and less time in hotel rooms pondering being charged six bucks for a soda. Our e-business solutions help keep you off the road by putting the power of the Internet at your fingertips. They'll save travel time, money and possibly your marriage by allowing you to work with your customers, partners and suppliers on the net. . . . You'll be amazed at the people you get to know. Your family for instance.

And Digital Equipment, in December 1997, began running two-page spreads of a Little League game in progress, with the word "alex" in huge type. It quotes Allen Feryus, senior vice president and chief information officer of the New York Mercantile Exchange, on Digital's Multivendor Customer Service. "It saves money. It saves time. Time I can actually spend with my family. I like that. My five-year-old likes that."

All these ads paint a seductive picture of technology in harmony with our nature as parents, but the truth is far more mixed. First of all, technology as it's applied today complicates far more often than it simplifies. Some executives swear by their Palm Pilots, for example, while others swear at them. (I personally regard them as Tamagotchi electronic pets for grown-ups.) E-mail, too, has gotten way out of hand—and forget spam, I mean E-mail from people we know. At Computer Associates, CEO Charles Wang has forbidden it altogether during core work hours, having seen it degenerate into time-wasting busywork: "I am talking about people in one cubicle asking people in the next cubicle out to lunch."

More broadly, studies show tens of millions of hours of work time lost nationwide by people futzing with their computers. The operating systems and applications software become more complex every year, but does all this "feature bloat" increase their usefulness? Scott McNealy, CEO of Sun Microsystems, believes the bells and whistles have gone too far, judging by a 1998 interview:

> I tell you that if we had ASCII and HTML and Java readers on everybody's desk instead of Windows and Macintosh computers and forbade anyone to create an attachment and forbade anyone to use any more than backspace, cut, delete, paste, or print, we'd all have time to know our children. . . . If you give somebody a word processor with 4,000

features, the implicit instruction is: "This is a tool. I bought it for you. You work for me. You go learn it and learn as much of those 4,000 features as you possibly can because we don't want all that money we spent to go to waste."

From a family perspective, though, technology sometimes does the most damage when it works *efficiently*. It's "efficiency" that causes business dads to natter away on their cell phones at soccer matches, or cut short a bedtime story so they can catch up on their E-mail. Just a few days before this writing, my firm had our annual off-site strategy session, and the subject of our intranet came up. One partner complained that it was not set up for easy remote access, and asked, "Wouldn't everyone like the ability to spend three or four hours working on Sunday night, to get ahead on the week?"

The fact is, it *would* be nice to have that option, but it's all too easy for the options offered by technology to morph into obligations. *When technology does succeed at making our work easier, the end result is usually heightened expectations.* When technology helps us learn critical information sooner, it's hard to keep the noncritical information from flooding in also. When technology lets us function as businesspeople without trudging to the office, it makes our time fungible, so that we suddenly have fewer hours clearly devoted to family. With cell phones and pagers, we can never be "out of pocket" anymore, leaving us always "in pocket." Work has a well-known habit of expanding to fill the time available. As a result, for every new hour technology makes available for work, it threatens to subtract sixty minutes from our personal lives.

So by all means use technology, but use it wisely and in moderation. Let its efficiencies increase, not decrease or disrupt, the time you spend with your kids. Don't buy new gadgets just because they're cool, or use them just because you've bought them. Keep technology as the servant promised by all those ads, not the master it too often becomes.

For real solutions to the scarcity of bandwidth, we must turn elsewhere.

Time Management: Office Efficiencies

I won't spend much time on office efficiencies, since there are plenty of books devoted to the subject. The underlying principle, however, is to judge yourself (and persuade others to judge you) by your output, not your input. Don't spin your wheels. There's no sense in burning the midnight oil if the 6:00 P.M. oil would be sufficient for the task at hand.

Michael Pietsch, the skillful and humane editor of this book, shared the following recollection in one of his editorial comments. "I remember how hard it was to make myself start leaving the office at 5:30 after our first child was born, since I'd routinely worked until 7:30 or 8:00 for years. But I learned to get ruthless with many kinds of decisions, and I learned to leave. It turned out not to slow me down at all."

Multitask if you can, reading trade magazines and E-mail while you're on the phone. Never undertake a task unless you understand exactly the "bottom line" objective, and never waste time wandering from the "critical path" toward that objective. Touch each piece of paper that crosses your desk exactly once, return E-mails and messages instantly, break big tasks into discrete steps, delegate whatever you don't like or don't excel at, and you'll do fine.

Don't call meetings unless they're crucial, and don't go out for long lunches unless it will lead directly to revenue. Those events may help cultivate warmth and team feeling, but you need those at home even more. Which is more important, two-hour politicking lunches with your officemates every day, or getting home in time for dinner with your kids? If you want to make the work environment more coherent and familial, don't waste huge swaths of your day! Bond more efficiently *at your job* with "quality time." You can network about as well with a forty-five-minute deli lunch as with two hours over a linen tablecloth.

It's tough for any business dad to excel as a father if he does not run his work efficiently. Peter Marcus, the president of QFTV, told *Forbes* in 1998, "The first thing I do before starting a meeting is to be clear on the time we expect to finish it. If it goes on too long, I request that we teleconference it. As a single father, I often feel overcome with guilt because I have to leave work. But if I am not there, my child stays alone." So read the many books about efficiency—or skim them, to save time. If you still are not squeezing out those time-wasting habits, you might also consider hiring an "efficiency coach" for a couple of hours.

One problem: once you're operating at maximum productivity, efficiency tends to generate more work. People take too seriously that saying, "If you need something done, give it to someone who's busy." When offered work, many business dads seem to think it's a sin to turn it down, for fear they'll seem lazy, incompetent, inefficient, or all three. So they eagerly accept any and all assignments, with the result that they see their kids only about every other holiday.

The question is, where should the benefits of our efficiency go—to our careers, or to our families? If we accept every task at work and never see the kids, what purpose is all our hard work serving? It seems reasonable to split the benefits evenly, with half the time we save by working efficiently to be spent at home and the rest on "extra credit" work at the office. *If we really distinguish ourselves by the speed and quality of our work, no one can fault us for having a life as well.* And guess what? The changes of pace we enjoy with our kids will probably make us more efficient and effective at work.

Time Management: Home Efficiencies

Home efficiencies basically come in three varieties: trying to accomplish more household tasks in less time, trying to do office and household work simultaneously, and trying to spend quality time with our children. My saying "trying to" might tip you off that not all of those are possible. Our home lives are already so regimented, so chopped up into segments such as play dates, soccer games, TV shows, homework, bathtime, and bedtime, that we may have less control over our time there than in the office. The one thing we don't need is to become our own "time and motion" bosses, like the factory owners who followed the Taylorian management fad in the early part of the century.

If you try too many home efficiencies, the more you think you're achieving may actually be less. The kind of quick meal you might get the kids to wolf down, for example, if it's greasy or sugary, probably offers less nutrition than a more leisurely, balanced repast. A lightning-fast bath and bedtime story (you know, the "Once upon a time, they lived happily ever after" kind of sound bite) may prove much less meaningful or satisfying than if you took an extra ten minutes. In general, working under a rigid deadline doesn't mix well with kids, who don't appreciate being shoehorned into your busy schedule. Children are not made to run on office time. Trying to speed them up (or even keep them moving) introduces stress for both of you, so it's best to avoid when possible.

As a rule, the best kinds of household efficiencies are those where you can blur the lines between work and play. You may have enough income to hire other people to do much of your household work, but parts of it might be worth sharing with your kids instead. What's mundane to you may prove fascinating to them, especially if they can do it with you. I often used to let Benjamin, as a toddler, "help" by holding the tools when I was putting together shelves or toys—it made him so proud.

Another "efficiency" that succeeds by blending chore with fun: I take the kids grocery shopping more often than not, and we all have a great time. I regard it as an opportunity to enjoy being with them, not to get something done despite them. It may take a little longer when we play around along the way, but getting there is definitely more than half the fun. If I treated those expeditions as beat-the-clock ordeals, that's exactly what they would become. It's good to include kids in your world, observing people and places in your life, rather than have your time with them always focused on their world and their ways of having fun.

The pitfalls of home efficiency show themselves most clearly when we try to do office and child-rearing work simultaneously. Through a rare fluke, there may occasionally be synergies between the two. Bill P., a San Francisco CEO I know, recalls that he sealed the biggest single deal in his industry at a Leaps & Bounds play center. The story goes that the principals in the deal were three business dads (including Bill), all of whom had been traveling too much to coordinate with each other. The only time they could get together was over the weekend, but their travel had also kept them away from their kids. They agreed to meet at Leaps & Bounds, where they bonded further with each other while playing with their offspring, then retired to the Parents' Quiet Room to hash out the details (leaving the kids with their caregivers). They got some strange looks from the moms with magazines, but the deal got done.

That kind of success story, though, is clearly the exception. Updating your boss on the cordless (or, even worse, speaker) phone while feeding your toddler, for example, is likely to please neither one. It's a matter of simple courtesy: after all, would you even consider reversing the situation and whipping out your cell phone to check on the kiddies while having dinner alone with a client?

The most pernicious attempts at home efficiency, however, involve the whole idea of quality time. This term is so well known that it is even satirized by business advertisers. (One of the more amusing examples is a drawing of a man playing poker with his wife and young kids, green eyeshade and all, with the caption, "Thanks to the exceptional service offered by Williams Communications, Ed could share quality time with the family.") Basically, quality time is shorthand for small amounts of preplanned time, usually structured into specific activities and burdened by expectations that *this* is the time to bond or communicate. Focusing on quality time is probably the greatest single mistake that business dads make, with the worst impact on the lives of their children, so it's worth debunking in detail.

Quality Time: Too Little of Either

When in Rome, do as the Romans do. Unless you want your children to grow up too quickly, you're better off interacting within their frame of reference than within yours. Ken Blanchard's famous manual *The One-Minute Manager,* while useful for the office, should have come with a warning label, "Do Not Try This at Home." As we've already discussed, "child time" by its nature meanders, and kids' enjoyment of any activity tends to correspond directly to their not feeling pressured to begin and end precisely on time. (Kids do follow television's rigid timetable slavishly enough, but I believe that's because TV is not really an activity.) Kids aren't conditioned to take meetings, which is in fact one of their more refreshing qualities.

Quality time means trying to accomplish more in the same period. *The more rushed the time is, however, the less enjoyable and worthwhile it becomes—that is, the lower the actual quality.* Children are, moreover, unpredictable creatures. If you have a rigid schedule for interacting with them, how do you know they'll be in the right frame of mind when the time comes? The existence of time pressure by itself may be enough to put them off. You need enough flexibility in your schedule to deal with their mood cycles, unplanned delays (like extended bathroom visits), your own emergencies (so you don't make them promises you can't keep), and serendipity (so you and they have the freedom to act on spur-of-the-moment inspirations, which often produce the highest-quality times of all).

Relying too much on quality time poses problems with older kids as well. Just knowing that *you* are heavily invested in a particular "special" activity could make them feel obliged to act happy and "bond" even if they'd rather be doing something else. If they feel self-conscious and pressured to perform, quality time will not exactly improve the closeness of your relationship.

Face time belongs at home. Coke's most successful slogan of the 1990s, I suspect, has been the simple "Always." Does Big Red know something about your kids that you don't? They need you to be a presence (physical or mental) all the time—not just on special occasions, not just on alternate Tuesdays, not just in months with an *r,* but *always.* What kind of message does it send them about your place in their lives if you interact mainly during preset, premeditated, prefab periods? Would you expect your employees or clients to react well if you had quality time with them once a quarter but were too busy the rest of the year? A week in a three-year-old's life is like a year in an adult's, so you need constant contact to keep your family connections healthy.

"It was the best of times, it was the worst of times." That's how Dickens began *A Tale of Two Cities*, but it shouldn't be how your kids think of you. Sure, it's important to be there for the best of times (graduation, basketball victories) and for the worst of times (illnesses, basketball losses), and those occasions do give you acceptable excuses to rearrange your work schedule. The heart of childhood, however, is all the times in between, when they're merely hopeful or worried, thriving or struggling, proud or downcast. If you miss that, you miss seeing them grow up.

It's ironic that face time is so common at work, when it's really home that needs it. Lotte Bailyn of MIT's Sloan School of Management has put it succinctly: "Quality time belongs at work. Quantity time belongs with the family."

Catch the everyday miracles. We're citizens of a media-dominated society, so it's understandable that our images of parenthood have been shaped by what TV and the movies can capture. But the best moments of childhood, the most rewarding for you and the most important for your kids, are not the Kodak moments. What are they? They include the quiet interlude when your toddler, not trying in the slightest to please you, breathes peacefully in her bed; the split second when your son, long intimidated, decides he can make it to the top of the jungle gym after all; or the fleeting instant when your daughter, leaving for her first date, runs back impulsively to kiss you.

Remember when you were a teenager, and you couldn't wait to get a life? Now you've got one. What are you going to do with it? John Lennon said, "Life is what happens while we're making other plans." We can't predict when our greatest fatherly thrills, or our children's most startling transformations, will occur. If you spend *quantity* time with your kids, you'll have a greater chance of actually being there when life happens.

Eternal vigilance is the price of fatherhood. Yes, I know Jefferson said that about liberty, but it applies to fathering just as well.

Like it or not, your chief responsibilities as a dad include monitoring and protecting, and it's awfully tough to do that in scheduled tidbits of quality time. It takes unstructured, rambling back-and-forth, when everyone's guard is down and no one's looking at his watch.

Quality *quantity* time wins every time. Saying that quantity counts, of course, does not mean that quality plays no role. Bulking up the time you spend with your kids by vegetating in front of the TV together, for example, is a poor substitute for true interaction. According to *Newsweek*, the average American spends 15 hours a week watching television, compared to 6.7 hours for social activities, 2.8 for reading, and 2.2 for outdoor activities. With numbers like that, it's not surprising that TV is one of the major obstacles for business dads in connecting with their kids.

If you've managed to set aside real quantity time, don't waste it through overbooking. Some terrific joint activities do require pre-planning, but being busy 100 percent of the time is not the same as being fulfilled. If you schedule yourself to rush from one activity to the next, you'll find yourself more exhausted than refreshed, more drained than renewed. Instead of approaching those periods with a businessperson's single-minded goal of throughput maximization, set yourself the unprofessional goal of not having a goal. Remember, when it comes to fathering, everyone's an amateur.

Your kids, by the way, can benefit from the same philosophy. Many ten-year-olds these days lead lives as busy as their parents', Filofaxes and all. They have incredibly fragmented schedules, what with extracurricular activities, organized play dates, and (if you allow it) rigid TV schedules. If you think that overscheduling makes *you* tired and cranky at the end of a long day, think what it does to your children. Kids need time just to play, without the timelines, deadlines, and worry lines of adult life. If you can help them keep flexibility in their schedules, it will help you as well, since you'll have more options for when to play with them.

Use your free time together, at least once in a while, to do "nothing." Play it by ear. Go with the flow. Plan not to plan. Think about *being* with your kids, rather than *doing* with them. It's the being that needs your attention; the doing will take care of itself. In a funny way, spending quality quantity time with kids (especially younger kids) can sometimes make you feel as if you have more time in the day, not less. Their experience of time is so dense that seeing life through their eyes for a while may actually help you feel you're getting more out of an hour.

Whether it's humdrum stuff like bagging your lawn clippings or pure pleasure like reading a favorite storybook, you'll both get more out of it if you stay "in the moment." Letting your mind wander to work problems or overdue bills has the effect of reducing your presence, and your kids will sense that you are just "phoning it in." If you need to think about business issues while you're home, save them for a specific time rather than letting them permeate your whole evening. That way, *all* the time you spend with your kids can end up being quality time.

Time Management: A Design for Living

The question of how to use quantity time is moot, of course, if you never find the opportunity. For that you need a final kind of time management, namely the right design for living.

The right system of being, the right way to live your life, is—did you really think *I* could tell you? The puzzle has a different answer for every player. Every business dad is different, and so is every family, so there is no one optimal solution. Setting your particular priorities will take some intense, lengthy, personal reflection. What I can tell you, though, are some specifications you can and should try to build into your own unique design.

The objective is to ensure that you'll have the time you need for your kids, your wife, and yourself, all while succeeding professionally. Your kids need you regularly like vitamins, interacting both one on one and all together. They also need to see you interacting with Mommy, which means spending at least some of your quantity time as a family. If you constantly switch off with your wife so there's never more than one of you with the kids, you're reducing your parenting to what *The Father's Almanac* calls "shared custody in the same house."

Once the kids are asleep, you probably won't immediately dive into your office work or start cataloging your bottle-cap collection. Your wife needs you too, after all, and you need her back. Each of you has a life, dubious though that may seem sometimes, so each of you is experiencing new thoughts, new events, new hopes and frustrations. When the couple down the street breaks up because they've grown apart, it's partly because they haven't managed to keep up with all the changes in each other. (Question: What made the Palm Pilot the most popular PC peripheral ever introduced? Answer: the neat, quick way it "synchronizes" with your computer, catching up and exchanging data. Don't play the Apple Newton to your wife's PC.)

You'll want to devote time to your relationship—not just infrequent weekend getaways but coordinated nightly sessions, even if that includes time doing the dishes or brushing your teeth together. When you're with her, leave enough time not just to debrief about the kids and the house, but also to explore the kinds of subjects you dallied over when you were first falling in love.

To be good company for your family, you'll also need to plan some time for yourself—for quiet contemplation and for changes of pace, to catch up with friends or catch up on exercise. Instead of taking the subway home, bring shorts and jog home, with your work in a backpack. Take time off from parenting while you're home, just as you might occasionally need to take a break from work while you're at the office.

Cultivate a hobby if you feel the urge. It may even be a hobby that aids you at work, either because it helps you network or because it cultivates useful attitudes or skills. But make sure that your hobby takes a distant third place to family and work in your priority ranking. This book, for example, was eked out in tiny scraps of time on airplanes, during kids' naps, and in the (ever shrinking) intervals between their bedtimes and mine. My rule was basically never to write while I was home with the kids awake or while I still had office work to do.

Once you know how much time you intend to spend with whom, your next step in sketching out a design for life is to assess the true costs and benefits of different activities. That is not a simple task. When I worked at City Hall, we had to bring in a high-priced accounting firm's "activity-based costing" team just to figure out how much it cost to fill a pothole. (Turned out it cost much more in some boroughs than others, which raised *other* interesting questions.) What do you gain and what do you lose from one more camping trip with kids, one more business junket, or one more night out with your pals? Or for another example, does the increased efficiency you gain from doing office work before the kids' bedtime, when you have the most energy, offset the time you lose with them? (Although worthwhile, cost-benefit analysis can be a complicated exercise. You will need to use your judgment about the short-term *and* long-term effects of your missing either business or family events. Also, your colleagues and family will not look at any one event in isolation, but rather as part of an ongoing pattern.)

Having estimated the costs and benefits of various design elements, you must stack them up according to your priorities. If you are completely clear about what really matters to you, you will minimize what Stephen Covey, in *First Things First*, calls "the gap between the clock and the compass," meaning the difference between how we think we ought to spend our time and how we actually do. Once you have established priorities, you are ready to design your life.

Business Dad: Man with a Plan

Draw a blueprint. I'm being almost literal here. Take a pencil and paper (or use our companion Web site, www.businessdad.com). Add up how much time you think you need with your kids each week —not the structured time like brushing their teeth, but the quantity time when you and they are free just to be together. Then add up your actual discretionary time. If the two numbers don't fit, think hard about both and revise until they do. If you put priority on the important things, the little things will fall into place around them.

Follow that blueprint. Once you've committed to a design for living, one of your priorities has to be living up to that commitment. If you keep your priorities in mind, you can resist letting the apparently urgent distract you from the genuinely important. In the heat of the moment, you might become convinced you "don't have time" for your family, but that's just another way of saying they're a lower priority, at least for the present. Perhaps you're having a tough month or two (like an accountant in tax season). Once that condition starts stretching into years, though, it's time to compare the life you're living with the life you've designed. J. M. Barrie, author of *Peter Pan*, wrote, "The life of every man is a diary in which he means to write one story and writes another; and his humblest hour is when he compares the volume as it is with what he vowed to make it."

If your priorities change, it behooves you to change your design for living as well. Checking that you're living the life you want is not something you do once a decade; you have too few decades for that. It's good to take some time away from work and family every few months, just to compare the clock to the compass. Are you spending time, out of habit, on activities that no longer have real value for you?

Eliminate wasted materials. *A business dad without priorities is like an enterprise without a clear business plan.* The reason good entrepreneurs function so efficiently is that scarcity of resources forces them to maintain what former Lotus CEO Mitch Kapor calls "ruthless focus in the face of insurmountable opportunities." If you try to succeed at everything, you'll fail at everything. But pick the few things that really matter, exclude everything else, and chances are you'll succeed where you care the most.

In practice, this means "ruthless" measures like cutting your losses on friendships that aren't working any more, reading more reviews and fewer books, and narrowing your nonfamily pastimes down to the essential one or two—for as long as your kids need you.

For example, Bill P., the San Francisco CEO I've mentioned earlier, has a motorboat in which he loves to putter around the bay. In the summer of 1997, though, he was so focused on launching his business and spending time with his daughter that he never used the boat once. "I went to check on the boat at the end of summer, and the battery was dead. I feel like such a schmuck, but it was the right decision."

Install a few locks. In your design for living, give your top priorities some of their own private space. Work already has a fairly secure place in your schedule, occupying as it does about half your waking hours. Try to include regular, predictable dates with your wife and kids. That is the basic concept behind the Judeo-Christian sabbath, in which each week has a holy day, off limits to work and worldly concerns, devoted to prayer, contemplation, and family togetherness. You don't have to be religious to give your priorities the protective structure of a regular Saturday night out with your wife, a regular Sunday brunch with your kids, or other reliable "time shelters."

Every family, of course, will find different shelters to their liking. Peter K., for example, does debt restructuring for a major investment bank, helping his clients minimize the cost of hundreds of millions or even billions of dollars of debt. His work gives him a lively appreciation for the value of time and commitments, so he makes every Saturday a "sacred" day to be with his wife and two-year-old daughter.

Ted F. runs sales and marketing for a young software company in Ohio. He works seventy to eighty hours per week, yet still feels he has a healthy engagement with his wife and their three-year-old son, Austin. How does he do it? By keeping to a fixed weekly schedule whenever possible. Austin doesn't expect to see Daddy on Tuesday and Thursday nights, because they are reserved for late meetings or trips. On Wednesday and Friday, Ted makes it home in time for dinner, though he may do some company work after Austin's bedtime. Saturday, Ted works at home most of the day—time he prizes for the kind of uninterrupted concentration that hectic weekdays make difficult. Sunday, Ted makes a point of not working at all if possible.

And Monday—Monday is "boys' night out," when Ted takes Austin for adventures indoors or outdoors, depending on the season, and gives his wife some time alone. If an emergency requires Ted to miss boys' night out, Austin always asks why, and Ted is careful to make it up later in the week. With Ted's emphasis on regularity, Austin feels that his dad is a dependable part of his life, and Ted's long work hours don't interfere unduly with his fathering.

Don't forget the alarm system. Along with your locks, you will need a system of alarms that can tell you when you are straying too far from your larger priorities. What counts is not merely how much time you are spending at work or with family, but how you are spending it and whether you are meeting the needs of the moment. If you focus too much on time allocation, you may miss important cues from employer or kids that you are shortchanging them.

I find it a constant struggle in my own life to hit the right balance; the only way I can attempt to stay on course is one day at a time. The trade-offs between work and family time can vary daily based on what's been happening where, who's in what kind of mood, and what your track record has been lately. It's worth taking thorough stock of the situation at least once a month, either alone or with your wife.

If you find that you can't make the math work when you try to draw that blueprint, if your design for living can't accommodate your priorities no matter how many times you sharpen your pencil, your situation may require a more fundamental redesign. When you build a house, you typically start with some property. If the contours of the property don't fit the house you have in mind, you've got to either change the landscaping or find yourself a different piece of land. Likewise, if your design for living isn't working, change it. The change could be as simple as getting up fifteen minutes earlier each morning, or as drastic as changing your job.

If you're skillful and lucky, you may be able to change your job without leaving it. But you can avoid the need entirely if you do your due diligence on company culture before accepting the job in the first place. Newly minted M.B.A.'s are following that strategy more and more often. This is clearly one reason that the big management consulting firms are having such trouble recruiting: the M.B.A.s are turning them down despite the high starting salaries, explicitly because the firms require too much travel. The travel schedule doesn't ease up much with seniority, either: Paul Laudicina, an A.T. Kearney consultant, told *Fortune* that he exchanges more information with his seventeen-year-old son through E-mail than face-to-face.

As suburbs continue their out-of-control expansion and commuters risk seeing less of their kids than some divorced dads do, you may find that you can increase your family time dramatically by changing not the kind of work you do, but something so simple as where you do it. Thom H., for example, spent twenty years managing municipal bond offerings at Morgan Stanley, commuting daily from his home in Connecticut down to Wall Street. Three years ago, he decided to launch his own business, arranging tax-exempt financing for transfer depots and other buildings in and around airports. He notes that his financial picture as an entrepreneur depends entirely on his success in networking and making deals happen, so he no longer has the "hedge" of getting paid well because Morgan Stanley had a good year. That makes the time conflict between work and family that much more direct. On the other hand, his office is now only a few minutes from home, so he spends significantly more time with his kids, ages thirteen and fifteen. He even contributes 30 percent of his time to running the New York office of a men's self-help organization. (That volunteerism has actually deepened his commitment to fathering: he estimates matter-of-factly that more than 75 percent of his members' problems, whether drinking or drugs or mental health, spring directly from troubled relationships with their fathers.)

Road Warriors

Rick J. is a successful executive straight from central casting. Tall, slim, with swept-back graying hair, he's run several large companies, as well as a multibillion-dollar chunk of IBM. He married late before siring a six-year-old, a four-year-old, and two-year-old twins. "I was a math major," he reports, "and it *does* get exponentially harder the more you have." Even harder for his wife, actually, because Rick has always been on the road at least three days a week. "She knew what she was getting, but she's a saint." He's in between jobs when I meet him, being wooed by countless headhunters, and he's traveling more than ever so that he can choose a new job quickly. The CEO slot I'm interviewing him for would require a cross-country commute. "My wife says I'm just looking for a job that'll get me back on the road." He pauses. "She's probably right."

There's no denying that business travel has its secret satisfactions. Sure, the excitement palls quickly, it's hardly glamorous, and it can be frustrating at times. On the other hand, it offers such splendid isolation, such reassuring constancy, such attention to our superficial needs. There's no use pretending that it's *all* a wearying grind. I'll admit it: when I settle into that business-class seat on American to California, with that familiar, vaguely upbeat boarding music, I feel a certain peaceful anticipation. I can use the next five hours however I choose. Even if I'm just catching up on work, I can do so without interruptions. The phone won't ring, the kids won't need attention, and just before landing, without fail, there'll be fresh-baked cookies. Will I have one, or maybe two? Hmmm, such decisions.

Yes, business dads and moms know the guilty pleasures of frequent flying. If we make it *too* frequent, though, the guilt begins to overshadow the pleasures. David W., the New York investment banker I mentioned earlier, told me, "At parents' night, the teachers always say, 'Your son has told us all about what you do, and how much you travel.' And they always give me this look."

Why is travel so tough on our children, especially the young ones? They're so helpless without adults, there's nothing they can do to stop us from going, and they're not absolutely sure we're coming back. Think about it. In any relationship—with your parents, your girlfriend, or your company—it's always easier to leave than to be left. Which would you prefer when you change jobs, to quit or to be fired? In your dating days, did you feel better being the dumper or the dumpee? Toddlers get dumped, in a sense, every morning, and when Daddy has suitcases packed it looks pretty permanent.

Leaving gets a bit easier once your kids accumulate enough data points to know you'll return. Still, the more you travel, the longer it takes that sense of abandonment to diminish. In addition, travel takes time away from both home *and* office life, so it can be tough catching up when you return. It usually introduces stress for your wife, who must handle the unhappy children while you're gone. And however old your kids may be, by traveling too much you may miss key parts of their growing up, and so cease really knowing them.

But moan though we may (when we're not thinking about those fresh-baked cookies), business travel is a necessary evil. Whatever your line of work, there are times when nothing substitutes for being there. The challenge, therefore, is to *manage* your travel, making it as painless as possible for you and yours. Luckily, being on planes gives you plenty of time to think, and I've racked up enough miles myself (over a million) to have some thoughts in this regard.

Frequent-Flier Fathering

• **Avoid useless travel.** In a 1998 special issue on frequent business travelers, the *New York Times Magazine* described the scene at United's first-class lounge at O'Hare.

> There's sushi for lunch and only two travelers in evidence. One is on the floor, waving his legs in the air, doing yoga. The other is a grouchy-looking middle-aged guy in tasseled loafers, slacks and a duffel coat he hasn't bothered to take off. He sits hunched, moodily sipping red wine, quite oblivious to the serene first-class space, with its subdued motif of the Orient. He's trying to control his temper.
>
> His name is Tom Stiffler. He sports a green-faced watch with golf clubs crossed at the stroke of noon, and he's a top executive for an automobile company. He's on his way to

Germany and he has just about had it. He has come in to Chicago today from St. Louis. He was supposed to be flying through Atlanta on TWA to Stuttgart but there was a cancellation. Now, if nothing else goes wrong, he'll be landing at 6 A.M. in Frankfurt, where he'll jump into a car for a high-speed autobahn drive to make a meeting he doesn't believe he needs to attend. "My trip today is happening because it makes someone feel better when they can touch someone," he says. "But if you need to see me once a week, you don't need me. You need a baby-sitter."

I ask if he enjoys travel and he rolls his blue eyes toward the ceiling and explodes with laughter. "No. No, no, no. I used to, quite, but now I view it only as a disruption, an irritation. When you've traveled as long as I have, as frequently as I have, it wears you out."

He says he once sat down and did the math. He figures that three years of his adult life have been spent on the way to and from airports, in airports, on airplanes. "On average, I'm home three nights a week. I have one boy just graduating college, and another still in college. They're assessing their futures in light of my life. On any given day they'll say, 'We're not gonna do what Dad did,' and I can't say I blame them. But it's what you sign up for when you join an international corporation."

That is as vivid a description of the sad, empty futility of excessive business travel as I've ever read. Here's a guy with two sons, forced to choose between raising them and raising his corporate profile.

Seems to me there's got to be a better way. It's all about making a commitment to assert *control* (that word again!) over where your body goes, cutting travel to the absolute minimum. Once you have that control, you can honestly tell your family and yourself that you *have* to be on this trip, that it's genuinely useful and not corporate busywork.

Stick to day trips when possible, even if it brings you home late at night: it will help your kids just knowing that you'll be there when they wake up. Don't book the cheapest route (or don't let the company book it for you) if it keeps you away an extra night. Use technology, when you can, to avoid traveling—those phones, faxes, and videoconferencing systems must be good for something! Do your kids tell their friends that Daddy works on an airplane? Being absent by necessity is a fact of life, but being absent by choice is a shame.

Rocco Maggiotto, senior vice president of Pricewaterhouse-Coopers, goes to extremes to minimize his travel time, as he recounted in a 1998 *Forbes* interview.

> One way to be around the kids more often is by taking one-day trips to Europe. I will fly out at 7 P.M. from JFK, sleep on the plane, work all day in London, and catch a 7 P.M. flight back home. I will never be a tourist in a foreign city. I have flown back from Europe on a Friday night to be with my family on the weekend, and flown back to Europe on Sunday. It is well worth it.

• **Way to go!** When you have no choice but to travel, at least take your leave without making things worse. Never, for example, try to avoid a tearful parting by sneaking out without saying good-bye. Once kids get the idea you might be gone without their knowing it, they'll never feel quite secure when you *are* there, and they'll keep checking on you. I learned the hard way that Benjamin wants me to say good-bye—even if I'm leaving at 5:30 A.M. and have to wake him up to do it.

Make sure the kids say good-bye back to you, so you know they're acknowledging your departure. For younger kids, it may help if there's some ritual connected with your leaving, such as a special kind of hug or loan of a favorite toy (yours or theirs). They might sometimes prefer not to think about your trips, but, by registering each going, they'll be quicker to internalize the knowledge that you always come back.

• **Play it straight.** Don't overdramatize your departures, because it could make your kids overreact. Tell them you'll miss them, but don't spread doom and gloom, or they'll pick up your cue and do the same. On the other hand, don't insist your trips are no big deal if you know they matter a lot to your children. Ignoring or questioning those feelings will exacerbate them, not make them go away. Be straight and matter-of-fact, treat each trip as an unpleasant interlude that will soon be over, and your kids should survive, despite a little sniffling.

• **Stay on their radar screens.** Knowing you're away will be easier for kids if they know where you are, why you're there, and when you're coming back. Explain it to them before you leave, using an atlas or the Internet on the *where* part, simple stories on the *why*, and kid measures of time (two dinners, not two days) on the *when*. To connect those expectations with reality, show follow-through, making sure to stay in touch with daily updates. Try not to let your travel schedule make you miss a day. If time zones require it, I will even excuse myself from a business dinner in order to speak with my family each evening, if only briefly.

A lullaby sung over the phone (even a picture phone, despite those AT&T ads) is a pale imitation of your presence, but at least it lets them know you still exist. The more time you can devote to real communications in phone calls, the better. Find out about their day from your wife first, for example, then show your kids you know and care about it. Photocopy their favorite storybook, and read it to them over the phone. Tell them about your own day, so they have some context for your absence. Depending on your communications infrastructure, you could also contact them through prerecorded cassettes, fax, E-mail, or snail mail. If you go out of your way to communicate while in out-of-the-way places, you'll avoid settling for what the social theorist Amitai Etzioni mockingly calls those "quality phone calls" whose gist is, "Kids, I won't be home. I love you."

• **Pack your shovel.** Don't neglect your personal need for a little uninterrupted rest and relaxation, but do reserve some of that blessed empty time for keeping up with your office responsibilities. Paper, E-mail, and voice mail don't disappear just because we're not there to receive them, and only sometimes are we lucky enough to return when we can no longer do anything about them. The rest of the time, they just pile up, like an avalanche waiting to hit the moment we get back to our desks. If we don't find a way to keep shoveling while we're gone, that avalanche is bound to get us— either swamping us in snowy drifts or blindsiding us with hazardous debris, or both. Even worse, we'll probably spend the evening before we return to the office, when we're supposed to be getting reacquainted with our family, preoccupied (in the literal sense of the word) with wondering what surprises the avalanche has in store.

So remember to pack that shovel. That could mean taking all your accumulated paperwork with you, and having new batches forwarded if you're on an extended junket. It could mean checking into voice mail several times a day, and doing your best to reply from the road. (Except when I'm on vacation, I never record one of those "extended absence" greetings, because I try to return calls nearly as quickly from the road as I do from the office. It's a great way to keep exchanges short and sweet, besides, since people know you're traveling.) Lastly, it could mean bringing your laptop or finding Internet access points from which to read and answer your E-mail. If your kids are old enough to have E-mail, you can take a few seconds over the same connections to let them know you haven't forgotten them.

• **Home again, home again, jiggety-jig.** Don't be surprised if you get a cold shoulder or two upon your return from a lengthy trip. Kids get genuinely angry at being left behind, and at some ages they also dislike the vulnerability of admitting they missed you. It's more than okay, though, for you to admit *you* missed *them*. Don't slink off to wait until they're more welcoming. Hug them, kiss them if they'll let you, but above all pay attention to them. You may even want to make plans together for some fun joint activity upon your return.

Do not, however, yield to the twin temptations of every traveling dad. Number one, do not buy them presents wherever you go. It may sweeten your absence to do so occasionally, but making it a constant expectation smacks of bribery, confuses love with gifts, and gives them all the wrong reasons to look forward to your return. Number two, do not try overcompensating for your absence by becoming lax in your discipline. I know you don't want to spend your first hours together playing the heavy, but consistency matters. If your kids find you incredibly lenient upon your return, they might decide that your travel and your discipline must both be discretionary—your travel because you wouldn't appear so guilty about it otherwise, and your discipline because you couldn't turn it on and off like a switch otherwise. Do you want them to reach either of those conclusions?

- **Is home a hotel?** Hotels try to offer all the comforts of home (except the human ones). That does not mean you should start confusing the two. When you get to your real home, bear in mind that your spouse has been holding the fort alone for the last x days and probably can use a break. Luckily, although you may be tired from the road, the change of pace you'll get from taking over with the kids often proves refreshing. Do what you can to pitch in with the household work, and you'll feel like part of the family once more.

- **You *can* take them with you.** In order for kids to understand that you're not vanishing off the edge of the earth, they need to know at least a little about traveling. The more you expose them to the world of travel, the more comfortable they'll feel with your solo excursions. Start with family pleasure trips, but, when they're old enough, you might also consider bringing them along on business. If so, make sure there's plenty to do while you're in meetings (including homework if necessary), but plan to make yourself available for dinner and at least a few daytime adventures. If your meeting falls on a Friday or Monday, why not stay the weekend with them and make a holiday out of it?

Phil Anschutz, the private, churchgoing billionaire who made his fortune in oil, real estate, railroads, and now telecommunications, has been married thirty years to the same woman, rare among billionaires. He is close with his three children, partly because he would fly his whole family to join him whenever he had to be away on business for long. Of course, we're not all billionaires, but there's nothing wrong with implementing the same strategy on a more modest scale.

The Wonderful World of Work

A couple of weeks after Beth B. started in an important position at my firm, I asked how she liked her new job. She said everything was great, but her five-year-old daughter was upset. How come? Because she hadn't been to visit Beth's office yet, so she had no mental picture of where her mother went each weekday. "Mommy," she said, "when you go to work, I don't know *where* you *are*." The next week Beth was able to bring her in, and later told me her daughter now felt much more secure.

For numerous reasons, it behooves businesspeople to make sure their children understand what they do all day, and where they do it.

- As with Beth's daughter, kids experience the world in very physical, concrete ways, so they often need to see before they can understand.
- Work is an important part of your life. The work you've chosen, and how you do it, say something about you. The better kids understand your work, the better they'll know you.
- The more kids comprehend what your job requires of you, the less they'll resent your necessary absences and occasional preoccupation.
- They might benefit by fully understanding the example you're setting of hard work, dedication, and meaningful employment.
- The media are already filled with antibusiness ideas and portrayals, since most writers and artists misunderstand, fear, or look down on mere commerce. You may be surprised to learn, for example, that businessmen are shown committing far more TV murders than any other demographic category. With all the media your kids consume, it can't hurt to offer a little antidote of reality so they don't turn against your way of life (any more than adolescence itself requires).
- If your kids don't have the inclination or talent to become writers or artists, musicians or athletes, then business is as good a professional choice as any. The country certainly has enough lawyers, and there's even an oversupply of certain types of doc-

tors, but a really good businessperson can *always* make the world a better place.

- If you should happen to lose or switch your job, your kids will be somewhat less jolted if they understand how business works, that Daddy is not defined by his job as a fireman or policeman might be, and that there's more than one job in the world available to him.

Neil S., the San Diego entrepreneur I've mentioned previously, has two kids, both old enough to understand his work. He really enjoys what he does, and he wants to share it with them. "Business is sexy. If you love what you're doing, your kids will get it. They get what I'm doing." If you're fortunate and enterprising enough to find or create a job you love, you'll be able to say much the same as Neil.

Never glorify play at the expense of work, or give your kids the false impression that work is yucky. They should always understand that you work for money *and* because it adds fulfillment to your life—but don't go too far and start them worrying that you enjoy working more than being with them. One way to tread that fine line is to say something like, "I'd always rather be with you but, since I also have to work for a living, I'm lucky to have a meaningful job that I enjoy." Don't act as if work is purely a bowl of cherries, either. When you're experiencing frustrations or concerns, let your kids know (in a nonfrightening way), so that they can get the full picture of business life, understand they're not the only ones with problems, and learn from your example in dealing with tough issues.

There are plenty of ways to include your kids in your other life. The most obvious is to take them to the office occasionally, and perhaps even let older kids sit in on routine meetings. To the younger ones, your office itself will seem as entrancing as Disneyland, filled with mysterious playthings like staple removers and binder clips. Take them one at a time, to make the experience more manageable for everyone. (Take Our Daughters to Work Day is fine as far as it goes, but there certainly should be something similar for sons.) Let your kids "help" in the office, so they'll feel useful and possibly see themselves following your example one day. Rob G., the Baltimore call-center outsourcer I mentioned earlier, has a conference room next to his office. When his eight-year-old daughter visits, he installs her there and puts her name on the outside as if it's her office.

When you take your kids in, prepare them carefully for what they'll be seeing and how they should act. You don't want them asking in a loud voice who that funny-looking woman in the corner office is, or why the people near your office have to sit in those funny boxes you call cubicles. As a cautionary tale, remember George Banks in *Mary Poppins*, whose children accompanied him on a seemingly harmless outing to his bank and ended up fighting the chairman over their tuppence, provoking a run on the bank, and ultimately costing George his job.

As an alternative to taking your kids to the office, you can take your office to *them*, in the form of samples, promotional videos, brochures, pictures, and anything else that tells them what you do or make. Or you could take one of their stuffed animals with you and let it tell your kids all about its day at the office. Barney, at least, is less likely to spill coffee on your boss in a meeting. Lastly, now that our office extends to so many parts of our lives, you can "include" them in a meeting by letting them listen (silently) to conversations you have on the car phone.

Matthew Sulik, the president of Red Hat Software, took Brendan, his nine-year-old son, to the CEO's house one weekend afternoon before signing on; he wanted Brendan's approval. Nicholas Graham, the CEO of Joe Boxer, told *Forbes* in 1998 of some creative ways he's found to involve his eight-year-old son in the business.

> I am happy I am in a fun business because I can spend some extra time with my son while working on ideas for the business. He helped me in sending a pair of underwear into space last year. He was my co-commander on that one. My friend built a 28-foot-long rocket, and we sent a pair of Russian underwear and a pair of Joe Boxers into outer space. We were trying to set a record of how high a pair of unmanned underwear could go. And I've just launched an un-

derwear vending machine. You get a joke with each pair, so my son gave me some of the jokes.

Back to Work

However much you strive to find the right balance, however assertive you are in standing up for your family when work pressure threatens, however skillful a "time architect" you become, you'll never be able to eliminate entirely the conflict between work and home. You can, however, prevent it from becoming a zero-sum game. *The more you hone your skills as a father, the better you can do in your professional life.*

Why do successful fathers also tend to be successful businessmen? Why does Stephen Covey say he learned his "seven habits" at home before seeing their application to business? Because fatherhood is similar, only harder. Fatherhood reminds me a bit of that song *New York, New York:* if you can make it here, you can make it anywhere—including the office.

The key skills I listed in the second chapter, once forged in the flames of fatherhood, can also make you a more powerful figure in that other place—the one with all the desks, where you spend half your time. Here is a sampling.

On-the-Job Training

• **Empathy.** Old soldiers never die, General MacArthur said, they just fade away. That's exactly what has happened in the nineties to the old military-style "command and control" hierarchies that used to dominate the business landscape. Successful managers are expected to maintain close-knit teams, understand and collaborate with other groups within the enterprise, and devise win-win solutions in dealings with other companies. Knowing what makes customers and colleagues feel good is a major strategic asset. In the

New Economy, the "sensitive man" is no longer seen as a wimp, but as a smart and effective operator—as long as his sensitivity means empathy rather than crying at the drop of a memo. The empathic skills you develop with your kids will help you navigate through the corporate world just the way bats use sonar to wing their way through the darkness of a summer night.

• **Creativity.** In a world of corporate change and lateral threats, "out of the box" thinking becomes a critical defensive and offensive skill. You need to question assumptions, perceive trends before they fully emerge, and figure out new ways of staying ahead of the competition. All work and no play makes Jack a dull boy; think of children as your sharpeners. They help you stay in touch with the childlike side of your own character, which in turn keeps your creative juices flowing. The more time you spend with your kids, the stronger that wonderful effect will be. That is, you should understand, the *only* way your "inner child" can help you at work.

Albert Schweitzer wrote one of the most perceptive comments I ever read: "The tragedy of life is what dies within a man while he still lives." The creativity and sense of wonder we had as children must survive if we are to be truly vital as adults. Too often, we let them atrophy and wither, but our own children can help us keep them strong.

• **Crisis management.** One of my firm's portfolio companies was recently going through some very tough times, and it was clear that radical changes were needed. Sales weren't coming in (despite great products and excellent results from the beta tests), top executives were at war, and nearly every senior employee had started sending out résumés. The company was in danger of imploding. The board needed to take swift action, so on two days' notice we all convened at the company's offices. I flew across the country and back in twenty-four hours.

Once gathered, we made some tough decisions (including a high-level departure) and then called a meeting of all the employees. So far, so good. Then one of my fellow directors (childless, I might add) kicked off the discussion. With the best of intentions, he nearly ruined it. He started to sugarcoat the truth, to accentuate the positive, talking only about his faith in the company's future and the value that everyone's stock options might have after the eventual initial public offering. I could see people shifting uneasily, getting more and more puzzled, wondering what this meeting was really about. They knew there was a crisis going on, but they weren't hearing about it.

I knew something was missing, but I wasn't sure what. Thinking back to crises past, in my career but especially in my family, I suddenly realized that only bare-faced honesty could win the employees' trust, and without their trust we could never improve their morale or their effectiveness. "Look," I jumped in, "let's face it. This company may have more potential than ever, but its problems have grown even faster. We've got problems of execution but, worse than that, we've got interpersonal problems. This is no secret." The employees began nodding. "The reason this board has come together on two days' notice is not to tell you how great you are, but because there's a crisis here—a crisis that could kill this company if we don't address it. That's exactly what we're planning to do, and we'll tell you how in a minute—but we're going to need your help." From that moment on, the meeting got easier, and we came away at the end feeling that things were finally back on track. (And as of this writing, they still are.) Experience at fathering helped to make the difference.

• **Efficiency.** As stated earlier, a conscious commitment to fathering almost forces you to become more efficient at work: it causes you to recognize the true value of your time. In an age when technology has made our time more fungible, since we can now work anywhere, the natural barriers protecting family time have fallen. To protect quantity time with our kids, we must set our own limits on work, focusing on what's really important and staying away from work with limited upside. Combined with our ambition and competitiveness, as well as our "multitasking" practice at home, those limits cannot help but increase our efficiency.

• **Negotiation.** The key to successful negotiation is separating emotion from interest. Because negotiations with children usually tend toward the emotional, learning to overcome that tendency will make you a stronger negotiator at work. You will learn to recognize how seemingly logical back-and-forth begins to spin out of control, how to spot the exact point of departure from rational to irrational, and how to put the negotiations back on a productive track.

Fatherhood may make you more empathic, but it also toughens you, which in turn makes you a more effective disciplinarian and negotiator. Many businessmen desperately want to feel liked, or at least understood, and can give in too early as a result. Once you've lived through your kids' toddlerhood or adolescence, however, you've probably developed a much more philosophical attitude. You're used to not being popular all the time. Moreover, if you have a family to love you (most of the time), you're probably less dependent on the approval of strangers in the first place.

• **Authority.** Cynthia Wick is a partner in Aspect Ratio, a leading producer of movie trailers and posters. A 1998 *Forbes* feature quoted her on how lessons from home have helped her in business.

> I apply the knowledge of being a parent of a 3½-year-old to dealing with difficult people. A baby will continue to cry because it learned, "If I scream and cry and break things, I'll have my needs met." The prima donnas do the same thing. You have to teach them that ranting and raving and breaking pots will not get mommy's attention. So to the prima donnas I say, "If you continue to scream, I'll walk out; if you want me to hear you, you have to calm down."

In business it takes all types, and dealing with those types can be challenging. Developing your own style, your own quiet, confident, centered sense of authority, is one of the key business benefits of active parenting.

Authority also requires coordination and teamwork with your spouse. The increasing trend toward co-CEOs following mergers tests the same skills. Michael Hammer, corporate consultant, has commented, "We're asking people who are products of the traditional 'do it or I'll shoot you' model of leadership to change the rules on themselves."

The day after the announcement of Citicorp's 1998 acquisition by Travelers Group, in which John Reed was named co-CEO with Sandy Weill, Reed told the *New York Times*, "I think we must work effectively together and, most importantly, be seen by our people to be working together. It's like Mom and Dad in one house. If they differ on a single question, the kids know how to exploit it very well." As of this writing, the jury is still out on how well that particular corporate couple is coordinating.

• **Tolerance.** Although raising children makes you a tougher negotiator and more powerful authority figure, dealing with all their helplessness and emotional confusion can also make you a more loving, giving, patient, positive person. Children are imperfect beings, who often can't want what they should or can't do what they want, but you have no choice but to love them. Sometimes, you need special resolve simply to accept them as complete packages, flaws and all. At work, if you apply those lessons, you won't frustrate yourself and others by pushing your good employees too hard, and you'll earn their trust by demonstrating that you're thinking of them as well as yourself.

• **Team building.** I recently lived through a very ugly fight between the two top officers of one of my firm's portfolio companies. The whole company was divided, with vitriolic E-mails flying back and forth, leaks to newspapers, and even acts of sabotage. It's been resolved now, but the theme that kept resurfacing throughout was how childlike much of the behavior was. One top salesman just wanted to get on with his job and wished his colleagues would "stop acting like kindergarteners." A fellow board member compared the troublemakers to a "clique of rebellious teenagers." That was a real-world situation (all too real for my taste, believe me), and experience with sibling rivalry (my own kids' and others') definitely came in handy. (Our first step was to give one of the executives a time-out in the form of a suspension.)

• **Leadership.** Although it's unfortunate that our prime career-climbing years coincide so closely with our children's time of need and development, there is an incidental benefit: once we've helped build a vision and culture within our families, we begin reaching senior enough positions at work to be called upon to do the same there. Fatherhood can give us a certain presence and air of command just when we need them at the office. Fatherhood and marriage together make the crucible that forms our adult characters, and it is by the content of our characters that we will be judged as leaders.

Modern corporate leadership includes not only articulating a vision and pushing your followers to realize it, but also serving them and giving them the tools they need. Men traditionally have not been raised to think of themselves in service roles, one advantage women managers have in today's workplace. To the extent fatherhood trains you to include service in your repertoire, you will rise higher and faster in business, and your subordinates will rise with you.

Because fathering is harder than business, when a committed dad steps up to the plate at the office, he's like the batter who's been preparing himself on deck by swinging two bats at once — he can swat the ball that much farther. He may not weigh in with the same face time as his rivals, but his productivity, sharply honed people skills, and inner stability are nonetheless likely to win him his rightful place on the scoreboard. In companies where those qualities are rewarded, every day is Father's Day.

Closing the Loop

In this age of change, business and fathering both offer more opportunities than ever. Any finance textbook will tell you, however, that reward tends to correlate with risk. The business dad's battles never end; there are only lulls.

Office and home sometimes conflict with each other so directly that they seem locked in perpetual opposition. On the one hand, work is so consuming and hectic that it can be easy to feel we are only "careering" through life. Children, on the other hand, have so many needs and wants that they will crowd work (and everything else) out of our minds and lives as much as we allow. Who would have thought such small creatures would have such weight to throw around? At any one moment of stress and conflict, crushed between those two irresistible forces, it's tempting to groan that the term "business dad" is practically a contradiction in terms—that we can't possibly be good businessmen and good fathers.

The fact is, though, that the battle between work and home can be mediated with a little intelligence, planning, and consistent effort. As long as you keep your priorities in mind, it shouldn't take a rocket scientist to put them into practice. As An Wang, founder of

Wang Laboratories, once said, "Success is more a function of consistent common sense than of genius."

The two great challenges for the business dad are to raise a family, and to provide for that family in a changing, challenging world. Without the skills and abilities we hone in the latter effort, it's tough playing more than a biological role in the former. As this book has argued, work is a major formative force in men's lives, and the lessons of business apply equally at home. Just as our office skills can help us with our kids, moreover, practice at home can make us, well, not perfect but at least better at work. Not only that, but being happier in either capacity improves our performance measurably in the other, because it boosts our energy and confidence.

I hope this book will be helpful in your quest to be a successful father and a successful businessman, two goals that you may find conflict less than you previously might have thought. From time to time, though, and to some extent all the time, they will still conflict. The pie, bigger though it may be, will still have to be sliced. You will still need to make choices.

When those choices arise, please keep in mind the fundamental difference between your family and your job: family is forever—like diamonds, but even more precious. Companies go under, jobs get downsized, careers may lead you from employer to employer; but family, once made, can never truly be unmade.

In business, there's a saying that "there are no footnotes to the bottom line," but how much more permanent is the bottom line in child rearing! Is it exciting and worthwhile and satisfying to build a corporate empire? Of course! Is it something to be legitimately proud of? Yes! But attention will soon move on to the next empire builder. We live on in the memories of our children and their descendants, not in musty press clippings from ancient business sections.

Fatherhood, more than business, is almost always what shapes a man's personal legacy. Simply stated, it is the most important job we'll ever undertake. When done right, it is also the most enjoyable and fulfilling. In the words of Peter Lynch when he left Fidelity in 1991, "Nobody on his deathbed ever said, 'I wish I'd spent more time at the office.' " According to the *New York Times*, nature has al-lotted no more than about a billion heartbeats to each living thing, from mice to elephants. What will you do with your billion?

Turning one last time to that font of truth *Mary Poppins*, let us recall the gentle irony with which Bert the chimney sweep finally lifts the veil from the eyes of George Banks, the business dad:

> You're a man of high position, esteemed by your peers!
> And when your little tykes are crying, you haven't *time* to
>   dry their tears,
> And see them grateful little faces smiling up at you,
> Because their dad, he always knows just what to do.
> You've got to grind, grind, grind at that grindstone,
> Though childhood slips like sand through a sieve,
> And all too soon they've up and grown, and then they've
>   flown,
> And it's too late for you to give
>   Just that spoonful of sugar to help the medicine go
>   down . . .

It's not long afterward that George wises up, mends his son's torn kite, takes the kids to the park—and does better than ever at the bank, in part because he's found his sense of humor and humanity.

When I was growing up, my parents gave me a fascinating book called *Birds Do the Strangest Things*, by Leonora and Arthur Horn-blow. While reading it to my own son, I came across the following passage:

> Can you believe that a bird can build a house? Well, there is one that does. When explorers in New Guinea first saw these houses, they thought children had built them. But bowerbirds had built them. What wonderful bowers they are! Many have roofs. Some even have rooms. There are different kinds of bowerbirds. They build different kinds of bowers.
> One kind of bowerbird makes a garden of moss around a

tree. Then he builds a house of twigs. Sometimes he builds it six feet tall. He wants his house and garden to be pretty. He puts leaves and moss and ferns all around. He makes little piles of berries, stones, shells and flowers. When the flowers die, he throws them out and brings fresh ones. Bowerbirds are always looking for pretty things. They will even steal them from another bird's bower. . . .

The blue satin bowerbird wants his bower to be pretty. His idea of something pretty is something blue. He finds blue flowers and feathers, shells and berries. Everything he puts in his house is blue. Most amazing of all, the blue satin bowerbird can paint the inside of his bower blue. He makes his paint out of charcoal and berry juice. He even makes a paint brush out of a piece of bark. He holds the brush in his beak.

It may take a bowerbird months to build his bower. He would like to share it with a lady bowerbird. When one comes along, the male stops work on the house. He does a dance for her. After a while she goes in to see if she likes the bower.

But she never uses the bower for a nest. When the time comes to lay her eggs she flies away. She makes a plain nest for herself and her children. Her husband, the wonderful builder, does not help her. He does not even know he has children. All he cares about is looking after his bower.

Upon reading those words, I thought, "Wait a minute! I think I know some bowerbirds myself!" Don't we all? Haven't we all met business dads who keep score with material possessions? Who roam the world in search of "pretty things" they can collect? Who devote all their energy to erecting the grandest career structures possible, the better to convince the world (and themselves) of their own importance? Those one-sided human beings strive desperately to make themselves memorable to every business contact, yet they neglect the very people most likely to carry their memory into the future—their children.

And their wives? Surely they appreciate the hard work, together with the shells, flowers, and other accessories, but they know that young chicks need a different kind of warmth in the nest. The mothers assume the whole responsibility themselves, and so everyone loses: the chicks with only one real parent, the mothers forced to fly solo, and (perhaps most of all) the misguided daddy bowerbirds themselves, victims of a life-depriving edifice complex.

Don't be a bowerbird. Feather your nest, by all means. Build one of the nicest in the forest, if you can. But don't let your competitive and acquisitive instincts blind you to the greatest treasure life has to offer. Work and family can and do fit together, but only if you give each its due priority and transfer knowledge and skills between them. If this book helps even a little in thinking through these challenges, it will have accomplished its goals.

Now if you'll excuse me, I've got another early morning tomorrow. Let's see what the day holds: work out, help get the kids off and running, attend meetings at the office first thing, put out three fires, answer ten voice mails and thirty E-mails—all before lunch. As for after work, I can't even imagine what the kids will come up with by dinnertime to shock or surprise me, or the new family issues Julie and I will have to talk through afterward.

Will tomorrow be hectic, stressful, bewildering, challenging? Of course. Just another day in the life of a business dad.

And you know what? I wouldn't trade it for anything.

Appendix

———

Nuts-and-Bolts Books

The Daddy Guide: Real-Life Advice and Tips from over 250 Dads and Other Experts. By Kevin Nelson. Lincolnwood, IL: NTC/Contemporary Publishing, 1998.

The Father's Almanac Revised. By S. Adams Sullivan. New York: Doubleday, 1992.

How to Father. By Dr. Fitzhugh Dodson. New York: Signet, reissue 1992.

Early Fatherhood

Baby Tips for New Dads: Baby's First Year. By Jeanne Murphy. New York: St. Martin's Press, 1998.

Crib Notes for the First Year of Fatherhood: A Survival Guide for New Fathers. By Everett De Morier. Minneapolis, MN: Fairview Press, 1998.

The Expectant Father: Facts, Tips, and Advice for Dads-To-Be. By Armin A. Brott and Jennifer Ash. New York: Abbeville Press, 1995. See also Brott's 1997 book on the first year and his 1998 book on the toddler years, Abbeville Press.

The Joy of Fatherhood: The First Twelve Months. By Marcus Jacob Goldman, M.D. Rocklin, CA: Prima Publishing, 1996.

General Guides

Becoming a Father: How to Nurture and Enjoy Your Family. By William Sears and Paul Froelich. Schaumberg, IL: La Leche League International, 1998.

The Five Key Habits of Smart Dads: A Powerful Strategy for Successful Fathering. By Paul Lewis. Grand Rapids, MI: Zondervan, 1996.

The Gift of Fatherhood: How Men's Lives Are Transformed by Their Children. By Aaron Hass, Ph.D. New York: Fireside, 1994.

The Seven Habits of Highly Effective Families: Building a Beautiful Family Culture in a Turbulent World. By Stephen R. Covey. New York: Golden Books, 1998.

The Seven Secrets of Effective Fathers. By Ken R. Canfield. Wheaton, IL: Tyndale House Publishing, 1995.

Balancing Work and Family

Marathon Dad: Setting a Pace That Works for Fathers. By John Evans. New York: Avon Books, 1998.

Working Fathers: New Strategies for Balancing Work and Family. By James A. Levine and Todd Pittinsky. San Diego, CA: Harvest Books, 1998.

Humor and Anecdotes

The Book of Fathers' Wisdom: Paternal Advice from Moses to Bob Dylan. Edited by Edward Hoffman. Secaucus, NJ: Birch Lane Press, 1997.

Fatherhood. By Bill Cosby. New York: Berkley Publishing Group, 1994.

Lessons from Dad: A Tribute to Fatherhood. Edited by Jean Aho Ryan. Deerfield Beach, FL: Health Communications, 1997.

Zen and the Art of Fatherhood: Lessons from a Master Dad. By Steven M. Lewis. New York: Plume, 1997.